A PASSAGE THROUGH PAKISTAN

a PASSAGE
through PAKISTAN

by

ORVILLE F. LINCK

Professor of English
Wayne State University

Detroit—Wayne State University Press—1959

Library of Congress
Catalog Card Number 59-15364
Copyright © 1959
All rights reserved
Wayne State University Press
Detroit 2, Michigan

Grateful acknowledgement is made to the following:

Mirror Publications, Karachi, Pakistan, for permission to quote from Zeb-Un-Nissa Hamidullah, *Sixty Days in America* (1956).

Sayyid Abul Ala Maudoodi for permission to quote from his book, *Towards Understanding Islam* (5th ed.; Lahore: Tarjumanul Quran, 1954).

The Macmillan Company for permission to quote from Keith Callard, *Pakistan: A Political Study* (1957).

Miss Frene Talyarkhan, editor, for permission to quote from Indira Sen, "The Human Side," in *Trend* (June 1957).

The Manchester Guardian, London, for permission to quote the editorial on Ayub Khan (June 18, 1959).

The Macmillan Company for permission to quote from Frank Moraes, *Yonder One World* (1958).

To my wife

Preface

This book is written for the general American reading public, not for scholars or specialists. It is based on my experiences as a Fulbright lecturer during the academic year of 1956–57. My wife was with me every step of the way, and, though I have done the writing, the work was really a joint enterprise. The photographs (with a single exception) are one of her tangible contributions; the intangible ones are more important.

The need for such a book has been dramatized in the last few years by events in the Muslim world; more specifically, it was emphasized for my wife and me when we received letters overseas from American friends addressed to "Pakistan, India." The letters were delivered, but the Pakistanis were justifiably annoyed about such an error. The confusion is, perhaps, understandable, but it is high time that it be cleared up. A twelve-year-old nation of some eighty million people, an ally of the United States, deserves to have its existence better recognized and its significance better understood.

The United States Educational Foundation in Pakistan was officially responsible for our welfare. However, the services rendered to us and the personal interest taken in us by its staff went well beyond the formal call of duty. We wish to express our appreciation particularly to the Executive Secretary of the Foundation, Dr. John Withall, and Mrs. Withall; to Dr. Syed M. Jafar, Deputy Executive Secretary; and to Mr. Mohammed Salam, Financial Secretary.

The Karachi staff of the Asia Foundation was always helpful.

Dr. Mohammed Ihsanullah Khan, my principal at Abbottabad Government College, was invariably understanding and cooperative. We have come to regard him, not as an official, but as the warmest and most generous of friends. We are deeply grateful to him and to the students and faculty of the college.

We also owe an unusual debt of hospitality to the following: the members of the Abbottabad Club, military and civilian, British and Pakistani; Dr. Mazher Ali Khan, head of the English Department, University of Peshawar, his faculty colleagues, and his students; and Father F. Scanlon and his staff at Burn Hall School, Abbottabad.

From our early correspondence with the Pakistan Embassy in Washington before we left the United States to our last dealings with the customs men in Karachi on the way home, all of the people of Pakistan with whom we had any official or personal relations were courteous, cooperative, and interested in their foreign guests.

As for India, we wish to acknowledge similar debts of hospitality and friendship to the faculty and students of Patna University, to the faculty and students of Jain College, and to our hosts during our short, but impressive, visit to Maharajah College.

A special note: Mr. Kanhya L. Kaul of the Delhi University Library was a guest librarian at Wayne State University during the academic year of 1958–59. At the invitation of the Wayne State University Press, he graciously undertook to read the manuscript of this book. I have profited from his intimate knowledge of Indo-Pakistani culture, for he possesses the unusual combination of a sensitive understanding of intercultural relations and a critical objectivity in respect to both India and the United States. Of course, Mr. Kaul must not be charged with any errors in fact which may appear, nor is he responsible for any of the value judgments herein expressed.

The spelling of Pakistani proper names is as varied as Elizabethan spelling—and as troublesome. Professor Keith Callard observes, "There are at least five common variants of the English spelling of Muhammad."* In the face of this difficulty, I have spelled names as I have found them recorded in newspapers, in letters, and in an "official" list of the Abbottabad College faculty made up for me by the college office staff. In many cases the individuals involved might choose to spell their names differently. Like Professor Callard, I hereby apologize to those whose names are not spelled as they would choose.

O.F.L.

* See "A Note on Pakistani Names" in *Pakistan: A Political Study*; see also my Note 2, Chapter VIII.

Introduction

Our assignment was to the Abbottabad Government College, District Hazara, the Northwest Frontier Province, but in the course of the year, by virtue of attendance at professional meetings, lecture trips, vacation trips, and just plain necessary travel, we spent some time in Karachi, Lahore, Rawalpindi, Peshawar, Nathia Gali, Murree, and Dacca, the capital of East Pakistan. This is to say that we got to know most of the important places in Pakistan, and, altogether, we were able to get a pretty good idea of the country as a whole. Moreover, before, during, and after my Fulbright year, we did considerable background reading about Pakistan; in particular, we read the Pakistani press with close attention. However, our most valuable experience was living from day to day as working members of a Pakistani community for a unit of time, a cycle, which has provided a solid basis for the understanding of the nation's culture.

Without claiming profound or authoritative knowledge of Pakistan, I think that this book offers more than a mere tourist's travelog. The United States has had good reason to be sceptical of the worth of accounts written by short-term foreign visitors, and the awareness of the arrogance and superficiality of these commentaries has induced an intellectual humility in me which, I most prayerfully hope, pervades the whole of this book. Although this is less than the "big picture" which only years of devoted study could provide, it is something more than "once over lightly" reportage. For I have tried to write an account which should have the virtue of immediacy, but I am more concerned with the *meaning* of what happened than with the fact of ego. I suggest that the insights expressed here will hold good while the present patterns endure, and most of them, in my judgment, will endure for some time to come.

Nothing very sensational happened to us. We did not see any tigers except in zoos; we did not find any cobras or scorpions in our bathrooms or bedrooms; we were not shot at by tribesmen, although we saw plenty of Pathans in and around Peshawar, fully equipped with bandoliers and home-made rifles, looking as if they were quite ready and willing to shoot; we were not assaulted by fiercely anti-European mobs either in Pakistan at the height of the Suez crisis, or in India, when the Kashmir issue was coming to a boil in the UN, with the United States on the unpopular side. But this very absence of the Great Adventure is an advantage, not a disadvantage. The sensational tends to eclipse the typical. Moreover, what is commonplace in Pakistan is not commonplace in the United States, and I have no fear that this account of life in a strange culture will lack intrinsic interest for American readers. For a curious Westerner, any day in Pakistan can be a real adventure until he comes to take the pattern for granted. The problem is to see the "ordinary" freshly and in perspective.

A word about point of view: My wife and I are Americans born and bred. We cannot escape our conditioning, but, insofar as possible, I have tried to recognize and to make due allowance for our Western primary prepossessions. Subconscious, built-in ways of seeing and judging are admittedly difficult to control. However, I have not made any bland assumptions about the superiority either of American culture or of Americans as human beings. I have tried to understand our Pakistani friends in their own terms and then to examine both cultures from a detached (not "higher") point of view. In the end, it was only natural that we should come to a fresh appreciation of American values. We feel that we know our own country—both its strengths and weaknesses—better after a year abroad.

Since this book contains one chapter on India, a necessary point must be made: one can be pro-Pakistani without being anti-Indian. Most Pakistanis would probably disagree with me, I regret to say. I do believe that Pakistan has a strong case in respect to the plebiscite which has not been held in Kashmir, but this fact does not make me anti-Indian in any fundamental sense. However uncomfortable the political relations may be between the United States and India, we were received there as individuals with great cordiality, and this in a tense period.

There is another ground for making this point. Like millions of mature Americans, we have grown up in a tradition of sympathy for India in its struggle for self-determination. Before 1947, Americans made no sharp distinction between Muslims and Hindus in India. We find it hard to do so even now. This long-standing sympathetic concern for "India" and "Indians" still endures.

This is to say that we are pro-the-peoples-of-the-Indo-Pakistan subcontinent. To put it simply, we are pro-people.

CONTENTS

ILLUSTRATIONS

Chapter One

On the Way to Abbottabad

Karachi, Overloaded Capital: Camels and Chevrolets

We entered Pakistan in September 1956 through Karachi, located on the Arabian Sea, near the mouth of the fabled Indus River, about three hundred miles east of the Iranian border. Karachi is West Pakistan's only seaport, and the city's modern airport is an important base on the long air routes to the Orient and Australia. Since 1947, when Pakistan was established, Karachi, the nation's capital and the nerve center of its industrial, commercial, financial, and political life, has been one of the fastest growing cities on earth. In 1956, its population was well over a million, and it is destined to become one of the world's important metropolises.[1]

But, for all its weight and significance in Pakistani and world affairs, it is not a pleasant city. Once a placid provincial capital, reputed to be the cleanest town in all pre-partition India, today it is a raw, young, rapidly reproducing organism, much too big for the

1

old municipal britches, and it floods out into the encircling desert. Showing the strain of its terrible load as the improvised capital of a new nation and as the home of hundreds of thousands of Muslim refugees from India, it has the characteristics of both an industrial war-time boom town and a refugee camp. Greenery is rare. The climate is murderously hot and humid in the bad months. At its best, during the winter months, it is not one of the world's garden spots. As a rule, people do not choose to live in Karachi; the choice is forced on them.

Recent reports indicate that the current Ayub regime will shift the capital of Pakistan from Karachi to Rawalpindi, the big army center a thousand miles to the north. One story on this theme appeared in the *New York Times*, March 1, 1959, headed "Pakistanis Seek New Capital City." This account, summarizing the many good reasons for the move, points out that the population of Karachi has grown from 350,000 in 1947, the year of partition and independence, to *over two million in 1959*! A later report, in the form of a personal letter dated August 7, 1959 from our able Fulbright successors, relays information from Americans in Rawalpindi to the effect that the process of moving the capital has already begun.

Nevertheless, despite its liabilities Karachi is an amazing and fascinating place—in short doses. In the suburbs are walled stucco villas containing every modern amenity, which look from a distance like ocean liners sailing over seas of sand hills. Watching from one of these villas (the home of John Withall, Executive Secretary of the Fulbright program in Pakistan), we were electrified to see a large camel caravan moving slowly out into the Sind desert. The camel caravan is one of the oldest and loneliest sights on earth; yet, not many miles away on the other side of the city, there is a General Motors Chevrolet Assembly plant.

This juxtaposition of the old and the new is the hallmark of Karachi. There one lives in two worlds at the same time: in the old Islamic world of the camel, the ass, the ox, and the human beast of burden—with water buffalo thrown in for good measure—and in the new world of the truck, the motorbus, the automobile, the bicycle, and the motorcycle. All of these are on the streets at the same time, with the latest-model airliners flying regularly overhead. For public transportation in Karachi, you may have your choice of streetcar, bus, automobile-taxi, motorcycle-taxi (at your own risk), bicycle-rickshaw, or horse-drawn tonga.

The streets in Karachi do not belong to the motor vehicle as a matter of course as they do in the United States. On American roads or streets, we feel fundamentally aggrieved if we encounter a horse cart; we feel that it does not "belong." Not so in Karachi, nor in the rest of Pakistan. There the next turning will reveal burdened camels, loaded-down asses, or the ubiquitous oxcart or buffalo cart, and you must drive accordingly.

Another factor which adds to the hazards of the road is that the people are not yet conditioned to motor traffic. In the United States, we tend to respond instantly to the sound of squealing brakes and automobile horns. These sounds are not fully comprehended by Pakistani pedestrians, and their reactions are unpredictable. It is for this reason, in addition to the need for maintaining face and status, that American missions require their motor vehicles to be driven by Pakistani nationals and that most foreign civilians employ Pakistani chauffeurs.

In the heart of metropolitan Karachi, the contrast between the old pastoral world and the new motor world is accentuated by the number of water holes filled with wallowing buffalo. These amiable and docile beasts, mainstays of the Pakistani domestic economy, furnish meat, milk, fuel, transportation, and power, but, to the Westerner, they are a strange and peaceful sight in the middle of a big city.

The two worlds existing side by side are also clearly manifest in the clothes of the people on the streets. You will see orthodox Muslim women covered from head to foot in the *burqa*, an all-enveloping hooded garment equipped with eye-holes or built-in screens to afford some limited vision. This outer garment, dictated by a fundamentalist interpretation of the Koran, may conceal the loveliest of feminine costumes, for all the observer can tell. In public, these orthodox women in their shrouds are in sharp contrast with their more modern Muslim sisters who do not wear the *burqa*. In the lobbies of the fashionable hotels, for example, one may see the emancipated women in many variations of the graceful, time-honored sari or in the *salwar* and *kameez*, the pajamas and long overtunic which West Pakistani women also prize. These clothes are invariably worn with a shawl or head covering which is more of an ornamental part of the total ensemble than a protection against the eyes of men. You will see some female faces in Karachi or Lahore; you will not see many in Abbottabad or Peshawar. It may be noted in passing that Hindu women (not very numerous in West Pakistan) do not wear the *burqa* at all.

As for the men, the variety in dress is even greater. Their attire

3

may be divided roughly into three classes. The first is composed of flowing shawls worn over every conceivable combination of long-tailed shirt, sleeveless waistcoat, and pajama-type pants, very full at the waist and very narrow at the ankles. The second is composed of the "national dress," basically a long-skirted frock coat with a high collar which hooks up at the neck, thus eliminating the need for a necktie. This *achkan*, usually well tailored, is a dignified garment reminiscent of the bygone glories of the Prince Albert and Edwardian modes; it is worn with the same kind of white pajama pants described for class one. Such a black frock coat with white trousers was the required uniform for students at Abbottabad. This national dress is accepted as the equivalent of dinner jacket or tails at formal affairs. The third class of clothes is composed of standard sack suits tailored on English lines. Many Pakistani men wear tweed jackets and slacks.

Headgear in Pakistan is a continuing delight in its variety and color. Men from the hills or the countryside often wear class one clothes, and they sport turbans of all colors and shapes, a flat pancake version of the beret called a Gilgit cap, or the high-sided, trim, boat-shaped Jinnah cap in cloth or karakul. Men who favor class two clothes, the national dress, which is often worn as a symbol of the rejection of Western ways, wear a Jinnah cap or a smart turban to top off the ensemble. The men of class three, business men, many government officials, many teachers and professors, and most army officers, usually wear Western headgear, if any. Officers in mufti can usually be spotted by their regimental ties and smart felt hats which smack of Ivy League styling. We would call them pork-pie hats, but pork is an unpleasant word in Muslim countries.

In Karachi, all of these types of dress will be seen. Karachi, though a new and roaring city, is a place where the old Muslim devotion to classic Persian and Urdu poetry is still strong, yet I attended a learned lecture on William Butler Yeats at Karachi's new university. It was delivered to a class of M.A. candidates by a young man who had just the right kind of donnish, intellectual, weary arrogance one might expect him to bring back from Cambridge, but his manner stood out in sharp ironic contrast to his beard and his frock coat, which quietly affirmed his deliberate commitment to Islam and the Muslim world. The lecture was held in a dingy classroom, itself a symbol of the hard lot of the new Republic, and it overlooked one of the unbelievably squalid refugee quarters which checker the city. At the same time, a mile or so away, a team of professors, working un-

4

der an ICA (International Cooperation Administration) contract with the University of Pennsylvania, was conducting a successful program of training in Public Administration.

Karachi is a modern city, with new factories on the outskirts; with miles of small shops and biggish stores carrying all kinds of familiar brand-name consumer goods; with the ever-present Bata shoe chain; with the Singer sewing machine; and with a few show-rooms and service stations for the automobile—all the signs which give every big city around the world a common denominator, a sense of sameness. Yet, in other out-of-the-way quarters, you will find bazaars like those of Fez, Marrakech, Damascus, or Baghdad—narrow lanes lined with cubbyhole shops, dammed with tongas, ox-carts, rickshaws, and people. In these shops, you will find all the goods painfully crafted by man before the machine took over: cop-per and brassware, pottery, jewelry, rugs and carpets, leather, em-broideries, textiles, and the like. Some of this merchandise comes from far-away places like Bokhara and Samarkand. In these streets, the twentieth century is far away. The rhythms of life are not synco-pated, and the methods of doing business are not IBM. The curious crowds will press upon you while you shop, but nobody will press you to buy.

It is different in the Empress Market, the nearest approach to a supermarket which Karachi provides—excluding the commissary of the United States embassy. There you will be charged by a brigade of coolies all wanting to carry your purchases, for no true sahib or memsahib will stoop so low as to carry anything in Pakistan. There you will find everything edible which the country provides for sale: fruits, vegetables, meat, chicken, fish, bread and such staples of Pakistani life as ghee (which is distilled butter) and grains of vari-ous kinds—all this with no refrigeration and millions of flies. For the spirit, you may buy birds which are not for eating: song birds, para-keets, and iridescent redbirds caged up by the hundreds. The Em-press Market is a trial for Western sensibilities, but it is a place to see nevertheless.

Dominating everything in Karachi is the presence of the Muslim refugees from India who present the primordial problem of the dis-placed person, a problem which Pakistan has faced in Lahore and elsewhere. Conversely, India has faced it in Delhi and Calcutta with the Hindu and Sikh refugees. The governments of both India and Pakistan have battled it manfully, but neither one has been fully

5

able to cope with it. Their resources are too small and the numbers of people are too great. In the cities, the refugees are everywhere. In Karachi and Calcutta, they sleep in the streets.

These people are on the consciences of both nations, because they made their choice deliberately according to their religious convictions, and they have a right to life and a chance to work and to carve out their own destinies. But such opportunities are not yet the birthright of the inhabitants of this vast subcontinent. A Muslim or a Hindu may love his brothers in principle and may approve heartily of the decision which brought them to Karachi or Calcutta, but when the older inhabitants of these cities have to deal daily with thousands of their brothers—poor, hungry, sick, and unemployed—there is a great strain on the family tie, and exasperation followed by callous indifference is the consequence. The same pattern holds good for refugees in West Germany. Ultimately, nobody seems to care except the "government." It is true that refugee housing is being built in Karachi, but it is pitifully inadequate, and the result will be, I fear, that much temporary housing will become permanent, as has happened in the United States since World War II. It is likely that the terrible refugee camps in Karachi will be a distinctive feature of the urban landscape for some time to come. Still, the refugees contrive to exist; they find some kind of work; they get some help from the government; and in time—a painfully long time—they will be absorbed into the national blood stream.

Despite all the disadvantages of climate, overpopulation, the perennial health problem, and the absence of the usual municipal conveniences of a well-ordered city, the European business man, the staffs of the foreign missions, and the well-to-do Pakistanis manage to live in reasonable comfort in Karachi. They establish domestic fortresses in their walled compounds with large staffs of servants; they have automobiles—badly needed in a city which sprawls for miles along the sea and into the desert; and the official foreigners, notably the Americans (but excluding the Fulbrighters), have access to commissaries where staple goods are relatively inexpensive and cigarettes and liquor are cheap. Good clubs are available for tennis, cricket, riding, and other sports, and the seashore affords opportunity for swimming, boating, and picnicking. Movies are plentiful, and there is a good deal of give-and-take entertaining. But, as usual, Karachi is a city in which life is difficult for the middle classes and the poor.

From all this, it is obvious that Karachi is not likely to become a favorite spot for tourists, but a visit there for a few days would be an enlightening experience. Tourists can get in and out of the city on any one of several good airlines—among others, SAS, BOAC, Pan-Am, Air France, KLM, or Pakistan's own PIA—and, of course, by sea. Tourists will find the hotels interesting and adequate. The hotels furnish bed tea, breakfast, lunch, afternoon tea, and dinner for a set price which is expensive in Pakistani terms, but not out of line with standard tourist prices elsewhere in the world. Some hotels are even air-conditioned. Since Karachi is a boom city, the hotel situation is bound to improve because there is money in the business.

The Metropole is the best known hotel; centrally located, it is the hub of the city's business and social life. The Beach Luxury is some distance from the business and shopping districts, but, as its name indicates, it is on the beach, and is a favored place for parties or "functions." It is an education in itself to observe the flow of national and international life through the lobbies of these hostelries.

As for other attractions, tourists can live in two worlds at the same time: they will find the hotel bars sufficiently cosmopolitan and lively; they can meet the new international set of ICA and UN technicians as well as foundation personnel and business carpet-baggers; they can shop for true indigenous items in the old bazaars or in the good handicrafts shop run by the APWA (All-Pakistan Women's Association) with its fixed prices; they can ride a camel on the beach; or they can simply walk the streets and ponder the problem of Asia: too many people and too little food. Altogether not a bad two or three days' harvest.

However, if we can make a distinction between tourist and traveler, other areas of Pakistan like Lahore, Peshawar, and the Kaghan Valley have great potential for those who are tired of the obvious and have a little adventure in their souls. In time, the Pakistan government will exploit this potential; it is already making some progress in this direction.

As for us, we were tourists with a purpose: to learn as much about Pakistan as we could before undertaking our assignment. We spent two weeks in Karachi to our great profit. Having done considerable reading about Pakistan's history and culture (with the generous help of the Pakistani Embassy in Washington which sent us valuable materials), we received an additional thorough briefing from the officials of the United States Educational Foundation, the administrative agency for the Fulbright program in Pakistan. Living with John Withall and his family, we also got a practical course

7

in Pakistani domestic science. Our baggage was cleared through the customs (which is no mean feat) by the Foundation's efficient financial secretary, Mohammed Salam. Because of a polio scare we took shots and listened carefully to the medical advice offered by the able and conscientious doctor who served the American Embassy: drink only boiled water, eat only cooked food; no salads; fruit dangerous; no milk; take your malaria pills regularly; take your vitamin pills regularly; and keep your shots up to date. There was more advice of a hair-raising variety. We were willing and eager to follow the doctor's orders, but if you are to live with any people for a year, you eat and drink what your hosts do. Therefore, we followed that stern medical advice whenever we could, but on many social occasions we had to violate the doctor's precepts.

Neither my wife nor I had any serious illness resulting from our Pakistani experience. However, the earnest doctor was not a professional alarmist; considering some of his own embassy cases, he had good reason for his tough attitude. East of Suez it is easy to get amoebic dysentery; friends of ours in the Orient have had hepatitis; malaria is still endemic in parts of Pakistan; the TB rate is frightening—largely as a result of malnutrition; the sun itself is a dangerous enemy at times; and the daily impact of disease and death is stronger than it is in the United States. No one should decide against going to the Orient because of health reasons, but it is wise to be on guard there all the time.

With these warnings on our minds, we left Karachi gladly in the middle of September 1956. The sun had been a physical burden during the daytime, and the nights, although cooler, had been unpleasantly humid. Psychologically, we felt (whether justifiably or not) that we were already veterans of Pakistani life. We had seen the two extremes of relative luxury and direst poverty; we were pretty well prepared for whatever would happen; and we were cheered by the unanimous opinion that Abbottabad, our destination, was one of the pleasantest places in all of Pakistan. And so one evening we took off for Lahore in a Pakistan International Airlines plane.

It was a good, big plane, a "Connie." The hostesses were efficient and very attractive in their uniformed version of the *salwar* and *kameez*—the feminine flowing pajamas and long tunic overskirt— and the pilots were also good. This point is worth making because there is a general tendency on the part of some Westerners and even of some Pakistanis to ridicule and derogate all aspects of Pakistani effort. For example, we heard a story to the effect that a PIA plane

8

left Cairo, developed trouble in one of its four engines, and, instead of going back, continued on to Karachi with only three. This story was cited as an instance of the cavalier way of Pakistanis with machinery.

Months later, on our way home, at a pleasant Karachi party, I mentioned the story to two American Pan-Am pilots who were on detached service (as we used to say in the Army) training Pakistani pilots for commercial airline duty. They heatedly denied the whole tale, saying that the culpable pilot had not been a Pakistani, but a foreigner who was no longer with PIA for obvious reasons. Furthermore, they were warm in praise of their students who were "sharp," trustworthy, and good enough to earn and hold instrument ratings. Both of my compatriots struck me as being hard-boiled, competent types. I liked them for their patent earnestness and their devotion to the job. Therefore, what they had to say about the incident was all the more convincing.

At any rate, our Pakistani pilots on the Lahore trip landed their big plane on a flare-lit runway as gently as a mother putting her child to bed, and this initial sample of their skill held good for all of our subsequent flights via PIA from Lahore to Rawalpindi, from Peshawar to Lahore, and from Dacca to Lahore.

Lahore, the Paris of Asia: a Living Past

But, after the modern conveniences of the Karachi airport, the Lahore airport was a different story. The field was being reconstructed, and, in the middle of the night, we were dumped out into a big crowd, had to scramble for our baggage which was somewhat unceremoniously deposited in inches-deep dust, found a tent serving as the airlines office, and searched in vain for either a taxi or a bus. Things looked bad for a couple of American pilgrims in a strange Asian city until an American consular official, who was at the airport to welcome a visiting VIP (Fulbrighters are *not* VIP), rescued us from the dust, the heat, and the crowd, and took us downtown to Faletti's Hotel.

Faletti's, like Dean's in Peshawar and the old Cecil in Delhi, is one of the famous hotels of the Indo-Pakistan subcontinent. For the traveling American, it is an experience in itself, quite different from the Karachi hotel pattern except in the matter of servants. It is on one floor and occupies a block or so of land. A typical "double room," which is opened with a huge ancient key by a turbaned room bearer,

9

is composed of a large sitting room equipped with elephant-sized furniture, a bedroom containing two huge beds, two dressing rooms, and two baths. The ceilings are immensely high, and large-bladed, electric-powered punkahs (fans) disturb the 100° heat with some success. In cold weather, small fireplaces in bedrooms and sitting rooms take off some of the chill—if you are willing to pay for the fuel, an expensive item in Pakistan.

It is true that the furniture was old and worn and that the plumbing was nineteenth century in vintage and doubtful in performance, but, on that very hot September night, the place looked good. As shabby as the rooms are at Faletti's, one can still see how it must have been for the sahibs of Kipling's day when they came to town. For all this faded grandeur plus a ballroom-sized dining room, servants constantly underfoot, bed tea, breakfast, lunch, afternoon tea, and dinner, the cost is about ten dollars per night per couple—a sum which is still considered too high by old Pakistani hands. Faletti's also has an air-conditioned bar for which the traveler has to buy a permit certifying, in effect, that he is a chronic alcoholic and can't do without the stuff. The number of cheerful alcoholics in Lahore—Muslim, Christian, Hindu and godless—was, it appeared, sizable.

Lahore is the pride of Pakistan. In 1948 its population was estimated at one million.[2] It is much larger now by virtue of natural growth and the influx of Muslim refugees. Several people told us, with an understandable nostalgia, that it was formerly known as the Paris of Asia, implying a night life which, possibly as a consequence of Islamic puritanism, is not as flourishing as it was in prepartition days when Lahore was a favorite city of Sikhs and Hindus as well as Muslims.

Whatever the truth of the view that Lahore is not quite what it used to be, it is no mean city. It is in striking contrast with Karachi, the raw, new center of the nation's political, industrial, and financial life. An old sophisticated city, Lahore is still primarily the cultural center of the nation and *was* secondarily the political capital of West Pakistan, the One Unit made up of the old provinces of the Punjab, the Sind, the Northwest Frontier Province, Baluchistan, and some other semi-autonomous units. In Karachi, the new tends to overwhelm the old; in Lahore, the old gives way unwillingly to the new. Karachi is a seaport built in a desert; Lahore is the Queen City of the Punjab, the fabled land of the Five Rivers, once the granary of all India, now fighting a losing battle to maintain its old fertility. In addition to its ancient bazaars, Lahore has wide, tree-lined streets, parks, and

10

gardens which, even when parched by dry weather and 115° heat, are pleasing to the eye after the blazing yellow-white of Karachi's sands. The pace in Karachi is fast; in Lahore, the pace is slower. One can still see elements of grace in Lahore, derived from traditional Muslim culture and from nineteenth-century British mores. There is not much of a sense of history in Karachi; in Lahore, the past is more nearly an organic part of the present.

Karachi is not yet a writer's city; Lahore is still the city of Rudyard Kipling, who, aside from his Empire bias, was a marvelous reporter. I re-read *Kim* in Pakistan and found many illuminating insights which are good for both India and Pakistan even today.[3]

The living quality of Lahore's history was brought home to us by a young Pakistani staff man from the United States Information Service who was asked by his chief to serve as our guide for a tour of the city. He enthusiastically performed this function, as did the Pakistani driver of the USIS car. In us, they had an attentive and appreciative audience, and they made the most of it. Through their eyes and their reactions, we received a vivid impression of how desperately a people needs a tradition to be proud of—a base to rest on—particularly when the going is rough as it is now. With them, we saw the Shalimar Gardens, not at their best because water in Lahore was at a premium, but still a miracle of line and proportion. These gardens brought home to us two of the reasons for the best in Islamic art: the Koran's prescription against anything smacking of idols and the age-old affinity of the Muslim mind for the classical purity of mathematics. "Euclid alone has looked on beauty bare," wrote Edna St. Vincent Millay, and I think that the Muslim artist would agree with her. The Shalimar Gardens have an uncluttered purity of line and deceptively simple geometrical patterns which are also characteristic of the great Badshahi mosque (a "must see" in Lahore) and of Jehangir's tomb in the outskirts of the city. We came upon the wonderfully moving spectacle of the latter at twilight. Surely it is one of the finest works of man on the whole subcontinent.

My enthusiasm for the best of the Mogul seventeenth-century art tradition as exemplified in the tomb, the gardens, and the mosque (as well as in the delicate court paintings which we later saw in a Delhi museum) led me to ask an important question: what has happened to art in modern Pakistan? After all, these achievements are not so very old; one might expect to see first-rate modern versions of them as one sees evidence daily in Japan of the continuing vital force of a tried and tested esthetic married to modern technology.

11

The fact seems to be that, insofar as art, architecture, and handicraft design are concerned, Pakistani artists and artisans have no significant relationship with their own past.

Iqbal's tomb, for instance, is right next door to the great Badshahi mosque. Iqbal is Islam's greatest modern poet and philosopher.[4] He is regarded as the father of the "idea" of Pakistan. He is venerated in Pakistan and all through the Islamic world, and, as I was later informed, his intellectual and esthetic achievements are highly valued by non-Muslim Indians as well. There is nothing particularly wrong with his tomb—it is simple enough—but there is nothing impressive about it either. Nondescript is the word for it, as for most of the new buildings we saw in Pakistan. At first sight, the new buildings of the University of Peshawar in the Northwest Frontier Province are impressive against the background of the mountains which hem in the Khyber Pass, but a closer look reveals that they really have neither the authentic hallmark of tradition, nor the functional virtues of contemporary international modern; they are neither in the spirit of Jehangir nor in that of Le Corbusier's new capital for Indian East Punjab, now being built at Chandigarh.[5]

As for the artisans, the situation is much the same. The Pakistanis are good craftsmen and many people believe that the utilization of their skills on a cottage-industry basis is one answer to mass unemployment. The All-Pakistan Women's Association is attempting to carry on such a program. But there seems to be too much reliance in this program on machine-made rather than on hand-made embroidery designs. There is little point in competing with mass production processes. The glory of handicrafts lies in distinction of design and quality of workmanship. These qualities can be seen in abundance in the All-Indian handicrafts center in New Delhi and, in some degree, in the APWA shop in Karachi.

Here I am not arguing for mere imitation of the past. I do not believe that university buildings should be Neo-Gothic or Neo-Taj Mahal; that paintings should be imitation Reynolds or Gainsborough; that pottery, brass and copper artifacts, home-made textiles, or jewelry should be outright imitation of museum pieces. What is needed is a creative synthesis of the finest of the old with the functional qualities of the new. What is needed is a restoration of the sense of confidence in design on the part of the individual village workman, coupled with high standards of execution. The silk saris of Banaras and the cotton saris of Dacca are cases in point.

To exemplify the creative synthesis I have in mind, I might mention the products of Zarena house which we discovered during our stay in Karachi. The Zarena fabrics enterprise is run by Dorothy Habib, an American lady married to a Pakistani psychiatrist. Mrs. Habib, utilizing Pakistani craftsmen, has developed a line of intriguing textile designs for curtains and draperies based on the archaeological discoveries made at Mohenjo-Daro and Harappa.[6]

In the field of the arts, as distinguished from crafts, another Western lady who is married to a Pakistani, Mrs. Anna Molka Ahmed, the head of the Fine Arts Department of the University of the Punjab in Lahore, is also doing notable work in revitalizing the Pakistani art tradition. It was pleasant to note that something like a renaissance was going on, especially in the field of painting—a phenomenon which is also observable in India. That is, a number of Indo-Pakistani artists, sensitive to and aware of Western styles and techniques, are recording these new insights in their own terms. Anyone interested in this aspect of culture should consult Jalaluddin Ahmed's essay "Art in Pakistan."[7]

The tour of Lahore was a labor of love for our two likable young Pakistani guides. The city is the cultural capital of Pakistan not only because of its historical monuments cited above, but for other reasons. It is the chief publishing center and an important seat of learning. Here one finds the University of the Punjab, probably the best of the nation's institutions of higher education, notable for its strength in physics and chemistry; the best regarded medical college; institutions like Forman Christian College, founded by missionaries and held in great affection by its graduates; and several other institutions for the education of both men and women. One source lists eighteen institutions of learning affiliated with the University of the Punjab in Lahore itself.[8]

It was in Lahore that we first realized the importance of the Indo-Pakistan institution of the cantonment (pronounced cantoonment). In the United States, a cantonment is simply a big army camp. During the old days of undivided India, under the British Raj, the cantonment was the place where the English military and civil officers lived with their families. In those brave old Empire days, the military took care of the civic housekeeping—water, sanitation, street paving, schools, and the like. Today it appears that the armed services and the Ministry of Defense perform these functions with the aid of civilian cantonment executive officers and engineers who are relatively high-level members of the civil service. At least, we found that they were considered as "gazetted officers," a term that will recur often in this book.

The importance of the cantonments lies in the fact that they are generally better run than their adjacent or surrounding municipalities. The cantonment address is the "good" address; it is on the right side of the tracks; the streets are cleaner, the water is safer, the gardens and parks are greener, the avenues are wider, and the schools, separately administered, are better equipped and better staffed than their civilian counterparts. We have heard that the cantonments "ain't what they used to be," but they are still visibly the best residential parts of Pakistan's cities.

Let us finish with Lahore by saying that, although no one we encountered really loved Karachi, everybody who knew Lahore had an affection for it. Lahore may no longer be the Paris of Asia, but surely it is the Paris of Pakistan.

The Land of the Five Rivers: Plain Tales from a Plane

We took a PIA plane from Lahore to Rawalpindi, a city universally referred to in Pakistan as 'Pindi and hereinafter so termed. 'Pindi is some two hundred and fifty miles from Lahore, and the trip was pleasant and uneventful, but it was also revealing.

We had not seen much of Pakistan up to this time. Karachi is not Pakistan any more than Chicago is the United States, and we had flown to Lahore at night. But on the plane for 'Pindi in the early afternoon, the whole land was laid out for our perusal, only partially obscured by the terrible haze of the heat. We read some fundamental truths from the landscape. In the first place, Pakistan, like India, is a village-centered land. In the United States, an air trip reveals a pattern of towns and cities, of course, but the farms themselves are single units, family units, which, despite parity payments, are still largely operated in the spirit of individualism. On the contrary, the Pakistani farmers huddle together in the spirit of community. Their villages, however small in population, are internally as crowded as the bazaars in Lahore and Karachi. This tendency to hive together, to be at home in crowded quarters, so different from our own pioneer quest for space and lebensraum, seems to me to be a fundamental psychological pattern in both Pakistan and India. Furthermore, the average holdings of a Pakistani village—the amount of land between one village and another—will not be, in general, as big as one average Iowa farm. Our farm vocabulary of quarter-section, half-section, section, township, and county, would be incomprehensible to the average Pakistani. To him, "forty acres and a mule" would be the equivalent of the King Ranch in Texas. The Punjab is a large and fertile region, somewhat like our flat wheat states. As of 1954, it had an area

14

of 62,245 square miles as compared to Kansas' 82,276. But the Punjab had a population of 18,828,000 and Kansas (as of 1950) had a population of 1,905,299.[9] Again, too little land and too many people, and the tragedy is that, under Muslim laws of inheritance, the holdings grow smaller.

From the air, one can clearly see that the farmer is dependent on water derived from canals which in turn is derived from the rivers which give the Punjab its name, "The Land of the Five Rivers." There are wells, of course, but they do not do the heavy work of irrigation. And when one then recalls that the head waters of these rivers are in Kashmir to the north, now controlled by India, the Pakistani obsession with the Kashmir problem becomes easier to understand.

The Punjab, the heartland of West Pakistan, looks pastoral, peaceful, and fertile enough in the shimmering afternoon heat, but it is nevertheless a troubled land. Our commuter's hop from Lahore to 'Pindi was uneventful, but with these considerations surging through our minds it certainly was not commonplace.

In the late afternoon we landed in 'Pindi, a city of approximately 250,000 population. 'Pindi is one of the most important military bases in Pakistan, and, therefore, the locus of much high-level staff activity. From it, important routes run to Peshawar, to Abbottabad and Azad ("Free") Kashmir, and to Murree, the hill station which is West Pakistan's swankiest summer resort. 'Pindi is also the point of departure for air travel to such fascinating isolated outposts as Hunza and Chitral, semi-independent mountain states, tucked up in the Himalayas between the USSR and China. These places, almost inaccessible by road, are, in the large sense, part of Pakistan. 'Pindi always was an important commercial center, and, since 1947, it is also becoming increasingly important industrially.

We chatted at the airport for a while with a likable Canadian engineer on leave from the Warsak Dam Project not far from Peshawar. When completed, the dam will be of major importance to the economy of the Frontier. This enterprise is organized under the Colombo Plan as a joint Canadian-Pakistani undertaking. I make a point of this casual meeting with the Canadian because it is typical of what happens to the Western alien in Pakistan all the time—encounters with technicians from many different countries, working under both private and governmental auspices.[10] But more about these people later.

After leaving the pleasant company of our Canadian cousin, we took the airlines bus to Flashman's Hotel, a second-rate Faletti's,

15

located in the cantonment area. It is another of those citadels for the growing foreign colony in Pakistan. Then we paid a courtesy call on the missionaries of Gordon College, an institution somewhat like Forman Christian College in Lahore; had dinner with a lonesome American engineer who was very generous with his precious American cigarettes; and the next morning hit the road in a Chevrolet station wagon for the last lap to Abbottabad, some fifty miles away.

It was a surprising trip. We had half expected the road to be at best a jeep track, but it was a "metalled" road, which is British-Pakistani usage for broken stone and cinders rolled down into a smooth surface. The only objection Americans could make to it was its English width. In fact, we found all the main routes in northwest Pakistan to be perfectly navigable by standard American cars despite their huge (relative) size. The road system is one of the great British contributions to the subcontinent. Parenthetically, it is quite feasible to drive from Karachi to Lahore across the arid Sindhi plains, although I was told that the trip is not pleasant. However, a motor trip from Lahore to Peshawar, such as we took later in the company of a very congenial and considerate ICA grain expert, is a very rewarding experience indeed, and, from the point of view of the prospective tourist who really wants to see the country, preferable to air travel.

On the last leg to Abbottabad, we had a good road, a competent driver, a sunny day, and two good companions. One of these was a Pakistani army officer in well tailored civvies returning to his post after leave. The other was an enterprising Pakistani business man from Karachi. He was a sales agent for Ovaltine, and he was going to Abbottabad to donate as much of his product to the Pakistan Olympic team (in training there) as it would care to consume. All he wanted in return was the right to advertise the fact that the team was using it. This encounter served to remind us that imaginative salesmanship is not an American monopoly. This salesman was a sportsman with a couple of tennis racquets in his luggage, a gentleman, and, like all educated Pakistanis we met, highly respectful of professors and learning. Later during his stay in Abbottabad, we enjoyed dining with him.

The trip took about two hours and a half. The road traverses the last few miles of the hot Punjab plain, and then it begins to climb. At approximately the point where the plains and the hills meet, we encountered a huge monument to a bygone British military action. In its loneliness, it only served to emphasize how completely dead the British Raj is today. When we asked our Pakistani officer friend about it, he simply shrugged his shoulders and smiled.

At last, twisting and turning upward from the plain to an altitude between four and five thousand feet, we came upon Abbottabad, which looked very attractive in its setting among the hills. We drove up to what was to be our home for the year, the Palace Hotel, its grounds a riot of flowers. We were put into a battered suite; had tea on the lawn with Mr. Ovaltine; received a punctilious courtesy call from the hotel manager, Durrani, who later became our friend; and then we assumed that our tourist days were over. But they were not, as it turned out.

We had arrived on September 15, and the college did not open until October 1. With no duties to perform until then, we had time to go on up to Nathia Gali and Murree.

Summer Resorts, Pakistani Style: Nathia Gali and Murree

Nathia Gali is about seventeen miles from Abbottabad, and Murree is twenty miles farther. But the distance stated in miles is most deceptive. The mountain terrain makes it at least twice that much. As I have said, the main routes in northwest Pakistan are suitable for modern automobiles, and, in a way, this is true of the Nathia Gali road. Cars and buses travel on it daily, except in the winter, but I would not like to drive it myself. We went by bus, and these mountain bus drivers are especially trained for the job by the Government Transport Service. They should be. Along the seventeen miles of the route, the road ascends from Abbottabad's 4,010 feet to Nathia Gali's 8,040 feet.[11] There are tight turns along sharp ridges all the way, for the road is carved out of the mountain sides. It is a comfort to know that, in theory at least, the traffic is only one way. It is supposed to flow alternately up and down, morning and afternoon, with barriers manned to make sure that nobody goes the wrong way at the wrong time. But, apparently, there are exceptions. It is nerve-wracking to come around a right-angle turn, leaning on six or seven thousand feet of crystalline empty space, and to meet another vehicle going the other way. Moreover, no road barriers can control the oxen and other hazards of the road, such as the hill folk on foot. The complete absence of any fences on the empty side is not conducive to peace of mind en route, either. Still, everybody was very calm on this trip; the driver didn't turn a hair; the local passengers didn't get excited; and the accident rate is something less than 100 per cent.

17

After an hour or so, we became as philosophical as the rest of our shipmates and concentrated on enjoying the views—one narrow valley after another full of tall, straight pines, villages perched everywhere in unlikely places, and every inch of available flat land cultivated carefully on terraces.

As we crawled upward to Nathia Gali with much whining of gears, it was hard to realize that, as the crow flies, Srinagar, the capital of Kashmir, was only seventy-five or eighty-five miles due east. In order to get there legally, however, one would have to go all the way back to Lahore, enter India at Delhi or Amritsar, and proceed to the Vale from one of those points. In the old days, one could go to Kashmir via Abbottabad, Mansehra, and Muzaffarabad, the capital of Azad ("Free") Kashmir, to the north of Nathia Gali. That is the route which the Frontier tribesmen took in 1947 when they invaded Kashmir. They got pretty close—as far as Baramula, about twenty-five miles away from Srinagar. Today, the border is closed, and it will, no doubt, remain closed until the Kashmir question is settled.

The village of Nathia Gali is sufficiently high, but the Pines Hotel, our destination, was even higher by a couple of hundred feet. To get there, we walked up steep gradients, followed by the coolies with the baggage. There are no elevators or escalators, but, like the bus trip, it was worth the effort. The Pines, an altogether fitting name, is a long, narrow, one-floor line of rooms stretching along the top of a ridge which commands a wonderful two-way view. We were told that, from a certain point nearby and on a clear day, one can see Nanga Parbat, one of the most impressive peaks in the whole Himalayan complex, a legendary peak which has a great hold on the imagination of all the people we encountered.

The Pines has no running water and no flush toilets, but, in the old-fashioned way, its staff of bearers and sweepers take good care of basic human needs like bath water and toilet facilities. Altogether, the hotel is comfortable and well run, with the best food we found in any hostelry in either India or Pakistan. Much of the credit for the general excellence of the Pines' service is due to its manager, Zaman Khan, an impressive looking Pathan whose headgear alternated between a very expensive golden-brown karakul Jinnah cap and a very colorful turban.

It was near the end of the season; not many guests were in residence; and therefore Zaman was able to pay more attention to us than he might have been able to do with a full house. He said that the secret of the hotel's good cooking was that he spent some time

18

every day in the kitchen himself and that he did not hesitate to eat with his own staff. He arranged a special Pakistani dinner for us one evening—very good it was, too. Then, at his suggestion, we rose very early the next morning and, under his guidance, took a walk to the Government House about a mile away. He wanted us to see the place and the view at sunrise. This establishment is a kind of summer White House reserved for only the highest officials. The "incharge" was proud of the fact that the governor general of All India had been in residence there in times past. It is in a magnificent location, and its grounds and gardens are beautifully kept. After a conducted tour of the house and its grounds (which evoked memories of the imperial glories of the British Raj), we were honored with the crowning touch: flowers, still wet with morning dew, presented to us by the staff gardeners who were justly proud of their work and its results.

Our fellow guests at the Pines in those last days of summer were representative of its clientele at the height of the season: the wife and son of an English engineer working for the Pakistan government at the ordnance depot of Wah, which is down on the superheated plains; the wife and children of an English meteorologist in the service of the Pakistan government in Peshawar; a Pakistani lieutenant-colonel of artillery with his charming, photogenic wife; and a couple of Pakistani business men from 'Pindi.

The English wives and children had been at the Pines all summer. Others like them had recently departed for their winter homes. It is traditional in India-Pakistan for those who can afford it to take to the hills in order to escape the heat of the plains, which at times goes as high as 115–120° Fahrenheit. Murree and Nathia Gali are the Pakistani equivalent of Simla and Darjeeling in India. Here, again, Kipling's tales of hill station society come to mind. From the health point of view, these summer sojourns are good for women and children; the husbands come for weekends when they can. But Nathia Gali, although a pleasant place, is not very exciting. There is little to do except to walk, look at the mountains, play tennis, and talk. A society without men has obvious limitations. The European women, therefore, lead a lonely and circumscribed existence, but it is better than enduring months of furnace heat. For this and other reasons, life in India and Pakistan is psychologically hard on expatriate Western women.

In some ways the Pakistani army officer and his wife were typical. He was a good example of the career officer, youngish, intelligent, very British in clothes, manners, and speech. Like many others whom we met later, he had done postgraduate work in his field in the United States—in this case, at Fort Sill. His wife, a handsome young woman, exemplified the more advanced army wives in that she was not in purdah; she was quite at home in mixed company; and neither she nor her husband objected when pictures were taken of her in her Pakistani clothes—and she made a lovely picture. In these respects, she was atypical of most women of good family and social position in the Frontier province.

During our stay in Nathia Gali, we made a one-day trip to Murree, about twenty miles away. Murree, in season, is a bustling place with all the stigmata of a mountain resort—hotels, tourist shops and new villas going up apace. In fact, we found it somewhat too resortish; we preferred Nathia Gali. The highlight of this excursion was a visit to the Murree outpost of the United States Information Service which was almost ready to close up for the winter. This outpost, basically a library which was quite good, was in the hands of an energetic and competent young Pakistani, obviously devoted to his job. We had a profitable coffee hour with him, and then went back to the Pines by bus. The trip did not seem to be so perilous this time.

The days passed quickly at Nathia Gali, and we left with pleasant memories of Zaman Khan, the hotel, the pines, the mountains, and the Government House splendors. But the most important result of our expedition was the acquisition of that peerless bearer (the Indo-Pakistani term for servant), Ali Khan. He was a little man, barely five feet tall. He lived in a nearby village, and during the summer he worked for Zaman Khan, who recommended him to us. After the Pines closed for the winter he came to work for us in Abbottabad. He is a story in himself which will be told in due course.

And so, a couple of days before the end of September, we returned to Abbottabad, where my wife set about the business of turning the hotel suite into a home. And when the college opened on October 1, we were no longer tourists; we were full-fledged members of a Pakistani community.

Chapter Two

Abbottabad

The Town

The town of Abbottabad lies in a large bowl surrounded by high hills. It is about fifty miles from 'Pindi to the south; it is approximately one hundred and twenty miles east of Peshawar, the gateway to the Khyber Pass; and Muzaffarabad lies forty-eight miles to the north. Geographically, it is one of the strategic points in northwest Pakistan. As already noted, the tribesmen marched on Kashmir in 1947 by way of Abbottabad and Muzaffarabad, an event which is still green in the memories of the people of the region. In Kipling's *Kim*, Abbottabad is mentioned in Chapter XIII as one of the probable and logical places where the enemy agents might have been able to enter India. Today the town is on the regular route taken by the nomad *powindahs* in their yearly treks from Afghanistan (where they spend the summer) to the plains around 'Pindi (where they spend the winter). They travel without interference on the part of the Pakistan government, and they are a fascinating spectacle on the roads in October and November.

To the north can be seen the snow-capped peaks of the Hindu Kush, dwarfing the intermediate high hills, and this perennial sight is one of the loveliest aspects of the town's location.

The name Abbottabad looks strange to foreign eyes, but actually it is very simple. Abbott was an almost legendary nineteenth-century English officer, and "-abad" is a standard suffix for "place of," akin to our "-ton," "-town," and "-burg." In Pakistan, facts are sometimes hard to come by and dates seem not to be really important, but the stuff of legend is everywhere. The townspeople did not tell me much about Abbott, but one story was that he had liked the site, that he had drained a lake, and had established the town on its former bed. An even better story says that Abbott was the father-confessor for the region; that he used to hold audiences for his troubled people; that, when individuals were in financial need, he would tell them to go and dig under a certain tree at midnight, and infallibly, money would be found when directions were followed. It's a fine story, and why should I take the bloom off it by research?

Abbott's town does not have much of the flavor of antiquity. It is a flourishing place of roughly five thousand inhabitants. It is the administrative seat of Hazara District, and therefore it has three different courts, three judges, a full complement of police, and a busy post office.

As for commerce, Abbottabad's bazaar (the generic term for shopping district and market) is big and bustling. Along with many food stalls and textile shops, the bazaar contains: three gas stations; a liquor store (an interesting phenomenon in this fundamentalist heartland); two sporting-goods shops; many chemist shops (drug stores to us); several photo studios (the Pakistanis are great camera fans); two Chinese bootmakers; many small restaurants and tea shops; local outlets for Bata shoes, Pfaff and Singer sewing machines, and standard typewriters; several different news stands and book stalls; two big movie houses; and a couple of bus stations. The local branch of the Bank of Pakistan is always busy because, in addition to the normal commercial business, it takes care of army payrolls.

On the institutional side, Abbottabad has a public hospital; a government college for boys—my college—and one for girls; government high schools for boys and girls; middle schools; a forestry research center and training college (which was to be moved to the University of Peshawar); a prep school called Lower Burn Hall, run by a Catholic order (the Mill Hill Fathers) ; and a church center for Protestant missionary activity, run by a cooperative American oganization called TEAM.

In the old British days, Abbottabad was a Ghurka training center, and the military tradition is still very much in evidence in the cantonment part of the town. There, along the clean, tree-lined streets, are the large and impressive houses of senior army officers and civil service officers—all carefully labeled with full titles on the gates; the headquarters of the station commander next to the post office; the cantonment "model" school; the cantonment reading room, which is a library open to the public, but rarely used; the adjacent cantonment public park, trim and well kept, which *is* used; the Frontier Force Regimental Mess with its outlying quarters for officers, somewhat like our motels; the Officers' Club with two fine tennis courts, swimming pool, and gardens; an old Anglican Church, now down to a congregation of five or six communicants, but physically still the dominant building of the community, set in its carefully tended grounds and gardens; and, directly across from this monument to an imperial past, the Palace Hotel, our home in Abbottabad.

Some three or four miles out of town is Kakul, the big and sprawling army training camp which contains, as one of its autonomous components, the Pakistan Military Academy, the West Point of Pakistan. Along the roads to Kakul are the indications of all the various functions which the modern army, that state within a state, must perform: reception centers for recruits; veterinary posts; an army music school then headed by a British officer; maintenance depots for tanks, trucks, jeeps, and command cars; EM quarters; NCO quarters; parade grounds; football and hockey fields; volleyball and basketball courts; canteens; hospitals and clinics; and unit signs to denote the headquarters of all members of the military family—the police, the engineers, the medics, and the like.

And out along the Mansehra Road, which heads across the valley floor to the snow-topped peaks of the Kaghan Valley and Azad Kashmir, are the rapidly increasing numbers of big bungalows built by the well-to-do who find Abbottabad a pleasant place to retire to or to spend summers in. These large establishments show that not everybody in Pakistan is poor. Another reminder of this fact is the presence, a few miles out of town, on the Mansehra Road, of Upper Burn Hall, where the older brothers of the lads of Lower Burn Hall, go to school under their English and Dutch Catholic teachers. Burn Hall, taken altogether, is often referred to as "The Eton of Paki-

23

stan." It is attended by Pakistani sons of privilege, by a scattering of pupils from such distant places as Thailand and Iran, and by an occasional English or American boy whose parents are temporary residents of Pakistan. Burn Hall has established its reputation in Pakistan by its success in preparing its students for the standard Cambridge examinations (something like our "college boards") the passing of which is one way of gaining entrance to Pakistani and British universities and colleges. Its graduates can speak and write English relatively well, an accomplishment which is still important in Pakistan for both career and snob reasons. The Eton-Harrow character of Burn Hall is further illustrated by its emphasis on sports. The institution's cricket pitch, hockey field, basketball court, tennis courts, and swimming pool are all—as the Pakistanis would say—quite "up to the mark."

Our friends in Karachi were right when they said that Abbottabad was one of the pleasantest places in Pakistan. What makes it so, in addition to the location, is its climate. It is true that we had a few days of hard rain in the early part of October, a rather depressing beginning to our stay, but they passed, and we enjoyed the luxury of playing tennis in the sun right up to the time we left for India in late December when the college closed for some two months. On our return, we were told that it had been a hard winter in Abbottabad: it had snowed three or four times! There is no central heating in Abbottabad, and 30° or 35° Fahrenheit in the mountains seems to be ten degrees colder. There are only small fireplaces to hold off the chill. In fact, for the average man, fuel of any kind is a luxury. However, chilly though it may be, the temperature never approaches zero. Conversely, it gets very hot in Abbottabad, over 100° on occasion, but it is a dry heat, quite bearable out of the direct rays of the sun, and the nights are always cool. On the whole, the climate is good.

The People

The District of Hazara is a transition area between the Punjabis of the plains and the Pathans of the mountains, and the people of the district are literally in the middle of a conflict between the two. This conflict, the product of historical regional developments, constitutes a continuing problem for the Pakistani state. The antagonism and suspicion which exist between Pathan and Punjabi is surprising to the foreigner. The situation is somewhat like that which exists in our own country between South and North. However, in Pakistan the tension is exaggerated by greater differences in culture, many of which can be accounted for by provincial or regional language loyalties.

The Pathan speaks Pushto (also spelled Pashto), a language which is markedly different from the Urdu which Pakistan is seeking to establish as the national language along with Bengali. Punjabi is not so sharply differentiated from Urdu; a Punjabi speaker can make himself understood to a person who knows Urdu whereas the Pushto speaker can not. The Punjabis (like the Sindhis) insist on the special qualities of both their language and their culture, as do the Pathans. They *feel* themselves to be different. The Pathans are proud of their separate language and of their tradition of independence, of the "fact" that they have never been conquered. They do not trust the Punjabis, and the Punjabis do not trust them. The plainsmen Punjabis tend to look upon the mountain Pathans as unlettered, unsophisticated savages, speaking of them with the same kind of condescension which, in our country, has been accorded American Indians or "hillbillies." This mutual antagonism is hidden beneath the surface, but it breaks out often enough to be disturbing to well wishers of Pakistan. For instance, Abbottabad college students, both Pathan and Punjabi, have made precisely the same charges to me against their co-nationals in almost precisely the same words: "What can you expect from a Pathan?" "What can you expect from a Punjabi?" "You simply can't trust any of them." I was told by my Fulbright predecessor at Abbottabad Government College that this rivalry had actually been the cause of a student strike at the institution a year or so before my arrival.

Since the Hazaris really belong to neither camp, they are in a difficult position. Many of the district people do not speak either Pushto or Punjabi, but a local dialect called Hinko. They have none of the strong local traditions nor the fierce regional loyalties of their neighbors, and it seems that they are not much respected by either. In my experience, the Punjabi or Pathan was affronted if identified as a Hazari, or even if asked whether he (in Pakistani idiom) "belonged" to the district.

The result of this situation is that Abbottabad has become a kind of minor-league melting pot, particularly in respect to language. It is only the person who has spent his whole life in one village who speaks but one language. The local merchants and professional men are likely to know several—plus English—as do the professional servants (the bearers) who get around Pakistan a good deal. Many

25

Pushto speakers know Urdu and some English; the Punjabis will speak Urdu and sometimes at least a little Pushto. The Pakistanis and the Indians are much better linguists than the Americans; they have to be. I think that, in the future, we too, will have to be.

Another way of putting the case is to say that there is no strong local stamp on Abbottabad. The community is made up of a primary core of merchants, lawyers, doctors, and their servants; of retired people on government pensions; of the military, a transient population—always different men in the same uniform; of the top civil service personnel, such as judges, district administrative officials, forestry officials, public works officials, and police officials, all subject to quick changes of assignment in accordance with basic government policy; of the faculties and teaching staffs of the educational institutions; of the inevitable sweepers and the laborers who do the dirty work of municipal and domestic housekeeping; of a small transient colony of Westerners, usually composed of British officers and War Department personnel, representatives of various American economic and military missions, a few foreign technicians, and a few American missionaries.

There is no real industrial proletariat in Abbottabad because there is very little industry. On any given day, most of the interesting people one sees around the court buildings awaiting their cases are from the country villages; they are not inhabitants of the town.

Abbottabad is too large and varied in its concerns to be labeled as a village, yet too small to be called a city. It is provincial and gossipy, a town very much like Winesburg, Ohio, Spoon River, Illinois, or Sauk Center, Minnesota. Transients aside, everybody knows everybody else and knows everything about everybody else. On the whole, it is complacent and contented. Cosmopolitan forces touch it in the form of the relatively advanced army officers and their wives, the tourists, the foreigners, and a scattering of Pakistanis who were educated overseas or in large cities, but the town remains largely unaffected. It is even more fundamentalist than the towns of our Bible Belt. In Abbottabad, the American frontier pattern is reversed: our frontier tended to be radical and unconventional; this Northwest Frontier Province, in its religion and culture, is highly conservative and conventional.

The Palace Hotel: A Study in Hierarchy

We lived in the middle of this community at the Palace Hotel, across from the Anglican Church, kitty-corner from the Post Office, with the Abbottabad Club a half-block down the road and the busy bazaar one block the other way. Behind the hotel, large bungalows were arrayed neatly in their compounds along another cantonment road which ran upwards toward the lovely hills.

The Palace was a two-story building shaped something like a Roman II. It had about thirty suites, almost evenly divided between singles and doubles. Basically, the hotel had possibilities. It was graciously set in gardens. The cloister-like front verandah commanded a fine view of the valley floor and surrounding hills, and the second floor sun-terrace commanded an even better view of distant snow peaks. The suites were large and particularly fine in the summer because of their high ceilings, screened windows (a luxury in Pakistan), and individual private porches or terraces. Moreover, the bathrooms had running *cold* water and flush toilets—things not to be taken for granted in Pakistan. The Club, for instance, did not have such facilities. Running *hot* water came on demand from the *bhisti*, or water carrier, who brought it in pails—often literally on the run.

The disadvantages of the Palace were the shabbiness and dirtiness of the furniture, the hard beds, and the absence of central heating. In cold weather, the guests huddled around small fireplaces in their rooms—and they paid extra for wood or "coals," expensive items. The greatest disadvantage was the poor quality and the monotony of the food, which was served in a morguelike, huge dining room, very depressing in cold weather. This is not merely an American opinion of Pakistani food; it was the unanimous opinion of our Pakistani friends as well.

The Palace had been owned by Hindus before partition. As a matter of fact, one of the first persons we met in Delhi at the Janpath Hotel told us that the Palace used to be his father's property. Only one sign of the former ownership remained: a bar on the second floor adjacent to what used to be a dance floor. Neither bar nor dancing area is used now. The bar has been converted into another room. There is no mixed dancing or public drinking in Abbottabad, except at the Officers' Club.

But, all in all, the Palace would bring a gleam into the eye of Conrad Hilton. It would not take much money to transform it into a really good tourist hotel, and the surrounding country would be worth any tourist's time and money.

As explained to us, there were two obstacles which prevented the Palace from being renovated. The first was that the government would lease the hotel to private operators only on a short-term basis, thus preventing any long-term development. The second was that the military had priority on its accomodations, and officers got special low rates. Therefore, it was always possible that, at a moment's notice, the entire establishment would be taken over for billeting.

However, we were never in danger of being evicted, although there was a constant flow of officers in and out of the hotel. The principal of Abbottabad Government College, Dr. Khan, had made very fair and reasonable arrangements for us with the management, so that we had a somewhat special semi-official status. Altogether, it was the best possible arrangement in Abbottabad, for we did not have to worry about the large staff of servants required to run a household in Pakistan; we were centrally located (almost *too* centrally located); and, even without an automobile, we had no transportation problem.

As for our personal quarters on the sunny side of the second floor, we had a large living room, a private terrace overlooking the town (a great asset in any weather, and wonderful in good weather), a large bedroom, a dressing room, and a bath. We had the hotel staff to serve us, and, above all, we had Ali from Nathia Gali to make us comfortable. We lived at the Palace from the end of September 1956 to May 1957. By that time, save for Amjad Ali, the manager of the local branch of the National Bank of Pakistan, we were the senior guests. At times, we three (Amjad, my wife, and myself) were the only guests.

During those months we became part of the hotel family. The current lessee of the Palace was a tall, grave, dignified, courteous gentleman of a well known Frontier clan, named Umar Khan Khattak. He was always gracious. The next in command was Durrani, the manager, proud of his descent from an aristocratic line which had originated in Afghanistan, which had furnished kings and noblemen for the region, and which still had numerous scions on both sides of the border. Durrani was an unusual chap. Active in local politics, he was highly regarded as an orator and student of literature. He was one of the speakers at the college on Iqbal Day, of which more later.[1] He commuted to and from the University of Peshawar, where he was taking a law degree. He lived in the hotel with his family, but he kept his wife in strict purdah, and we never saw her. He had a high respect for learning and letters (like Mr. Ovaltine), and we got along very well.

Next in line in the hotel hierarchy was an example of a familiar type in Indo-Pakistan, the subadar, an ex-non-commissioned officer of the old Indian army. We never knew his name; he was always simply "the subadar." A true Pathan, his native tongue was Pushto, and although he knew very little English, he was willing to learn. His chief job was to oversee the understaff of the hotel—the room bearers, dining room bearers, water carriers, and sweepers. He did not do this very efficiently. He seemed to spend most of his time on the verandah drinking tea. Nevertheless, he was an impressive and, on occasion, a decorative figure—six feet tall, ruddy complexion, blue eyes, military mustache, and handsome turban. A visiting foreigner might easily have mistaken him for the doorman, but that would have been a grave mistake; the subadar would have been insulted. He was the top sergeant, the intermediary between the commanding officers and the troops.

Directly under the subadar was the clerk (pronounced "clark," of course), a young man who was succinctly summed up by an American engineer friend of ours as the "Whine Boy." Next in rank came the two dining room bearers. Kuchal, the head waiter, a veteran of long service as a bearer, was particularly proud of his correspondence with one of his former masters, a high-ranking British army officer, and, in this respect, he was typical of many good servants on the subcontinent. Kuchal did his work with the pride of the craftsman; he sensed what we wanted before we spoke of it; and, above all, he had a keen sense of humor, with overtones of irony and satire, a rare thing in our experience.

In the late stages of our year, Kuchal fell victim to some form of creeping paralysis and had to retire to his nearby village. Sher Ahmad moved up from the second rank. Not quite as masterful as Kuchal in his control of the dining room, Sher Ahmad was a good servant and a good man. He had humor too, though his was not quite as penetrating as Kuchal's, but the most notable thing about him was his gentle face upon which the peace of God was indelibly written. There was a sweetness, a calm, a repose about him, which, I think, was the end product of his whole life and faith. I have seen just one other face like that in Pakistan: it belonged to an old man— Baba, as our Pakistani friends called him—who was the bearer for a rest house up toward the Kaghan Valley, a beautiful spot.

As a rule, the Pakistanis are pretty tough on servants, especially in public places. I am sure that they rarely, if ever, consider what the servants think about them—or what servants think about anything, for that matter. On the contrary, Americans may be a little too much at the mercy of waiters. If we are not worried about the waiter's reaction to us, we are worried about what other people will think of us in relation to the waiter. But, to the extent that this awareness stems from the proposition that servants are people, I'll take the American Plan. Over the months, Kuchal and Sher Ahmad seemed to drop their guard enough to give us some insights into their judgments on the clientele. On one occasion, we were even let in on a private joke at the expense of another bearer who, it developed, was called by his peers "The Buffalo."

We never could find out why he should be so labeled. He was not clumsy or awkward, nor was he big of build. We guessed that he did not belong to the right family group, for the bearers were very clannish. They stuck together, saw to it that their brothers and cousins or fellow villagers were employed, and they presented a solid front against the outsider. Good bearer jobs were scarce, especially since the departure of the British. The Buffalo was, in all likelihood, an outsider, and therefore a threat.

This solidarity was evident in the personnel of the underservants as well. When the time came for the monthly bucksheesh (the tips to the hotel staff), Ali, our personal bearer, always managed to remind us of the merits of the second cook and dishwasher. The water carrier, a simple, smiling individual, was one of the clan. When he fell ill one day, his twin brother took over, and we hardly knew the difference until they both appeared together later on. The old *mali* or gardener, a stalwart and picturesque figure with his henna-dyed beard and big purple turban, seemed to have a solid position in the inner circle of servants. So did the old sweeper who worked the opposite wing of the hotel; he found Memsahib's wrist watch on the hotel porch one night and promptly returned it. The young sweeper who worked our wing was accepted too, but the hotel roombearer for our wing was not accepted, in part because he was a thief and in part because he did not belong to the gang. And lastly, the *chowkidar* (the watchman), who spent his nights huddled up in his blanket-like robes on the hotel porch, appeared to be "in."

The hotel servants went out of their way to take care of us. During the winter, when the dining room was moved from The Tomb to a smaller suite which could be more easily kept warm, we were accorded the table nearest the fireplace. Kuchal and Sher Ahmad saw to it that special dishes were prepared for us. Since Memsahib could not stomach a steady diet of Palace curry, she got chicken and beef more often that the standard menu permitted. When they found out that we relied heavily on the custards and similar desserts for subsistence, special dishes of these dainties appeared on our table. The *mali* kept our suite filled with flowers in season; the *bhisti* used to knock regularly on our door at five-thirty in the afternoon to inquire whether we were ready for the hot bath water; the *chowkidar* used to remind us to keep our door locked, and was always ready to light us to our room late at night; and the young sweeper industriously raised a cloud of dust daily in our suite—under Ali's close supervision.

Surely one reason for all this attention was the monthly bucksheesh which we distributed to the staff, but the money was not the whole answer. We tipped a little better than the average Pakistani, but, under Ali's guidance, we did not throw money around like American millionaires. I think that the real reason for this devoted service was that we liked these men, saw them as individuals, and were interested in them. Basically, we were simply recognizing the universal dignity of man, not a difficult thing for Americans to do, for, to most of us, it comes almost instinctively. As a rule, Pakistanis do not do this with servants.

I know that it is very easy to confuse the professional behavior of servants with a personal interest in the master, which is as gratifying to the ego as incense is to a god. I know, too, that personal service of this kind, which Americans are largely unaccustomed to, can lead to a gratifying subconscious assumption of superiority—in short, to a Sahib Complex. Upper-class Pakistanis have it in full measure. I suggest that this pleasing state of mind is one of the major reasons why Westerners who have spent some time in Asia find it difficult to come to terms with life back home, and I further suggest that the absence of this kind of service is one reason why Pakistanis and Indians from the upper economic brackets are not necessarily happy abroad.

But, in spite of all these considerations, I still think that the hotel staff responded to us with unusual warmth because we responded to them as human beings engaged, as *we* were, in the common enterprise of living as best they could in a hard and uncertain world. I fear that the large promise of Islamic equalitarianism will not be borne out in Pakistani society until the masters recognize their inferiors as citizens of the cosmos and of the nation in practice as well as in theory.

Ali from Nathia Gali

The question inevitably arises: Why, with all these hotel servants, did we need Ali Khan as a personal bearer? I suppose that we could have done without him, but Abbottabad would have been far less pleasant. Furthermore, in our "position," we were rather expected to have a servant of our own. But more important than these considerations is the fact that having Ali was an experience in itself. We learned much from him, and an account of life with Ali will exemplify the life of the settled Westerner in Pakistan. It is nothing like the day-to-day routine of the average middle-class American household which simply cannot afford a servant other than a once-a-week maid. Ali served us as he had served Americans and English before us and as he will serve others in the future. He was a good example of the professional bearer, but better than most in his competence and in his scrupulous honesty. He preferred to work for foreign sahibs, and he rarely had trouble finding employment to suit him. He was our bearer from October 1956 until we left him on the railway platform in 'Pindi late in May 1957. During our two months' sojourn in India, Ali went back to his village near Nathia Gali on half-pay, a standard arrangement.

He was a little man, quick and graceful in his movements, and he generated more force than one expected from a person of his size. He wore a waistcoat, a long cotton shirt hanging to his knees, the full trousers, tight at the ankle, which are characteristic of Pakistani male dress, and either a turban built over a straw skull cap or the beret-like Gilgit cap. We never saw him with his head uncovered. He had worked as a bearer from the time he was ten years old. He had a wife and family back in his village—"two little she's and a little sahib," as he put it; there was a touch of gray in his hair; and we finally concluded from his work history that he must have been between thirty-five and forty years of age.

It was soon evident that Ali had status in his world. He was well known in Nathia Gali and Abbottabad. His fellow servants respected him. He was on a par with and perhaps superior to Kuchal and Sher Ahmad in the bearer hierarchy. In part, this prestige was due to the fact that he worked for us, the symbols of the rich and powerful United States and the potential sources of bucksheesh and chits (the written recommendations which all Pakistani servants carry in abundance). In part, his status derived from the fact that he was a pukka (genuine) Muslim with the moral authority which comes from a consciousness of rectitude. All this was reinforced by the indefinable power of his own personality.

What did he do? Literally everything he could think of. Ali did not need to be given instructions for each little task; he found his own work. When he walked in and took charge, the first thing he did was to assemble all our shoes and shine them. Every day thereafter he shined the shoes we had worn the previous day, and he whitened our tennis shoes after every game. He took inventory of all our clothes, and he kept track of every single handkerchief and sock. He invented a tie rack on which he hung up my ties neatly. He collected the dirty clothes and took them to the *dhobi* (the laundry man), carefully making out a list each time which he checked when the clothes were returned. He saw to it that our suits and outer coats were pressed regularly.

When we moved from our first suite to our permanent suite on the sunny side of the hotel, Ali supervised the operation, making sure that no article disappeared in the process. After the move, he carefully arranged all our clothes in two big wardrobes, and thereafter he kept them in order.

In the daily routine, Ali would appear at the appointed hour of the morning with bed tea, that pre-breakfast tea which is SOP in the hotels on the subcontinent, and a very sensible custom. At first, we took our meals in a crypt of a dining room, but, in cold weather, Ali insisted on serving most of our meals in our rooms before a fire, a much more pleasant arrangement. He seemed to like doing this despite the necessity for making many trips back and forth to the kitchen. Time made no difference to him. If we wanted to dine late after the hotel dining hours, Ali would make arrangements with the kitchen staff, would wait patiently, and would serve us in our suite at any hour of the evening upon our return.

After bed tea and before breakfast, Ali would bring the shaving things and a big mug of hot water to my bedside; it just would not do for Sahib to shave in a chilly bathroom standing up. When he observed that I liked a cigarette during the shaving ritual, cigarettes and matches were invariably at hand. He laid out my clothes for the day, meticulously matching up socks and ties, and he watched anxiously to see whether I approved of his sartorial judgment. He was pleased when I did, disappointed when I did not. Before my departure for the college, he used to look me over carefully to see whether I was up to his standards for the day. If it was raining hard, as it did from time to time, he provided a tonga for the trip, bargained with the driver for a fair price, and paid him.

Every day he reamed out my pipes. Once, when I was at the college, he noticed that all five pipes were on the shelf in the place he had made for them, and he realized that I did not have one with me. This would not do; Sahib surely was unhappy without a pipe. So he promptly hot-footed it out to the campus, stood outside my classroom windows until I noticed him, and delivered the briar as a matter of course. Another time, when it rained unexpectedly, he was in the same place with a raincoat, waiting until the hour was over. He did not have a raincoat and he absolutely refused to use one of ours at any time. It simply "wasn't done," as our English friends would say.

He bought and superintended the delivery of all the wood we used and made deals with the hotel sweepers for the wood and coals left over by other guests. For a rupee or two a month he contracted with the *mali* for all the flowers we could use. He did our household shopping in the bazaar, buying matches, pipe tobacco, tea, kerosene for the one-burner stove on which he used to boil our drinking water (he was very careful about this), cakes, rolls, and the like.

After the post-luncheon siesta (another sensible Pakistani custom), he served the ritual afternoon tea which he brewed himself, and he also served tea for our guests at all hours of the day, a custom observed *de rigueur* in Pakistan. No visit is complete and very little business is transacted without tea. When we had guests for dinner, Ali was in his glory. He served in our room, always with great interest and enjoyment. He had an insatiable interest in all our affairs. He seemed to identify himself with us completely, and I am sure that he listened to our conversations with careful inattention.

One of his greatest services was to get our letters mailed properly. In Pakistan it is wise to register any letter of even minor importance. It is charged by both Pakistanis and foreigners that post office employees, many earning no more than two rupees a day (about forty cents), have a habit of supplementing their incomes by appropriating stamps and then destroying the letters. Be it noted, parenthetically, that, on the whole, we had good luck with the mails. At any rate, we had most of our intra-Pakistan letters registered. The process takes a long time—what with excessively bureaucratic procedures, long lines of customers, a slow tempo of work, and the usual necessary gossip. Ali probably earned his keep at the post office window alone. It would have taken us untold man-hours to keep our correspondence alive.

Another important function which he performed was messenger service. There were very few telephones in Abbottabad. Social life is largely arranged by chits delivered by servants. Ali knew the town well, and he never failed to deliver messages punctually.

He also took upon himself the duties of doorman and receptionist. At first he arbitrarily screened our guests without our knowledge. If he did not deem visitors of sufficient importance to be admitted to the Presence, he sent them away with the curt statement that Sahib, or Memsahib, was sleeping or not at home. He had strong notions about the social hierarchy, and, after we firmly established an open-door policy, he used to register silent disapproval of some of our guests who happened to be students, or faculty colleagues, or local folk without exalted rank or station, or those who came too often. In this respect, he reflected not only the class consciousness of his own people, but also the attitudes of his former employers. Altogether, he had very little respect for most of his fellow nationals. Perhaps he was taking his revenge, subconsciously, for the manner in which they treat servants. Perhaps he simply enjoyed the exercise of a little power, an attribute not uncommon in servants and secretaries the world over.

At any rate, Ali would not work for Pakistanis (except Zaman Khan) if he could possibly avoid it. When our departure date approached, several of our Pakistani acquaintances expressed interest in hiring him, but he invariably said no.

I think he was genuinely puzzled by our accessibility, and I will never forget the tone of his voice when, upon being asked who was calling, he would answer scornfully, "Pakistanis." Once my wife tried to probe into this attitude, but Ali would not say much on the topic other than that Pakistani masters were "chinchy," which word we interpreted as meaning nagging, or, in our colloquial language, picky.

Ali loved to be the broker, the middleman, or the fixer. For him, the matter of getting a *dherzi* (tailor) to make a pair of white duck tennis slacks was an affair of high diplomacy, of bargaining and negotiation. Given a small domestic problem to solve, he was in his glory. Generally, he found good craftsmen, and he would oversee their every move. When we were getting a trunk ready to ship home, a major operation for the whole community, Ali arranged for two men to band it by hand with metal straps, an operation I did not think possible in Abbottabad. He also found an artist who painted our name on the trunk with fine artistic flourishes before an appreciative audience composed of almost the entire hotel household. Of course, all these subcontracts tended to build up his own power.

In Pakistan it is customary, for those who can afford it, to take a servant along on all trips by bus, rail, or automobile. In many cases it is necessary to take bedrolls along, inasmuch as rest-houses and

35

many hotels do not furnish bedding. This, with other necessary baggage, makes the total load considerable. Of course, no gentleman or lady ever carries so much as a small handbag. Under these circumstances, servants are very helpful indeed.

Ali made two such journeys with us: one to Peshawar for an educational conference after which we left for the winter vacation in India, leaving Ali to take the excess baggage back to Abbottabad; and the final trip to 'Pindi on our departure from Pakistan. Some hotels have quarters for servants as the famous Dean's Hotel in Peshawar does, but in 'Pindi our hotel did not. This did not bother Ali. As if it were a matter of course he spent the night sleeping outside our suite on the porch. On both occasions it was good to have him along.

And for all this service we paid sixty rupees a month, approximately twelve dollars. In addition, we paid five rupees a month for Ali's quarters in the servants' wing back of the Palace, and an extra three rupees a month for the rent of his charpoy (the rope cot-bed which is standard in India and Pakistan). Even so, we were accused, as are most Americans abroad, of overpaying him by ten rupees or so. With his salary, his power of contracting, his social position in the employ of a foreign Sahib, his expectation of a substantial bonus at the end of his term of employment (which he got and deserved), and his incidental windfalls of clothes, perhaps more important than money—with all these perquisites, Ali was an Aristocrat of Labor.

And what did we learn from him? In the first place, we got an insight into the grim battle for mere existence which is the lot of a vast majority of Pakistanis in the villages. The terrible inflationary spiral which plagues Pakistan as it does our own country was translated into graphic human terms by Ali in respect to the cost of staples in Abbottabad as well as in his native village: ghee, gur, gram, wheat, and the like. Then we learned the great social gap which separates the mass of Pakistanis from the relatively few at the top of the pyramid. We learned something of what Islam means in the day-to-day practices of a good and faithful Muslim: the obligations of charity; the ritual of prayer; the proper way to observe Ramazan, the month-long fast of Islam from dawn to dusk; the scorn of the true believer for those renegade Muslims who do not fast; the approval of the true believer for the deputy commissioner, who, during the days of Ramazan, shut down the cafés and restaurants of Abbottabad by executive fiat; the pride in the institution of purdah which prompted Ali to beam proudly and to say "Nice, Madam"

36

when my wife had a *burqa* made up to bring back to the United States; and the contempt which the pious Muslim has for thieves and cheats.

We learned that the good servant is not necessarily a sycophant; that he takes joy in his master's possessions and pride in his Memsahib's and Sahib's appearance; that he is essentially a craftsman who knows his job and does it well; and that he has no hesitation in suggesting to his employers what is right and what is wrong, particularly if they are foreigners.

We also learned a little bazaar Urdu, and we enjoyed some swordcuts of phrase in Ali's English. Once, in explanation of his delay in answering a call, he said, "Madam, coming—walnuts broking." He succinctly summed up his philosophy thus: "Lotta work—lotta happy." His universal phrase for a forthcoming interpretation or explanation was, "Madam, I show you." It was a great moment when Memsahib asked him the Urdu word for "tomayto." The answer came at once: "Tomahto." Upon leaving for the evening—he had a key to our suite—he would say, "I lock ups now." Referring to kindling for the fire, his phrase was, "A little wood morning time fixing." And a warm iron was, fittingly enough, "Little hot—little cold."

In India and Pakistan, there is very little belief in the Dignity of Labor, but we learned that, nevertheless, it was possible for men like Ali, Kuchal, and Sher Ahmad to achieve the dignity of man in their work. It is not mere sentiment which prompts the conclusion that, in fidelity to their own clearly understood values, these were among the best men we met in Pakistan. Their "betters" could learn much from them about living their faith and doing a job well.

Chapter Three

The College, the Faculty, and the Students

The College Itself

Abbottabad Government College, where I served for the academic year 1956–57 as a lecturer in English, was an institution made up of one large building, a faculty of twenty-four, and a student body of four hundred and twenty young men.

The building is just a few minutes of pleasant walking from the Palace Hotel—in our city parlance, about six blocks. Built at the base of some steep hills, it looks north across the valley floor to the far snow peaks, a view which, from the classroom, was always unexpected in its impact and grandeur and conducive to philosophical perspectives for lecture or discussion. The college grounds, cared for by a platoon of *malis*, appeared at first glance to be quite large and adequate, but closer inspection showed that they were cut up by ditches and hemmed in by roads, side roads, and lanes. Furthermore, the grounds were often pre-empted by water buffalo who exercised a kind of calm squatter's rights on the college grass, a pastoral reminder, almost as primordial as the mountains, of the eternal verities of man's existence. Keep off the grass? Not in Pakistan, for grass is life or death there. In fact, the college campus was somewhat like a village common.

The college boys could play badminton and volley ball on these grounds. Two basketball backboards had been set up—without nets or rims—and there was room to practice for some track and field events. But the boys did not have an adequate cricket pitch, hockey field, or football field. They had to rely on army facilities for these sports. There were two tennis courts adjacent to the student hostels downtown about half a mile away. Of course, there was no gymnasium; there are very few gymnasiums in Pakistan. Nearly all sports are played outdoors.

The college building was relatively new; it had been built in the early Fifties after partition. From the outside, it looked pretty good: a long, two-floor arrangement, with open galleries running outside the classroom doors. Bordering the galleries were two large, grassy, roofless courtyards which were often used for open-air classrooms. Although the college community thought well of this building, it was actually cheerless, uncomfortable, and highly inadequate. Undeniably cool in hot weather, it became instantly chilly, in fact, downright cold, whenever the sun was down or clouded over, or whenever it rained. The floors were stone, the furniture largely Spartan benches, and the lighting poor. In March, I found it wise to wear an overcoat while teaching. Most of my colleagues wore the traditional academic gown in the classroom, English fashion, and this added garment also served to keep them warm. I did not have a gown, but on state occasions, Dr. Khan lent me one of his.

The laboratories were barely adequate for basic instruction. I was told that the architects had simply overlooked the necessity for having sinks and faucets, necessary standard equipment, and that they had apparently not given a thought to the need for ventilation of the chemistry lab.

In these conditions, it was a wonder that any teaching could be done at all, but, with devoted zeal, the young science faculty conducted the great classic experiments and expounded classic concepts. These lecturers had tragically little chance to keep up with important recent advances in their fields, and research was simply out of the question.

The college library occupied one wing of the second floor. It was under the control of a former clerk, not trained in library science.

The library had a fair collection of basic works in various fields of learning, a collection which was reinforced by contributions from my Fulbright predecessor, Merle Akeson, from the Asia Foundation, from the United States Information Service in Lahore, and from myself. But, like most libraries in Indo-Pakistan, it operated on the closed door policy: the available books were kept in locked cases, and library circulation and library use were minimal. One reason for this sad situation was the fear of theft, a legitimate concern, and another was the examination system (to be discussed later) which tended to kill any student inclination to explore areas not required in the curriculum. However, the boys did read the daily newspapers and the magazines which were laid out on tables for their use.

The college had an assembly hall which was used often for various "functions." Every time there was an all-college assembly, benches had to be moved from the classrooms to the hall and then back to the classrooms again before instruction could continue.

One first-floor wing of the building was composed of the chief clerk's office, the principal's office, the bookkeeping office, and a faculty staff room.

Many of the things which are taken for granted even in our poorest country high schools or colleges would be considered luxuries in Abbottabad. Blackboards were hard to write on. The chalk was of the poorest quality. Maps and visual aids were practically nonexistent. Plumbing fixtures were installed, but the plumbing did not work, and the sweepers had to take care of the toilets in the age-old fashion. Furthermore, there was no central heating, so the college closed down in the middle of the winter. All in all, the college plant was probably the equivalent of a late-nineteenth-century American high school in a middling-sized town.

However, since the college is an outpost of learning on a primitive frontier, the mere fact of its existence is a striking phenomenon. In this respect, Abbottabad is comparable to Berea College in Kentucky: both institutions provide an opportunity for higher education in a mountain region for young men who otherwise would never get a chance. The Berea boys and girls are far more enterprising than their Pakistani brothers, but that is another story to be taken up later. The fundamental parallel holds.

The Teachers: A Gallery of Portraits

In this physical milieu, a faculty of twenty-four attempted to bring the light of learning to the young, or, to be more accurate, it

40

attempted to prepare the student body to pass examinations. This faculty was composed of the head, called the principal; a lecturer in economics, who was also acting vice-principal; four lecturers in English (including me); one lecturer each in Persian, Arabic, Urdu, and Islamiat; one lecturer in zoology; one in botany; two in mathematics; two in chemistry; two in physics; one in history; one in political science; one director of physical education; and three "demonstrators" (laboratory assistants) in various sciences. This list is in itself a profile of the college curriculum.

In Pakistan, the term "lecturer" denotes a specific rank in the educational system corresponding roughly to our senior instructor or, stretching it a bit, to our assistant professor. Actually, we do not have an exactly comparable rank; an instructor with tenure would be close. Fifteen lecturers on the Abbottabad faculty had M.A. or M.Sc. degrees. The demonstrators held at least bachelor degrees, and, occasionally, an M.Sc. as well. The members of the faculty were government employees, subject to transfer on short notice. A prime case in point is that Dr. Khan himself was transferred suddenly to Kohat Government College within a year after I left Abbottabad, much to his surprise and to mine. During my stay in the Northwest Frontier Province, lecturers were not yet considered "gazetted officers"; their colleagues in the Punjab were. The distinction is important: it meant that Frontier lecturers had an inferior social and economic status in the governmental hierarchy. Since West Pakistan was supposed to be One Unit, it was hard to understand why my colleagues should be discriminated against, and, when I left, they were agitating for equality. I hope they get it.

Lecturers at Abbottabad received salaries of something like three hundred rupees a month or approximately sixty dollars in American money. They could expect small increments and eventually a small pension, but most of them, although they were relatively young, had reached the end of the line. Chances for promotion were few. They were content, or at least resigned, to teaching the required curriculum to the end of their working days. There was little incentive for initiative in terms of salary, status, access to publications, or facilities for research. In consequence there was not much intellectual activity among the lecturers as compared with the almost compulsive, febrile intensity of American academics who produce learned articles, publish creative work, achieve eminence in professional organizations, or "do significant work in the community" in order to gain promotion or to become administrators. The explicit charge of intellectual apathy and laziness against the Abbottabad faculty was made to me by two of their own number, both of them respected by their colleagues. But my own observation was that, however true the accusation might be for the majority, some of the faculty taught with exemplary devotion to their disciplines and to their students.

The faculty in the abstract is not as meaningful as the faculty considered as individuals. Therefore, although it is not possible to give a biography of all twenty-four, I propose to give character sketches of those who, for one reason or another, struck me as being particularly significant.

The Angelic Doctor

Dr. Khan, that prince of principals and best of hosts, was not only the head of the college but its most interesting personality as well. In Pakistani fashion, I will set forth his full title as it appeared on his letterhead and on the sign posted outside his office.

> Professor, Major, Dr. Mohd Ihsanullah Khan, M. A., LL.B., (Allig.); Dr. Phil. (Bonn); Fellow of the Alexander Von-Humboldts Research Institute (Berlin), P.E.S.(I).

There is a good deal of biography in this sonorous roll call of degrees, ranks, and distinctions, and some important implicit social commentary as well. Dr. Khan held the official rank of professor, and there were very few professors in the whole Northwest Frontier Province. He held the rank of major at the Pakistan Military Academy, where he taught international relations and history before he took over as principal at Abbottabad Government College. He took the two degrees of Master of Arts and Bachelor of Laws and Letters at Aligarh University (usually spelled with one l) in the former United Provinces of north India (now Uttar Pradesh), the most famous Muslim institution of learning on the whole subcontinent. Aligarh was founded in 1877 in order to give Muslims a chance to compete with Hindus in the realm of higher education and in the civil services. At first, conservative in its political orientation, it followed a policy of cooperation with the British as the best guarantee of Muslim interests. Inevitably, it later became one of the centers of nationalist agitation against the British Raj, and in due course it produced many of the makers of Pakistan. The importance of Aligarh to the Muslim cause may be gauged by the fact that

Jinnah left a substantial portion of his fortune to it, despite the fact that, after partition, Aligarh was in alien territory.[1]

Dr. Khan, the only Ph.D. on his faculty, earned that degree at Bonn University in Germany where he specialized in Kant's philosophy. He spent several years in the Reich, completing work for his degree and getting out of the country in 1939, just in the nick of time.

The P.E.S. (I) stands for Pakistan Education Service, First Grade, and it means that Dr. Khan is a "gazetted officer" with a higher social and economic status than the rest of the faculty. More specifically, it means that the Doctor was invited to important functions to which his faculty was not invited.

Dr. Khan was then in his early fifties. A solidly built man, somewhat below average height, he had plenty of hair (like most Pakistani males), and very little of it was gray. He generally wore European clothes, and, on first meeting him, one might easily assume that he was a European because of his ease in the company of women, his continental, courtly habit of kissing a lady's hand on greeting and departure, and his engaging, sophisticated sense of humor which played, with keen perception, on the different ways of the world, East and West.

Nevertheless, the principal, for all his European experience, was a true Muslim Pakistani. He was proud of his Pathan heritage; his wife was in strict purdah (I never met her, but my wife, who did, reported that she was a charming and attractive lady), and he was also proud of his wife's descent from an aristocratic family of kings and warriors. Pakistani pride in family is comparable, it seems, to that found in England, Boston, Richmond, and Charleston.

He was a faithful follower of Muslim ritual, and he scrupulously discharged his obligations to his immediate family and to his numerous brothers, cousins, nephews, and nieces—family loyalty being a prime characteristic of Pakistani life. In his social attitudes, he took for granted the existing hierarchy in which he occupied a secure place. When he entertained us, as he did with gracious hospitality, the other guests were likely to be the highest ranking local military officers, senior judges, top civil service officers, the local MLA (Member of the Legislative Assembly), leading members of the bar, Father Scanlon (the head of Burn Hall school where the doctor's sons were students), and some medical doctors. Members of the college faculty were not much in evidence at these gatherings.

The fact that Dr. Khan spent some years in Germany is not wholly accidental. There is a strong affinity between Germans and

Pakistanis, and, in many respects, Dr. Khan and his peers in the Northwest Frontier Province were quite like antebellum Junkers.

Although the principal did not see very much of his faculty socially, it is not to be assumed that the faculty resented this; they did not. They liked and respected their head. In the words of one lecturer, his treatment of the staff was "angelic." However the principal was more concerned with the inner meaning of Immanuel Kant and with Islamic apologetics than he was with the practical details of college administration, concerns which also did not lower his prestige with either the community or his staff. His easy-going absent-mindedness was thought to be quite in keeping with his primary vocation. He was a philosopher, a professor, and a Ph.D., and they were all fond of him, including his former students at the Pakistan Military Academy. He has a formidable bibliography of learned articles, and any serious student of Islamic apologetics or of East-West intellectual relations would do well to consider his work.[2] Since my return to America, he has written me that he was recommended for a professorship in philosophy at Peshawar, but the budget for the university was cut and he was, therefore, not appointed. This is a familiar story in the United States as well as in Pakistan.

The Old Guard

From the point of view of Islam, the *raison d'être* of Pakistan, the most important group of the faculty were the four lecturers in Persian, Arabic, Urdu, and Islamiat. To know them well would have been to know the psychology of the nation from the inside. Whereas most of the faculty wore European-style clothes, these four men always wore the national dress. Three of the four sported quite impressive beards, and these three were generally suspicious of Western ways and Western values. As a group, they were gentlemen of the Old School, though not necessarily old in years. Unfortunately, an academic year of nine months is not sufficient time in which to break down the cultural barriers which prevent understanding. Moreover, two of the four did not speak English, and I did not speak Urdu. Still, we got along pretty well by virtue of exercising mutual courtesy, which in time became not merely polite gesture but the index of genuine liking—at least on my part. I came to know one of them, the lecturer in Urdu, Saghir Ahmad Jan, well enough to realize how much I did not know about the others and what they stood for.

Saghir deserves special attention for many different reasons. Physically, he was a tall, well built man in virile middle age, striking in his frock coat, Jinnah cap, and well kept mustache. He came from the University of Lucknow, a region where the purest Urdu is supposed to be spoken. He had remained in India after partition, but he was not comfortable there. He felt that a Muslim had little chance for advancement in the Indian university world. Therefore, he had cut his roots and migrated to Pakistan, a move which meant considerable sacrifice for him and his family. He had received some help from the Pakistan government which provided, at a reasonable rental, an Abbottabad home that formerly belonged to a Sikh or Hindu, and he had made peace with his life as a lowly lecturer in a government college. His attainments as Urdu scholar and poet, his conscientious performance of his teaching duties, and his quietly profound devotion to his faith all combined to make Saghir Ahmid Jan a highly respected member of the college faculty and community.

We got to know him better than his colleagues in Persian, Arabic, and Islamiat because he was our tutor in Urdu, a chore he undertook at the invitation of Dr. Khan. His own English was better than he thought it was, and, although his two students, my wife and I, did not learn as much Urdu as we might have (my wife did better than I did), Saghir taught us a good deal more than language. He prepared his lessons for us carefully in his own handwriting, and these lessons would have made quite a good little manual. Through him, I got some insight into the workings of Urdu poetry. He explained a couple of his own poems, which were distinguished for their concern with the metaphysical question of identity: "Who am I—who is this Saghir?" In contrast, most of the other Urdu poets I knew in Abbottabad (almost every literate Pakistani is a poet) dealt with love and nature in terms of late nineteenth-century sentimentalism.

Then too, though deeply convinced of the validity of Islam as a whole way of life, he had more intellectual curiosity about Western culture than most of his colleagues. He asked interesting questions, he listened to the answers, and he had some humor.

Saghir considered his task as our tutor to be a religious-ethical obligation, and he discharged it in that spirit, though he never tried to convert us to his faith. He is one of the relatively few persons I have met anywhere—Christian, Jew, Muslim, or whatever—who seemed to live his faith entirely.

The Young Guard

From the academic point of view, it was surprising to discover that, on the whole, the scientists were probably the strongest segment of the faculty. Despite the lack of adequate resources already commented on, they did pretty well in difficult circumstances. As a group, they were young, a significant fact in itself.

There was Manzur-ud-din, a physicist, the son of a former registrar of the University of Peshawar. His father, now retired to Abbottabad, was spending his days translating English scientific works into Urdu. The whole family was unusual. Manzur's wife, herself college-trained, taught at Burn Hall Lower School with my wife; his sister, an M.A. in political science, taught in the local government girl's college. At tea in their home, we found that the women were not in purdah, a notable exception to the prevailing rule on the Frontier. Manzur was one of the most conscientious teachers on the faculty. He was also the "incharge" of the college cricket team.

Another young scientist was Hamid, the chemist. He had degrees from a missionary college and from the University of the Punjab. He had done a little publishing in his field, a rare occurrence on that faculty; he was curious about the philosophical meaning of the English poetry he had read during his undergraduate days; and, like most Pakistani academicians, he had hopes of going abroad for higher study. He was one of the few among the faculty who permitted his wife, a charming and intelligent girl, to be seen in the company of the visiting Americans.

A third example of the young scientist group, modernist in their outlook though Muslim through and through, was Afzal Mirza, another chemist, a sensitive young man described to us as having come from a good family in Lahore. A poet in his own right, Afzal took part in the *mushairas*, those poetry symposia which are an important part of Pakistan's cultural life. He was much admired by his students, and, in just one year, he had so impressed his colleagues that he was elected secretary of the faculty. Unlike most of his co-workers he had a vital and informed interest in both world and Pakistani politics, and his attitude was far less defeatist than the faculty norm.

The case of John Khattak, a demonstrator in botany, highlights a pressing problem in both India and Pakistan: how to make good use of people who have received advanced technical training overseas. Khattak spent two years in Australia at government expense, studying food technology, a field of considerable importance to Pakistan which, in the Montgomery and Peshawar orchard districts, has great potential in the production of canned fruits and jams. When he returned to his homeland, the best he could do was to get a job as laboratory assistant at Abbottabad Government College—not even a lecturer's post. One of his responsibilities was to oversee the college gardeners.

Khattak was a good man, well trained, well mannered, loyal to his country—altogether a superior citizen. His skills were badly needed. Nevertheless, in spite of all his efforts to get a position in which he could use his training, it was over a year before he achieved any success. At last, he was hired under the joint auspices of the government and private enterprise to work at his speciality in Peshawar. Khattak was lucky at that. There appears to be a waste of high-priced, foreign-trained talent in both India and Pakistan because these countries have not established a clear policy to deal with the problem. An obvious reason for this state of affairs is the hierarchy in education and civil service. That is, the established officials obviously do not want interlopers to supersede them or to become their superiors. In consequence, returnees are often expected to take positions which they consider to be beneath their merits, like that of the botany demonstrator, for instance. In the long run, what happens is that returnees go into private employment; or they migrate to other countries, thus depriving their own country of their talents; or they lose their skills and become rusty and inefficient during the long waiting periods; or, perforce, they take work in fields unrelated to their training. In the end, they often become disgruntled, unemployed intelligentsia, and, perhaps, potentially dangerous.

This situation should be a matter of prime concern to our own government. Under various programs, we are educating numbers of students from India or Pakistan, partly or wholly at our expense, but there is little point in this training unless there is some assurance that it will be properly utilized when the trainees come home. We saw much of Khattak during his sweating-out period, and his account of the stresses and strains he experienced was illuminating.[3]

Outside of the ranks of the scientists, two other young men warrant special notice, the lecturers in history and political science. Arif, the historian, had an Indian background. Like Saghir, he had deliberately cast his lot with Pakistan. Arif's father was a lawyer, and the son had been expected to follow his father's profession, but Arif had quietly decided that his country needed teachers more than it needed lawyers. This decision probably cost Arif a good deal in terms of social prestige and economic status, and I have no reason to doubt that he was motivated by a sincere idealism. Surely he had the brains for law.

A personable young man, he taught modern history, concentrating

47

on the Islamic world and the subcontinent of Indo-Pakistan. The curriculum also required that he teach a couple of units in the American Revolution and the American Civil War, both of which interested him. He invited me to lecture to the History Club and to his upper classes in these subjects. Since we also had a mutual enthusiasm for tennis (he was the "incharge" of the college tennis club), we had considerable common ground, and we spent much time discussing these varied topics.

As might be expected, Arif, too, was fiercely devoted to Islam. He had a cordial dislike for the British, and he viewed the Indians with scorn and contempt—particularly for their alleged cowardice in war. He never called the neighboring country *India*; to him, it was always *Bharat*, a standard reference in the Pakistani vocabulary and in the press which seemed to connote a sneer for reasons I am not quite sure of, although there is nothing intrinsically derogatory in the term itself. This insistence on the use of the word "Bharat" may be in part the result of a desire to point out that India historically comprised both nations. Its employment by passionate Pakistani nationalists emphasizes once more the need of a convenient, neutral, objective term for the whole subcontinent, considered merely as a geographical unit. It will be noted that I have been driven to use the awkward terms "Indo-Pakistan" or "subcontinent." Ian Stephens has suggested the term "Delkaria," derived from the first syllables of Delhi and Karachi, but it has not gained any acceptance.[4]

Paralleling Arif's feelings about "India" and "Bharat" was his resentment of the term "memsahib." I judge that his reaction derives from associations of this form of address to a lady with the British Raj. At any rate, he insisted that Ali our servant, should say "begum" instead, but Ali was not having any part of this; to him, my wife was "memsahib."

During our frequent discussions, in which my wife regularly took part, Arif inevitably seemed to cover much the same ground. He constantly repeated the principle (never, of course, denied by us) that Islam was not merely a religion but a whole way of life. He defended the Muslim social patterns governing the position of women and seemed sceptical of the worth of Western patterns in this area. And he insisted almost daily that United States aid to Pakistan must be given on the basis of equal partnership between the two nations, without strings. This reiteration implied criticism of our foreign policy and our foreign aid programs. I was always willing to face up to the criticism, but, when I asked him to spell out just how we were

Street Scene in Abbottabad: sugar shops in the bazaar.

Memories of the Indian "Mutiny" of 1857 at Lucknow: ruins of the Residency, British stronghold during the siege, preserved as a park. The tonga taxi is typical.

Pakistani Summer Resort: father and son at Murree in the mountains. Note the differences in dress between the generations.

undermining the sovereignty of Pakistan, he had no specific answers. I finally concluded that the constant iteration of "equal partnership" was an emotional shibboleth stemming from a heartfelt nationalistic yearning for self-sufficiency and economic independence, two things which are, in fact, regrettably nonexistent and unlikely to be achieved in the near future.

Arif's way of looking at Pakistan-United States relations represents a widely held point of view in respect to the common denominators which tend to bind the two nations together: the United States has a democratic philosophy; so does Islam. Russia is atheistic; true Muslims can never be communists. In contrast, Americans are believers in the Book, or, at least, in *a* book, the Bible, just as Muslims believe in the Koran. Therefore, we are brothers under God.

In his emphasis on Islam as a total way of life, Arif gave me the feeling that he, like many of his co-nationals whom we met, surely believed what he passionately and earnestly said, but I also divined that he simply had to believe in Islam—that, without it, there would be nothing in his life, or in his nation's life, to give meaning to existence. This uncomfortable and desperate state of mind is, in part, also the consequence of Arif's thoroughgoing disgust with the political situation in Pakistan at that time. It amounted to political nihilism. It was expressed from *outside* the situation, not from the *inside*, and it meant that Arif, for all his idealism, had removed himself from the political process. On the grounds that there was nothing the individual citizen could do about politics, he seemed to shrug off personal responsibility for it. Politicians, to him, were "those people," as if they were strangers operating in another world. For all his fine qualities, for all his manifest devotion to his religion, this lack of faith and interest in the political process was one of the saddest phenomena I encountered in my whole Pakistani experience. Arif was all too typical of the Pakistani intellectuals we met, and I have stressed his scorn, contempt, and resentment of "politicians" because these emotions produced a disposition to settle for the "strong man" who will clean things up. As might be expected, Arif had great admiration for Nasser. He pointed out to me that Nasser had consistently rebuffed the Pakistani government, but that the Egyptian leader had with equal consistency corresponded directly with individual Pakistanis and organizations which had contributed to Egyptian relief or which had expressed their support of him—over the heads of their government. As Arif put it, this was deliberate policy, and he thought it a sagacious one.

There is one more important point to be made about him. Arif had no patience with the mullahs, the lay religious leaders of Islam who command strong support among the common people. Some mullahs may be compared to the nonconformists, those dissenting preachers of seventeenth-century England, or to backwoods preachers in the United States, men who are proud of the fact that they are unlettered and that they know only one book, The Good Book. Arif had something of the same fierce scorn for these preachers which is characteristic of Samuel Butler and Jonathan Swift in their corrosive satires on religious fanaticism. To him, the mullahs were ignorant men and dangerous in their ignorance. He also scorned *pirs*, or holy men, living or dead. He held that belief in or support of such men was contrary to the Koran, a view that has considerable justification in that the Koran does not allow for any intermediaries between God and man and in that the Prophet refused to permit himself to be worshipped. Nevertheless, much to my surprise, *pirs* do flourish in Pakistan, and, both living and dead, they occupy somewhat the same position that saints do in the Catholic Church.[5]

Arif's colleague, Zahurul Islam, the lecturer in political science, was the sole representative of East Pakistan on the Abbottabad faculty. As such, he was in much the same position as a man from the deep South would be if he taught in a small Minnesota college. The faculty liked Zahurul well enough; he was a youth with a perpetual smile, always warmly polite and eagerly interested in his fellows. But I got the feeling that they did not have much respect for either him or his native region. He would have been a very lonesome young man indeed but for his family who had migrated to Wah, not far from Abbottabad. He felt, with reason, that his colleagues did not understand either him or East Pakistan, and he was very pleased indeed when I came back from Dacca, after the winter holiday, and gave a favorable report of his homeland. He was also grateful for my sympathy and understanding. The relations between Zahurul and the rest of the faculty illustrate the difficulties of keeping a nation together when its two halves are separated by a thousand miles of alien territory and by widely differing languages and cultures. As I saw it, the only binding forces were Islam, anti-Indian feeling, and the English language.

More specifically, while I was in Pakistan, some politicians of the Eastern Wing made such extreme claims for regional autonomy that it was easy for their Western brothers to suspect them of secession sentiments. Zahurul was made the butt of such charges in

faculty staff-room discussions, partly in jest, partly in earnest. Zahurul used to deny these charges indignantly, and at the same time he
tried to convince his colleagues of the necessity for some measure of
local freedom of action for his distant and isolated Bengali-speaking
compatriots.

And what about my own English department? At first we were
four, but after "Ti" Farooq, a solid, hard-working chap, was suddenly
sent to Mardan Government College in mid-year, we were three doing
the work of four. The head of the department was F. D. Mahmood,
generally known simply as "F. D." He was a little man, very proud
of his warrior Rajput ancestry. He had a facile wit which was often
sharp and penetrating. He wrote short stories in Urdu, and he also
wrote a wonderful English purple prose which, though not a very
precise instrument of communication, was nonetheless interesting
and impressive in its way, for it married the excesses of Oriental
flowery rhetoric with the grandiloquent sentimentality of the nineteenth century. F. D. was a campus character, a Mr. Chips with an
edge. His faculty colleagues enjoyed his conversation, and his students liked him immensely. So did I; he took good care of his foreign
visitor.

The junior member of the department was Qasim Raza Rizvi, an
up-and-coming representative of the younger generation (F. D. represented the older). Rizvi had taken an M.A. in English at the University of Karachi, a degree distinguished by the fact that it had
included a paper, a unit of work, in American literature, an innovation
in Pakistani graduate study. In fact, Rizvi was the only Pakistani
teacher I happened to meet anywhere who had had any work in this
field. Moreover, Rizvi had a good deal more intellectual curiosity
than most of his colleagues. He read widely and thoroughly, and he
did not hesitate to ask questions. Like all Pakistani students in literature, he was very much interested in T. S. Eliot and in criticism.

Rizvi was a big-city product, and he was not particularly happy in
Abbottabad where cultural activity is not exciting. Like so many of
his generation, he had hopes of going abroad for more graduate work,
and I did what I could to help him. He worked hard and consci-
entiously with his students at Abbottabad, his first teaching position.
But, like Zahurul, he was a stranger in the area, and he was personally and intellectually isolated. I think that the college did not ap-
preciate his solid worth. Dignified in his bearing, independent of
mind, courageous in standing up for his rights in the face of authority, Rizvi was one of the most impressive young men I met in Pak-

51

istan. At last report, Rizvi had moved to the Pakistan Air Force Academy.

A Review of the Gallery

Here, then, is a gallery of selected portraits of the Abbottabad faculty. In it are some representatives of the older order whose tendency is to ignore the modern world insofar as that is humanly possible and to attempt to live from day to day according to the time-honored values of the Islamic tradition. But in it are also younger men, the scientists, plus Arif, Zahurul, and Rizvi, who are no less fundamentally committed to Islam and Pakistan, but who attempt consciously or unconsciously, either to harmonize Islam with the modern world or conversely to harmonize the modern world with Islam.

However much this faculty differed as individuals, they had a large common denominator. I found no radicals in politics, economics, or religion. I found none of that agnosticism or cynicism about religion which, back in our Twenties and Thirties, was incarnate in Mencken or Nathan and which, in the Fifties, rests upon intellectual scepticism of the new Fundamentalism preached by Billy Graham or the Wide and Smooth Path to Salvation preached by Norman Vincent Peale. It is true that mullahs and *pirs* disgust Arif and that Afzal, Hamid, and Manzur seek to know and to teach more science, but basically they are all conservative Muslims. As members of the middle class, they are bourgeois in their outlook on economics; the Communist panacea is not congenial to them. Intensely nationalistic, they are, nevertheless, fed up with an inefficient and bureaucratic government, but the result psychologically is not dynamic but defeatist. Intellectually, with honorable exceptions, they tend to apathy. They do not use the library resources much more than the students do. They teach their classes; they take care of their tutorial groups (each lecturer has charge of one) ; they do their duty as "incharge" of various student clubs and athletic activities; and they go home.

Socially, it seemed to me that the faculty did not have much to do with one another. As always, individual friendships were struck up, but, outside of the general college faculty meetings and "functions," there was not much social intercourse. That regular alternation of dinner parties which is so characteristic of the American college or university social routine was missing. One reason for this state of affairs is the institution of purdah. Faculty men may be close friends, but they will rarely, if ever, see one another's wives.

As a visiting professor from America accompanied by my wife, I was in a special position; an exception could be made for us. But in the whole academic year, I met the wives of just four of my colleagues: Arif's, Mahmood's, Manzur's, and Hamid's. My wife met the principal's wife, the economist's wife, and the botanist's wife in segregated circumstances, either at women's teas or in their own homes while I remained with the men. The closest friends of Hamid and Manzur may have been admitted to the company of their wives, but I am not sure of this, and I doubt that Mahmood or Arif ever permitted their begums to meet their colleagues. The rest of the faculty certainly did not.

A man with a wife and family could live a full life in the fortress of his home, but social life for the unmarried young man in Abbottabad was a drab and lonesome affair. They literally never had a chance to talk with women of comparable background.

For instance, Zahurul, Rizvi, Afzal, Khattak, and the boyish demonstrators were bachelors. Rizvi had charge of one student hostel, a dormitory, in return for which he got his quarters and meals. The others lived in cheap hotels or in cheap rooms. Barred from feminine society, what did they do with their leisure time? One might predict an outburst of feverish intellectual activity under such circumstances, but I saw no signs of this, with the possible exception of Rizvi. They had tea with each other, they went on walks, they played badminton, they went to the movies, they wrote letters, and they called on us at the Palace Hotel. In similar circumstances, in our own country, the young instructors almost certainly would have had access to the civilizing influences of their married colleagues' households. In Abbottabad, the women's world was largely denied to the men, and the men's world was denied to the women.

Another startling contrast with the small American college town and its faculty life was the absence of any community activity. Abbottabad had no Rotary Club, no parent-teacher association, no civic improvement club, no little leagues in sports (nor their adult male equivalents), no church groups, no boy scouts or girl guides, no young people's associations, no dramatic club, no teachers' association, and relatively little political activity.

The town did have a unit of the All-Pakistan Women's Association, in its potential a very important organization, but locally it was neither very big nor very active. There was a cultural club, but it conducted few programs; when it did give a "function," Afzal and Rizvi participated. And there was the Officers' Club with its fine facilities, but the teachers, not being "gazetted officers," were not eligible for membership, and furthermore they could not afford it.

Neither the town nor the faculty had what we would call "civic consciousness," and, apparently, no conscience about its lack either. That complex of voluntary associations for one cause or another, involving both women and men, which is so characteristic of our own society was notably missing. Such clubs cannot exist in Pakistan with women segregated as they are. In our country, these clubs and associations have provided a very good apprenticeship in citizenship and in parliamentary procedure for millions of our citizens, and I doubt that there will be much progress at the grass roots level in Pakistan until such movements as APWA[6] develop similar patterns of group cooperation.

At any rate, whatever the causes, the faculty, outside the college, was largely atomized; it exercised no leadership in the community; and therefore its total life was the poorer.

The Students

The student body of Abbottabad Government College totaled four hundred and twenty boys. The figure, of course, varies from year to year. It increases slowly, but not as fast as one might expect, considering the fact that the college is a badly needed outpost in a new nation with an appetite for education and a fast-increasing birth rate.

The boys struck me as being very young, but the ages of Pakistani males are difficult to determine from their appearance. The young may be older than they seem and the old often look younger than their years. The matter of age is also complicated in that, quite literally, many people do not know how old they are. Pakistan is not as careful about birth certificates as we are. However, it is reasonably accurate to say that, taken as a group, the age of these students was a year or two under American college averages, that is, from fifteen to nineteen as against our seventeen to twenty-one. The exceptions to this generalization are likely to be at the older end of the scale, not the younger.

The students may be divided into approximately equal groups: day scholars whose parents live in Abbottabad or in neighboring villages, and boarders from more distant points who live in the hostels. The day scholars either walk or ride bicycles to college; some of them, I was informed, pedal ten miles a day from their villages. On rare occasions, the son of one senior army officer was delivered to

54

the door in an automobile, but the automobile is a highly restricted luxury in Pakistan.

The hostels, situated in the center of the town, some four or five blocks away from the college, were generally regarded as disgraceful by all concerned. They were long, two-storied affairs which provided rows of cubicles (and very little else) for the inmates, two to a room. There was a good deal of grumbling about them, but nothing much was done about it. Some of the boys ate the hostel food; others, better off financially, patronized the local restaurants which, at best, were not very good. The quarters and the food together explain and justify the many absences due to "fever" (in Pakistani usage, a term which seems to denote generically almost all illness). These dormitories were under the supervision of resident faculty members, like Rizvi, who were responsible for the behavior of their charges.

One hostel, though not having any toilet facilities which we would consider adequate, had two tennis courts under the supervision of a professional, or "marker," who was paid thirty chips (approximately six dollars) a month. The marker, an able player, ran a sports store on the side; he had to.

From the American point of view, it seems strange that Pakistani students do not work their way through college. Things may be different in Karachi and Lahore, but, in Abbottabad, they would never think of doing so. Their culture does not permit this pattern which is such an integral part of the American way of college life. So far as I could see, the students did no physical work at all. Our notions of the dignity of labor are completely alien to the Pakistanis; work is for "peons," not for educated people. It follows, then, that however poor the students and their families were, they were at least marginal members of the middle class economically and socially—and many of them were very poor indeed. A few others were, by Pakistani standards, very well off.

The students were generally the sons of local mechants, professional men (doctors, lawyers, and college faculty), government officials, army officers, landowners from neighboring villages, retirees in Abbottabad, and *zamindars* and *jagirdars* (very large landowners) from more distant points, including wealthy, ruling families in Gilgit, Chitral, and Hunza, those fascinating mountain enclaves up on the Russo-Chinese border. Not a single student at the college was the son of what we would call a working man. In Pakistan, the sons of working men—farm or industrial workers—do not go to college.

For two reasons the students had much leisure time: they did not work for a college living, and, aside from attending classes, they paid little attention to academic work until examination time. Like many of their American counterparts, they spent their time on sports and on extracurricular student activities.

Student Sports

The college had a lively sports program. It differed from the American pattern in that it rested on individual choice, was not as highly organized as ours, and spectator interest was minimal. The college fielded teams in cricket, soccer football, and field hockey. It also sent some boys to Peshawar to compete in track and field (called "athletics") against other boys from colleges affiliated with Peshawar University. The two most interesting contests I saw were a football game against Swat and a cricket match played against Upper Burn Hall. The Swat game was notable because the students and faculty turned out in comparatively large numbers to see our side soundly trounced, and the Burn Hall match was considered important because our boys did pretty well against a side which made cricket a specialty. If the college had an athletic hero, he was the wicket keeper of the cricket team who was selected as a member of the Peshawar University squad, made up of players chosen from affiliated colleges. This lad, one of my favorites because he worked hard in the classroom too, wrote a graphic paper for me about his adventures on a trip to Sind University where the Peshawar University team was "robbed" of victory by biased officials—quite in the American tradition. For him, this experience was the equivalent of a trip to the Rose Bowl.[7]

Aside from these team sports, a few students played tennis on the college courts with Arif and me; more played badminton on courts set up on the college grounds; and volley ball was popular by fits and starts. The hard-working director of physical education had erected the basketball backboards I referred to earlier, but no games were played during my tour of duty; no nets, no basketballs. Table tennis was also a popular game.

One of the duties of the physical education director was to keep a record on each of the students and to measure their performance on certain standardized tests.

The bases for student activities other than sports were the Student Union, the tutorial groups, and clubs founded on common interests in subject matter, such as the Economics Club, the History Club, the Chemistry Club, and the like.

The Student Union

Of these, the Student Union was the most important. In structure, though not in operation, it was comparable to the Oxford and Cambridge student unions. It had an executive board representing the four classes—in Pakistan called first, second, third and fourth years rather than freshman, sophomore, junior, and senior. These executive posts were eagerly sought after, and campaigning was hard and hectic. Posters advertising the competing candidates were in evidence on the main streets of the town when we arrived.

The struggle for power was, however, purely a personal scramble for office. The parties were simply coalitions of individuals, not at all comparable to Labor and Conservative in England or Republican and Democratic in the United States. The Ins wanted to stay in and the Outs wanted to get in. In the national political situation, there was, unfortunately, no clear-cut meaningful party structure, and student political behavior in Union functions was quite like the practices of their elders in the West Pakistan and national assemblies.

The Union program for the academic year opened with a formal function at which the officers and board members were introduced to the student body and faculty and took the oath of office. On this occasion, the Union president gave his inaugural speech, copies of which had been printed and distributed to the audience. The one I heard and read was a hard-hitting document calling for improved hostels, better facilities for sports, and the advent of Utopia forthwith. The speech was addressed directly to the principal who replied in the usual manner of harassed administrators working with insufficient budgets: all these matters had already been taken up with the proper authorities through the proper channels, and, in due course, steps would be taken. It was a highly interesting occasion.

During the course of the year, the Union sponsored three other important events: one was a debate on the proposition that democracy is a better form of government than dictatorship; the second was the All-Pakistan Intercollegiate Debate (for which the Union acted as host) on the proposition that the Suez Canal should be internationalized; and the third was a student strike in favor of separate electorates for Hindus, Christians, and Muslims in Pakistan. The first two functions were approved by the college administration. The strike was not. As might be expected, the Union also was active in demonstrations in favor of Egypt at the time of the Franco-Israeli-British invasion of the Canal Zone, but these did not disrupt the college program as the strike did.

The Student Debate: Democracy vs. Dictatorship

The other events provided some rather startling insights into Pakistani values and public behavior. The debate called Democracy vs. Dictatorship began with a series of pugnacious points of order raised by the leader of the opposition within the Student Union (he was anything but "loyal"). He challenged the president on certain fine points of the constitution and bylaws. This was my first experience with the talents of the Pakistanis for extreme legalism and their use of *Robert's Rules of Order* as an instrument of guerrilla warfare. The president answered patiently and reasonably enough, it seemed to me: certain things had to be done, the machinery provided in the "law" had not yet been set up by the college administration, and the Executive Board had gone ahead. If the rules had been abided by, it would have been impossible to hold the debate at all. Here in the United States, under similar circumstances, the audience would have become impatient with the tactics of harassment and would have yelled, "Let's get this show on the road." The Abbottabad college boys and faculty, on the contrary, enjoyed the passages at arms, seemed to consider the opposition's hair-splitting objections as normal, and, on the whole, seemed to be more interested in how the president would endure his baptism of fire than in the program itself.

After a half-hour of this preliminary sparring, the debate got under way. I was one of the three judges; the others were a distinguished member of the local bar and F. D., the head of the English Department. The debate was not a team affair. Any student could participate and prizes were awarded for individual excellence. First an advocate of democracy would speak, then a proponent of dictatorship. Speeches were limited to something like three minutes each. Altogether about twenty students addressed themselves to the question.

The advocates of democracy leaned heavily on Abraham Lincoln, almost invariably opening their speeches with a definition embodying "of the people, by the people, and for the people." The advocates of dictatorship relied on the arguments that democracy had failed in Pakistan, that it had reduced the West to a parlous moral state, that the great heads of states historically had been dictators, and that people were generally incapable of making democracy work. There was much repetition on both sides.[8]

The speakers either used very extensive notes or tried, surreptitiously, to read prepared speeches. The audience was rough on all of them. At the first sign of hesitation or stumbling, the wolves would be in full cry. As long as a speaker could carry on without a break, he would be heard with reasonable attention. Since most of the boys were inexperienced, the percentage of complete breakdown was high. It would have been a grueling test for any parliamentary gladiator or street-corner haranguer.

It was also a trying occasion for this American democrat doing his best to render grave and judicious appraisals of oratorical performance. What made it almost unendurable was the highlight of the argument, the impassioned statement made by a second-year boy that Pakistani young men would never forget the immortal achievements of Adolf Hitler. Moreover, this pronouncement came from one of the most intelligent boys in school, and he meant what he said.

Later, I came to know him quite well. He was one of my better students, and he used to raise challenging questions in classroom discussion, much to my pleasure. From time to time, we discussed the proposition of the debate in extramural conversation, and he listened attentively and respectfully to my arguments which were, in essence, that democracy had not been tried in Pakistan yet and that Hitler and Hitlerism had done a great deal of harm to Germany and to the rest of the world. I doubt that I changed his mind. It was no accident that his father, one of the town's best M. D.'s, was perhaps the most bitter man I met in Pakistan. As our guest one evening, he was utterly pessimistic about Pakistan's future, and he talked about current education and politics in searing and virulent language.

But back to the debate. The climax came when the proposition was put to the house—that is, to the audience—a customary procedure. The defenders of dictatorship won an overwhelming victory both in terms of votes and volume of noise. In truth, the pro-dictator speakers, measured strictly by effectiveness on the platform, had done better than their opponents.

I was consoled by the fact that the best speech of the day (no judge dissenting) was delivered by an ex-cadet from the Pakistan Air Force Academy, an older chap named Durrani (not the hotel manager), who spoke for democracy with unusual calm, maturity, and historical perspective, even reducing that howling mob to comparative silence. Durrani, a senior, had been appointed the official speaker of the house by the Union Executive Board, though, on this occasion, he spoke only for himself, of course. Durrani had failed his course in cadet training because, as he told us himself, he could not master the mysteries of celestial navigation, but he could find his way around in any other field without trouble.

The All-Pakistan Intercollegiate Debate

With this experience behind me, I was much better prepared for the All-Pakistan Intercollegiate Debate for which I was again requested to act as judge, along with two local lawyers. The debate was on the question of the internationalization of the Suez Canal, and it came right in the middle of the Suez crisis, a timing which was not exactly conducive to a reasoned examination of the issues involved because all of Pakistan was heart and soul on the Egyptian side.

The label "All-Pakistan" was a misnomer. Debaters appeared from colleges in Lahore and Peshawar, but there were no representatives from the Sind, Karachi, or East Pakistan. Again, it was not a team debate. The competing colleges sent two speakers, one for each side of the question, but the judges were expected, as before, to choose the prize-winners on the basis of individual excellence. Abbottabad nominated Durrani (who argued for internationalization) and the pro-Hitler boy, the doctor's son (who, inevitably, advocated Egypt's absolute right to unilateral control of the canal).

The college hall was full, some dignitaries were present, and there were even some women in the audience, all properly done up in the *burqa,* watching the proceedings from the safe sanctuary of the purdah gallery.

As soon as the Union president rose to make his introductory remarks as official host, our old friend, the student leader of the Disloyal Opposition, went to work. Once more he challenged the whole procedure. The Union Board, in his view, had not acted in a constitutional fashion in respect to the Union budget, and, in substance, the All-Pakistan Intercollegiate Debate could, therefore, not be held legally. The President did his best to keep his head and the peace, but, for a time, it looked as if the debate would not get started until midnight. Finally a visitor, a city slicker from Lahore (eventually he won first prize) got up, and, in a fine, tired, urbane and sophisticated manner, suggested that the issue being debated between the president and the opposition might well be reserved for intra-Union discussion—and could we get on with the debate? For some inexplicable reason, this condescending approach worked, the opposition subsided, and the debate began.

60

During the speeches, it became sufficiently clear that the debate was a labor of love for the nationalists and a labor of duty for the internationalists. The city slickers from Lahore dominated the day. They emulated the casual, witty and ironic manner of the Oxford-Cambridge students who used to make mincemeat of their earnest American opponents before our intercollegiate debating loosened up somewhat. Durrani, as usual, made a good showing. He pointed out that complete control of the Suez by Egypt could, in the future, result in sanctions against Pakistani shipping as well as against "imperialist" shipping, but the audience was having none of that, and his speech, like others on his side of the question, was greeted by loud boos. Hitler's champion, the doctor's son, did not do so well this time. He was younger and less experienced than the others, and he had not done his home work.

The proponents of naked nationalism had a field day. They held that Egyptians had built the canal—thousands of them dying in the process; France and England had milked it for all it was worth; it was altogether in Egyptian territory and therefore belonged altogether to Egypt; and what about the Panama Canal?

The counter-arguments were, as might be expected, that Egypt could never have built the Big Ditch in the first place; that it was too important to all the nations of the world to be in the hands of only one nation; that an international agreement could be worked out whereby Egypt's national interests and sovereignty could be protected; and that Egypt had herself violated agreements.

In the end, the first four places went alternately to speakers from Lahore and Peshawar colleges, and everybody seemed satisfied with the judges' decisions. It was pleasant to discover that we were remarkably close together in our assessments. Privately, we agreed that Durrani should have been in the first four, but protocol and policy dictated that we should not appear to favor the home team.

Then the question was put to the house, and, with a great roar, the audience voted against internationalization.[9]

The Student Strike

The third event sponsored by the Union, the student strike, exemplified a problem which troubles the academic world in all of Asia. In the struggle against Western imperialism, students got into the habit of striking, and, now, with the hated yoke of the Western oppressor thrown off, they keep right on striking against their own constituted authorities. This habit is a matter of grave concern to university authorities in India and Pakistan.

This particular strike happened to be, ostensibly, in favor of separate electorates for religious groups. It was not really an issue in that part of the country because public opinion, largely fundamentalist and conservative, overwhelmingly supported separate electorates as protection for Islam against the infidels—despite the fact the Christians were very few and Hindus practically nonexistent in Hazara District and in the Northwest Frontier Province generally.[10] Furthermore, the strike was held against the expressed wishes of the principal.

As it worked out, the college had an unexpected holiday. The entire student body absented itself from classes. The boys, led by union officials, "took out" a procession with flags and banners, marched through the town, and finally wound up on the campus where I met them. It was obvious that this strike would not have much effect on the voters of East Pakistan where the issue was meaningful because of a large Hindu minority nor on the MLA's from the region who already saw eye to eye with the students. When I asked the boys just whom they proposed to influence by their action, I received no answer, and they looked rather sheepish. Later in the day, some of them told me privately that it was simply an excuse for another holiday.

The aftermath of this affair was a college assembly in which the principal, speaking directly to the Union president from the rostrum, charged him with violation of his oath of office, which included a promise to obey the college regulations. In effect, the principal threatened him with expulsion, and, perhaps with more impact, reminded him and all the other students that, by virtue of his right to give or withhold indispensable character recommendations, he held power of life and death over their aspirations to enter public service or professional schools. In the end, no action was taken.

With this case history in mind, I read newspaper accounts of strikes in other institutions in both India and Pakistan with more understanding. At times even the old Ghandi weapon of the hunger strike was employed on both sides of the border. The pretexts for these strikes ranged from the largest of international and national issues to purely local institutional matters. Students all over the subcontinent struck in favor of Egypt, and students, among others, burned down the British Information Center in Dacca. We saw the ruins later. Pakistani students struck against the refusal of the Indian government to take effective repressive action against a relatively old book which was alleged to insult the Prophet; whereupon Indian students struck against the Pakistani strikes. The complex language issues in both countries also resulted in strikes. Students at a Peshawar missionary college struck against the administration's refusal to include Islamiat in the curriculum, and I have read about sporadic local outbursts concerning the length of reading periods before examinations, the dates of examinations, the content of examinations, increases in tuition, and hostel conditions.

Some of these strikes could, no doubt, be justified by principle and hard facts. In fairness to the Indo-Pakistani students, it must be granted that they are at the mercy of an examination system which makes them or breaks them for life. But surely there is a law of diminishing returns applicable to the use of the strike weapon, and surely in many cases there should be a closer functional relationship between the chosen means and the intended end. That is, many of these strikes simply could not have any effective result. American students may be much too docile in respect to important issues, but it is possible to state the case from the reverse point of view: they are more responsible in respect to their academic work, and they are more mature because so many of them are self-supporting, wholly or in part.

Tutorial Groups

The second major base for student activity at Abbottabad Government College was the tutorial group. Under this system, each lecturer had charge of a group of students averaging between twenty and twenty-six in number. The groups met weekly on Sunday mornings which was a semi-holiday, but not a religious holiday. These meetings were held after the college general assembly. The program usually consisted of poems and essays "read out" by members of the group and followed by discussion. The groups each had a slate of officers, and minutes of their proceedings were kept by the secretaries. Like American students, Pakistani boys are very office-conscious; these posts were regarded as honors and were taken quite seriously.

Aside from their formal programs, the tutorial groups were important because they gave the students a sense of belonging. The lecturer was the academic father of his charges. Students went to him for advice and counsel. He had the power to grant leaves of absence from the college on account of illness or family affairs. He was also the intermediary between the administrative operations of the college disciplinary system and the students. At times, I suspect, certain lecturers even gave their boys financial help for the payment of fines levied for breaches of discipline, a common practice.

Not all the lecturers lived up to their full responsibility for their groups, but the majority did. The young men I knew best were really interested in their boys; I found incidental testimony to this effect in student themes.

In addition to the required Sunday sessions, the tutorial groups also organized picnics, hikes, and sight-seeing trips to nearby points of interest. At the end of the year, each group had a formal function, usually high tea at a local restaurant or at the Palace Hotel. The climax of the year's activities would then be achieved: the group photograph. Pakistanis are very photo-conscious, and "Old Boys," which is Pakistani-English usage for alumni, will have pictures of all their college groups and clubs hung on the walls of their homes. I was the honored guest at six of these functions, and I was usually called upon the give "good advices" or to lecture on character building.

Student Clubs and Functions

The third nucleus for student activity was the student club. In the course of the year, for example, I lectured to the Economics Club on American Agriculture and to the History Club on the American Revolution. At Arif's request I later lectured to combined history classes on the American Civil War. The Chemistry Club, with Hamid and Afzal in charge, conducted a tour of important industrial plants in the Abbottabad-Wah-Rawalpindi area, and the other clubs had similar programs.

The pattern for club functions on the campus was rigid. The occasion would be publicized by notices read in the classrooms. It would be held late in the afternoon on a day which would permit all the students to come if they wished. The program would be conducted with the utmost formality and punctilio by the club officers, and invariably tea would follow. These teas were a major responsibility for club officials. It was a common occurrence for students to come to me with chits (the universal idiom for notes of any kind) requesting that they be excused from classes in order to get the requisite ration permit for sugar from the local authorities, a matter of high import. Pakistani tea is largely milk and sugar.

There were three other important functions in the course of the year which do not fit into the structure described above. These were all-college functions: United Nations Day, Iqbal Day, and the equivalent of our Commencement or Honors Day. Each of these was revealing in different ways.

United Nations Day was held some months before the UN Assembly supported Pakistan's stand on Kashmir. Since that time, I think that Pakistan may feel more friendly to the world organization than it did before. On the day I speak of, the audience was distinctly unfriendly. The function opened with a lecture on the history of UN, delivered by our political scientist, Zahurul. After this, individual students were given the opportunity to express their sentiments—which they did with great heat and little light. Led by the president of the Student Union, they were, without exception, hostile to UN. In their eyes, the failure of UN to achieve a solution on Pakistani terms of the Kashmir impasse was enough. UN was clearly useless. These boys wanted action, and the clear implication of their remarks (not carefully thought out, of course) was that either UN troops should throw India out of Kashmir or Pakistani troops would do it. The possibility of a third world war stemming out of such actions apparently never crossed their minds. As the tirades went on, the principal, sitting next to me on the platform, leaned over and, very earnestly asked whether I would speak in defense of UN. I agreed, and shortly thereafter, I entered the argument with enthusiasm. I tried to point out that no one nation, including the United States, was ever likely to get all it wanted from UN; that UN constituted a world forum in which Pakistan's case could be presented with greater effect that it otherwise could; and that the long-range importance of UN consisted in its being the only agency through which a third, and probably final, World War could be prevented. The boys listened respectfully, but it is doubtful whether they changed their views. The one concrete result of this oratorical effort was that Hitler's disciple asked me to write down a summary of my remarks after the event—which I did.

That the students remained unconvinced was to be expected under the circumstances. More important, it seems to me, was the principal's desire to support UN as well as a pro-UN speech made by another faculty member, one of the young scientists. This illustrated what I found to be true later—that a substantial portion of the faculty (by no means all) did not share the students' extremist views. They felt deeply about Kashmir, but they were not prepared to advocate Pakistan's secession from UN on that question alone.

Iqbal Day

The Iqbal Day function provides a convenient pretext for reminding Western readers of the great importance of this poet-philoso-
pher in the whole Islamic world. It is not an exaggeration to say that
he is, to the Muslims, the equivalent of both Shakespeare and Aris-
totle. Any American or European who proposes to spend any time
in a Muslim country would do well to become acquainted with his
works. Iqbal's philosophy is well known to professional philosophers,
but in the West his poetry is not. It has not yet received the translation it deserves, and some scholar-poet could make a great contribution to Muslim-European-American cultural relations by doing this
job well. Our great foundations ought to look into the matter.

I had read some essays on Iqbal before going to Pakistan,[11] and,
as chance would have it, a week or two before his day, one of my
students had lent me a book called *Iqbal as Thinker,* a work made up
of a series of lectures by Indian and Pakistani scholars on various
aspects of his philosophy. Two days before the commemoration, I
was asked to take part in the program. I refused on the grounds that
I had no business to talk about Iqbal. I did not know enough about
him. But Afzal and a student delegation were insistent and finally
I agreed.

Luckily for me, my student's book contained considerable chunks
of Iqbal's poetry, and, even in a mediocre translation, some of his
unique force and fire came through. I was genuinely impressed. I
chose as my organizing theme those things in Iqbal which reminded
me of similar utterances from American and English poets: social
protest much like Markham's "Man with a Hoe," a poem which many
of the faculty knew because they had studied it in their undergraduate days; a Whitmanesque equalitarian poem; and most striking to me, a powerful poem challenging God himself in man-to-man
language strongly reminiscent of the personal immediacy to be found
in the religious poetry of John Donne and George Herbert. Prefacing
my speech with a statement of my inadequacies to the subject and
my necessary reliance on secondary sources, I gave my report to
the audience. This effort elicited a spontaneous and surprisingly enthusiastic response from both students and faculty.

For an understanding of Pakistani national psychology, I think
that this reaction is significant. The reasons for it are these: The
Pakistanis love poetry to begin with; Iqbal is not only a fine poet,

but a national hero, the philosophical father of the idea of Pakistan; they were delighted to have him grouped with American and English poets; they were pleased that I had taken the trouble to give them something more than polite clichés; and, above all, they responded warmly to the ideas of their Poet-Rebel.

On this occasion, the other speakers were Saghir, the Urdu poet-scholar; Afzal, the poet-chemist; and Durrani (the manager of the Palace Hotel, not the ex-Air Force cadet). Saghir and Durrani spoke in Urdu; Afzal spoke in English—for my benefit.

Commencement Day

Two aspects of the college's annual Prize Day and Commencement remain in my memory. In most respects, the function was quite like its American counterparts: many dignitaries were present; a spokesman for the third year bade farewell to the fourth year boys; Durrani, the ex-cadet, responded ably for the graduates; and the station commander, a brigadier general, distributed the prizes and made a workmanlike, though conventional, speech. Diplomas were not handed out because the University of Peshawar, not the Abbottabad Government College, conferred the degrees.

However, when the officers of the Student Union were being introduced, a troubled young man in the audience stood up and raised a point of order. Though he was one of two secretaries of the Union, he had been passed over, a fact which made him indignant. Apparently it was an oversight, not a deliberate slight, and although under similar circumstances the faculty had allowed the leader of the opposition to have his say, this time a couple of lecturers descended on the young secretary and reduced him to silence—and to tears. I sympathized with him, for he had lost his brief moment of glory, but I doubt that an American boy would have reacted in quite the same dramatic fashion.

The other aspect of the occasion which struck me as being strange was the audience's reaction to the prize winners. The applause was at best perfunctory. This was true even in the case of a well liked first year boy who had brought prestige to the college by scoring the highest marks on the university-wide examinations for his class.

This inability to respond warmly to the achievements of one's peers may be a complement of the wolf-pack psychology which I had earlier observed in the two debates and in my own classes. It is not an isolated phenomenon. I have read letters in the press, written

67

by Pakistani observers, commenting on and protesting against the same coldness of response in Lahore audiences.

Other Customs

To this list of organized student activities should be added one unorganized activity. Pakistani boys have a real love of nature in the Wordsworthian sense. They love gardens especially, and it is customary for them to spend hours in one of the local parks or on walking trips to the neighboring hills for the explicit purpose of communing with the birds, the bees, the trees, the flowers, the moon, and the stars. They are quite unselfconscious about this practice, and they are capable of reporting their observations in fresh and moving terms. American boys of comparable age would be reluctant to express similar sentiments for fear of being labeled "sissy."

There is one form of student activity popular in the United States which is necessarily absent from the Pakistani student program: there are no mixed social affairs—no J-Hops. The segregation of women prevents such pastimes. Our college was not coeducational, and it is highly unlikely that it will ever be. In fact, most colleges like it are not co-ed. It is true that graduate classes at the University of Peshawar are co-ed, as they are in the University of Karachi, but at Peshawar the girls come in their *burqas*, and there is a curtain down the middle of the classroom. In Abbottabad, the college boys never had any socially approved contact with the students at the neighboring girls' college, nor any clandestine relations that I ever heard of. In fact, the boys never had any opportunity for conversation with decent Pakistani women at all—excepting members of their own family.

In these circumstances, speculation about the sexual life of these four hundred and twenty young men is inevitable. Elsewhere in the world, male college students have often received their basic training in the facts of sexual life from prostitutes. There are well established red light districts in Pakistan's cities (although my students seemed to be wholly ignorant of this) but there was no such thing in Abbottabad. I was told that there used to be some local practitioners of the world's oldest profession but that the army had cleaned them out. I was also told that, on very rare occasions, students in the hostels had imported sweeper women from the town, but discovery and drastic punishment resulted.

It would seem to follow logically that, in a segregated community of over four hundred boys, the pressures of the biological urge would result inexorably in homosexual practices. This is a problem not generally discussed in Pakistan, and statistics are, understandably, not available. Here we are wholly in the realm of subjective conjecture. However, it seems to me, the whole pattern of Pakistani relations between males tends toward a tacit acceptance of homosexuality. The fact that Pakistani men and boys habitually walk down the streets together hand in hand is evidence only of a difference in mores, and the same point holds true of the Pakistani custom of warmly embracing male friends on meeting or departure—even though, to the Western observer, such embraces are embarrassingly sexual in connotation. But there does seem to be a basically different attitude towards sexual commerce between men, or at least between men and boys. Peter Mayne and John Masters throw some light on this attitude.[12]

Of course, homosexual practices in some degree will be found in any segregated group of males or females anywhere in the world, in jails, in schools, in camps, or in the armed services, but I rather suspect that the incidence of homosexuality in Pakistan is relatively greater than it is in the United States. One observer of our acquaintance, with long experience in the old Indian army and in prep school work, dismissed the problem with a laugh, asserting that homosexuality was the national sport. One of his colleagues, a much graver type, incapable of much gaiety or humor, indicated that in his opinion, homosexuality in school situations was a very serious problem.

I comment on this issue only because of the holier-than-thou point of view held openly by Pakistani students, and covertly by Pakistani elders, in respect to coeducation specifically and to the relations between the sexes generally in the United States and other Western countries. Neither group really knows much about these subjects, but this ignorance does not prevent them from holding strong opinions about them. The Pakistanis tend to be deeply moralistic, even puritanical, and, like some of our Puritans, they also tend to limit morality to sexual morality. In their minds, the mere presence of boys and girls together in a school situation or of men and women together in a social situation leads inevitably to mass sexual intercourse. Their prurient concentration on this image is in itself a measure of the repercussions of the Islamic social pattern which produces an intense obsession with sexual matters. My students, for example, were far less concerned with other aspects of morality such as financial honesty, stealing books, intellectual in-

69

tegrity in respect to plagiarism, or relative honesty in governmental administration. Indeed, it hardly occurred to them that these matters also involved considerations of morality.

There is a good deal of sexual play on American campuses. It is a phenomenon freely observed and freely commented on. Sexual practices on Pakistani campuses are not freely observed nor freely commented on. It is this absence of a systematic collection of social data which makes the running debate between Americans and Pakistanis a somewhat one-sided affair. They have the advantage of citing our own evidence, like the Kinsey reports, against us; similar data are not as yet available in Pakistan. I shall recur to this controversy in a later chapter.[13]

My own subjective conclusion is that, in respect to both psychic and physical well being, American students are healthier than their Pakistani counterparts.

Chapter Four

The Academic Program: Curriculum and Classroom

The College and the University

Our college was one of nine (at that time) which were affiliated with the University of Peshawar. The university itself was established in 1950. It is a graduate school in its own right, and, in relation to its affiliated colleges, it determines undergraduate curricula, sets examinations, grades examinations, and confers degrees. This control by the university leaves very little power in the hands of the component colleges. The system is common to both India and Pakistan. Today it is under attack by professional educators in both countries.

On the one hand, it is argued that the prevailing emphasis on the passing of university-set examinations as an end in itself makes education as a continuing process almost impossible; on the other hand, it is held in substance that the individual colleges—some private, some public—cannot be trusted to maintain proper standards on the local level. This is an important issue, and I shall return to it in due course.[1]

Abbottabad Government College was reasonably typical of this system in operation. Its four hundred and twenty students had been admitted to the degree program by passing the matriculation examinations set by the university, or the equivalent thereof. These examinations are referred to generically as "the matric." Matriculation status is the approximate equivalent of a diploma from an accredited high school in the United States. To achieve it, students have to pass examinations in five subjects: three subjects in Group I—English, mathematics, history and geography; and any two subjects in Group II—a Pakistani language, Urdu or Pushto; a classical language—Arabic or Persian; physics and chemistry; drawing; physiology and hygiene; and agriculture.[2]

Most of our boys at Abbottabad offered Urdu for matriculation rather than Pushto; in Peshawar, the reverse would probably be true. The university regulations made it possible to offer French or German in place of Urdu or Pushto, but I knew no student who had done so. One boy, after matriculation, was trying to study French by himself for the later intermediate examination. It was a courageous enterprise.

The English Curriculum

In the matriculation examinations, English was the medium for English, Urdu for the classical Pakistani languages, and either English or Urdu for the others. On this point, there is much debate in Pakistan. In part under the stress of nationalism, there are strong advocates for making the national languages the media for instruction and examination altogether. A stronger argument is that a student is penalized when he cannot deal with subject matter in his mother tongue. There is substance in this position, but, when it comes to the sciences, for example, there is also a real question as to the adequacy of these tongues to meet the demands of scientific terminology and the need for close definition of concepts. Historically, the Pakistanis have been out of touch with science and technology, but attempts are being made to develop vocabulary in the vernacular languages for these purposes. The reader will remember that Manzur's father was engaged in this work.[3] But it is doubtful that these efforts can be effective for some time to come.

However, in my observation, as Pakistan comes to take its nationhood for granted, the extreme nationalistic view in respect to the languages of instruction and examination seems to be meeting opposition. Many educated members of the older generation have lamented to me the decline in the standard of English since partition, and I take it that they would welcome better instruction in English all the way through the educational system.

Here the problem is to get competent English-speaking teachers on both the high school and college levels, and it is a real problem. Furthermore, there is a sensible recognition of the plain fact that the English language—though the mother tongue of the British—is one of the great international media of knowledge, if not the greatest. In short, English is perhaps the only means of access to what the Pakistanis must know in order to do what they want to do for themselves. Finally, however reluctant the country may be, there is some acceptance of the paradox that, in the face of regional and language cleavages, Islam and English are really the two most important common denominators which hold Pakistan together. Very few Pakistanis would put the matter in this way, but I have done so on occasion, and the proposition has been generally, although ruefully, accepted.

As the years go by, I should not be surprised to see both Pakistan and India reverse their policies of de-emphasizing English—at least to the extent of maintaining it as one of the required languages and continuing to use it as the medium of instruction in some important areas of higher education. But the nationalist reaction after independence was gained in 1947 has damaged the status of English in both educational systems, perhaps irreparably.

At Abbottabad, English was the medium of examination in all subjects except the classical and Pakistani languages. In these, the medium was either the classical language itself or a Pakistani language. In classroom instruction, because of the difficulties our students had with English, there was a natural tendency on the part of the lecturers to lapse into Urdu perhaps more often than was good for student command of English. Taken as a whole, the student body at Abbottabad, drawn from relatively isolated regions in large part, was not as competent in English as students in either Peshawar or Lahore. But it must always be remembered that English was a second language for all of them.

Once matriculated, the Abbottabad students elected either the arts or the science curriculum in preparation for the intermediate examination which normally comes at the end of two years of college work. At this crucial stage, the arts candidates (a majority of the student

73

body) had to write examinations on four required subjects and on one optional subject. The required subjects, under university regulations, were: English; one of the following languages—Arabic, Persian, Urdu, Pushto, French, or German; and two subjects chosen from mathematics, physics, philosophy, psychology, history, geography, economics, and civics. The optional subject could be selected from Arabic, Persian, Pushto, French, German, or Islamiat, provided, of course, that this choice had not been offered as a compulsory subject.[4]

However, Abbottabad gave no instruction in French, German, Pushto, philosophy, psychology, or geography. Everybody took English. The elections in the other languages were fairly evenly divided among Urdu, Arabic, and Persian. Since many of the arts students had no talent for mathematics or science, they chose history, economics, and civics from the required subjects and Islamiat from optional subjects.

The science group, who were as a whole intellectually superior to their brothers in the arts, comprised two divisions, medical and non-medical. The pre-meds faced examinations in English, physics, chemistry, and biology. The non-medics, largely embryo engineers, substituted mathematics for biology. Both science groups were permitted to offer an additional optional subject from among Islamiat, Arabic, Persian, and Urdu; the other optionals allowed under university regulations were not taught at Abbottabad.[5]

This intermediate examination is a big thing in Pakistan. Psychologically, it means more than two years of college work would mean in the United States. The intermediate certificate confers some status in itself, and it is needed for many jobs. To get it, the student has to pass all of his required subjects; the optional subject does not affect the final result. I observed at Abbottabad that there was a marked difference for the better between the third year boys who had passed the intermediate, and the second year boys who were getting ready for it. The mortality rate on the intermediate was evidently high.

My first and second year classes were very big. The third and fourth year classes were very small, but they seemed to be more mature than the difference of only one year would appear to warrant. I conclude that the intermediate examinations are a real screening process.

After the intermediate, the Abbottabad students stayed on for two years to prepare for the final university examinations for the bachelor's degree in arts or science. With minor modifications, the degree examinations followed the pattern of the intermediate examinations in subject area and structure. They were, of course, set by the University of Peshawar and read by examiners appointed by the university. Some of our faculty also served as university examiners; that is, they read papers written by students at other affiliated colleges. The university reports the statistics to its component colleges, and the chief examiners make reports on the quality of the examinations. Naturally, these are read with considerable attention because colleges and their faculties are judged by the number of students who pass.

I remember one such report on the English examinations, written by an Englishman attached to the University of Peshawar. It was a conscientious, literate, and lively document, but it had little relation to the hard facts of the actual teaching situation.

I also remember a visit to our campus by the woman principal of the Frontier College for Women at Peshawar who came as university examiner of the seniors in *viva voce*, or oral English. The lady was English, a dedicated teacher, completely committed to a career in the Pakistan Educational Service, and most sympathetic to her Pakistani charges. At dinner with my wife and me, she was quick to say that it was a mistake to send her to Abbottabad. Our boys had trouble enough with the English language in male company, and, in the presence of what certainly appeared to them as a very formidable female (and this in the heart of the Purdah Belt), they simply froze up.

A word about the grading system. Each examination paper on all levels, matriculation, intermediate, and final, was allotted a maximum number of points. Those who made 60 per cent or better on the whole battery of matriculation examinations were placed in the first division; those who made 45 per cent were placed in the second division; all below 45 per cent were placed in the third division. The minimum passing grade was 33 per cent. For the intermediate examination, the figures were 60 per cent for the first division; 50 per cent for the second; and 35 per cent for the minimum passing mark. For the degree examination, the figures were 60 per cent for the first division; 50 per cent for the second division; and 40 per cent for the minimum passing mark.[6]

I was in no position to judge the caliber of work required in such fields as Urdu, Persian, Arabic, and the like. I received the impression that, on a comparable basis with American colleges, the mathematics standard was fairly good and that, considering the quality of textbooks and laboratory equipment, chemistry and physics were as good as could be reasonably expected. The history standard was low, and the English standard was very low. But one thing I am quite sure of: by their lights, the examiners were tough.

Another feature of the system was the university requirement of attendance at a given number of lectures for each of the required subjects: for instance, a minimum of three hundred and eighty-five lectures in English in a two-year period. This stipulation meant that a student who fell below the given number had to make up the lectures before he could take his examinations.[7] It sounds like a reasonable regulation, but in practice it did not make much difference what lectures a student attended to round out the necessary number. In one of my first year English classes, four boys turned up from second and fourth year classes with written permission from the college administration to make up lectures on the first year level. This mode of operation would be the rough equivalent in the United States of sophomores and seniors attending freshman composition classes in order to qualify for hypothetical comprehensive examinations. At first, I was puzzled by this arrangement, and then I discovered that it was standard procedure. The boys, in turn, were puzzled by my failure to understand the commonplace, and they were even more puzzled when I set them to work on a review of their own class materials in addition to the first year class work. I also gave them some examinations on their required reading. Apparently, this simply was "not done," in that fine English phrase which settles matters with such finality, but, at least, I think they perceived the logic of my demands. At any rate, they went through the motions of complying with them.

As for the curriculum in English itself, I taught the first year boys a small anthology called *Fact and Fiction* which contained short pieces dealing with myth, legend, historical adventure, fictional adventure, and accounts of English schoolboy life. In another section, the first year boys worked with *The Adventures of Sherlock Holmes*. I taught the second year classes a novel by Arthur Quiller-Couch called *Poison Island*, an obvious imitation of *Treasure Island*. In the third and fourth classes, we worked over Milton's *Lycidas, Il Penseroso, and L'Allegro*; Addison's *Roger de Coverley Papers*; Drinkwater's *Abraham Lincoln*; Shakespeare's *Richard II*; and Hardy's *Mayor of Casterbridge*. My colleagues taught other items of poetry and prose, such as *Silas Marner*, selections from *The Golden Treasury*, and Shaw's *Arms and the Man*.

This list sounds respectable enough. In one sense, it is entirely too respectable. In the first place, the students did not know enough English to grapple with these materials; in the second place, the selections had little or nothing to do with their own way of life and their own culture.

This curriculum (remember that it was ordained by the University of Peshawar) is a watered-down imitation of the nineteenth century English academic tradition. It remains in force because of inertia and because many Pakistanis either were trained in that tradition in England or by exemplars of it in Indo-Pakistani universities— like one of my colleagues, F. D., who was proud of the fact that he had been a student of a student of Arthur Quiller-Couch, the famous "Q."

The basic objection to this curriculum as I saw it was that it made no distinction between the teaching of English as a language and the teaching of English literature. Let no one assume that I am about to suggest that English literature be tossed out of the curriculum. It is an admirable discipline, and I have spent much of my life teaching it. I would certainly like to see the Pakistanis keep literature in the English language as an important part of their educational system. But before literature can be taught in English, the language must be mastered. English is not well taught in Pakistan's schools for a number of reasons: it is not taught as a foreign language—as it should be; the teachers themselves do not know enough about English or about language as language; and the materials of instruction, like the college texts cited above, are so remote from the student's experience as to be almost meaningless.

At professional conferences in Pakistan and in conversation with my colleagues, I used to argue that instructional materials for the teaching of English should be based on good translations of classic short stories and poetry, selected from the rich storehouse of Urdu and Bengali literature, and that these translations should be printed side by side with Pakistani texts.[8] For that matter, why not use Iqbal himself in translation?

With such materials in hand, the Pakistani students would be psychically at home to begin with. English would not seem so strange to them then. Later on, they could be called upon to wrestle with those foreign giants of language, Shakespeare, Milton, and Hardy.

It is the greatest irony of my Pakistani experience that such notions, though listened to respectfully and politely, received the warmest support, not from my Pakistani colleagues, but from Dr. A. H. King of the British Council in Karachi.

I met Dr. King at a meeting of Pakistani secondary school educators in June 1957. The meeting was organized by the principal of the Karachi Parsi High School, Dr. Rustomji, a man of fabulous energy for whom those so-called American adjectives, "hustling" and "go-getting" were obviously invented. Principal Rustomji had summarily drafted me for the purpose of talking about the problem of teaching English in Pakistan's schools. There was no nay-saying to him. Hearing about this meeting, Dr. King, by virtue of his professional interests, invited himself, as he told me later, though he was clearly welcome.

In substance, I told the group what I have stated above, stressing the need for a sharp distinction between the teaching of literature and language, urging the use of instructional materials developed out of Pakistan's culture, and pleading for smaller classes, more written work carefully corrected, and greater emphasis on oral reading and class discussion. My Pakistani audience (not a big one) seemed to be impressed and disturbed. In turn, I was disturbed by what appeared to be a greater interest on their part in correct pronunciation rather than in competent control of English as a medium of effective communication.

At the close of the session, Dr. King arose, gave three cheers (in effect), endorsed everything I had said, and promptly invited me and my wife out to dinner.

At this dinner, much of it spent in mutual enthusiastic agreement, I got some understanding of the two paradoxes I had encountered: the first, an Englishman ardently applauding a proposal which would tend to de-emphasize the British literary tradition in Pakistani education; the second, the lack of enthusiasm on the part of the Pakistanis for a greater emphasis on their own cultural resources in the teaching of English.

As to the first, Dr. King is a linguist by training (as I am not). He had served on the faculty of Stockholm University, and he was also an honorary professor of English at Karachi University. At that time, he was head of the British Council in Karachi, a semiofficial agency of the British Government which performs the combined functions of our own Fulbright program, the USIS, and the Smith-Mundt program. As a linguist, Dr. King was anything but provincial in his outlook. As a consultant for the Pakistan Ministry of Education, he simply wanted to get the job of teaching English done effectively according to the best professional methods of doing that job and with the best interests of Pakistan at heart. This point is incarnate in the quotation which he put on the cover of his own *Background Paper for a Conference on the Teaching of the Recognized Languages (with Particular Reference to English) in Pakistan.* This quotation reads as follows:

> The emphasis during British rule on higher education, with English as the medium of instruction, is one of the many mistakes which can be traced back to that sinister figure (though probably quite unintentionally so), Lord Macaulay.

It was not a Pakistani or Indian who said this; it was Sir John Sargent, educational advisor to the Government of India, 1943–48.

Dr. King told me that he had been for some time one of the few voices crying out against the dominance of a belletristic, somewhat old-fashioned, donnish, British literary tradition over the teaching of English on the subcontinent; that is why he had been glad to hear what I said. Another way of putting our joint point of view is that we both wanted the position of English, as a necessary tool for the people of Pakistan, to be made stronger by more effective teaching.

But, assuming that such an end is desirable, as the participants in Dr. Rustomji's meeting did, why then should it be an Englishman and an American who should put the case strongly for a more realistic and national approach to the given end? I cannot speak about a majority of Pakistanis involved in the problem; evidently Dr. King had encountered a good deal of opposition to his well grounded, scholarly, linguistic views. But I suggest two explanations which I have deduced more from attitudes and by implications than from plain statements. The first is an unwillingness to accept the distinction between the teaching of literature and language. After all, these Pakistani educators had been reared according to old-school principles; they knew English well; they could pronounce it correctly—why shouldn't others do likewise? The second is, to put it bluntly, snobbism, a reluctance to give up the English "classics," which are manifestly the mark of the truly educated person, even though the proposed substitutes were Urdu and Bengali classics. I was surprised to find this attitude, but it was indubitably there, and I believe it went hand in hand with the disposition to think in terms of proper pronunciation as a mark of social status rather than in terms of a capacity for the functional understanding of English.

As Dr. King put the case to me in conversation, most Pakistani and Indian students who went to the United Kingdom avoided philology and linguistics, preferring literature and criticism. Likewise, as he says in the paper cited earlier, "Philology and linguistics were Western disciplines unpopular with most U.K. teachers of literature, who developed the subcontinental curricula one-sidedly."

Therefore, in his recommendations, Dr. King lays stress on the necessity of basic training in linguistics and philology notably in the training of teachers of teachers. In a letter of June 3, 1958, he told me: "Our language plans are going ahead here. We hope to have a language unit started in the Punjab University this coming autumn." I was very glad to hear this. In my experience, most Pakistanis who wish to do advanced study in literature would choose to work on the New Criticism and T. S. Eliot.

Let me illustrate these findings with my own experience at Abbott-abad. The English staff (aside from myself) was composed of three men. We lost one of these to Mardan at mid-year; he was returned to Abbottabad after my departure. The senior, F. D. Mahmood, was a beautiful example of the nineteenth-century "literary" orienta-tion. He had a Third Class M.A. (thus officially set down on the college roster) and a Bachelor of Teaching degree, taken *after* the B.A., and representing one year's work in a teacher-training insti-tution. The second, Farooq, the exile to Mardan, did not have a Master's degree; he was a conscientious chap with a particular in-terest in drama. The third was Rizvi, the Karachi University M.A.

Without exception, these men all worked hard, and I think that they were good teachers. But they had had no training whatsoever in language as language, they were not interested in this aspect of learn-ing, and they all subscribed tacitly to the outmoded prescriptive doctrine of "correctness" which still haunts much English teaching in the United States and which seems to dominate the Pakistani mind when dealing with English. Their own English was pretty good, but they, nevertheless, did not know much about the English lan-guage.

In the English courses, the students did not do any writing other than taking down dictation of plots of plays and stories and making summaries of the assigned materials, which were "read out" later for factual correction. I found this method of instruction to be standard, and, in my opinion, it is one of the greatest curses of Pakistani edu-cation. It obviates the need to read the works themselves to such an extent that few students even had textbooks in their own pos-session, depending on these teacher summaries and bazaar "notes" for the factual information needed to pass examinations. This pernicious

Pals in Pakistan: a familiar sight. Street ·scene in Abbottabad.

Sidewalk Salesman in Dacca, East Pakistan: his turban is a brilliant red, in wonderful contrast with the white wall.

Abbottabad Government College, District Hazara, West Pakistan. Photograph by Bobby Joseph, Abbottabad, Pakistan.

The Pine Ridges of Nathia Gali, looking toward the legendary peak of Nanga Parbat.

system is so well fixed that students protested when, in my innocence, I did not follow it.

It is true that English composition was taught at Abbottabad. Each student was assigned to a composition section in addition to his "literary" work. In theory, these sections met once a week for a double period of eighty minutes. The first and second year sections were much too big on the roll book, but, since the proportion of absence was greater in composition than in any other course, those who actually showed up were small in number. The standard procedure in composition was to write a paper in class and then to have it "read out" for correction. No homework themes were assigned. In the light of the total student load carried by the lecturers, this omission was understandable.

In the Classroom at Abbottabad

As for my own endeavors in this situation, let it suffice to say that I did what I could. I promised to read, correct, and return as much as my students would write. I tried to assign longer themes to be written outside of class. I assigned class themes on such topics as "My Favorite Sport," "My Choice of Profession or Vocation," "On the Significance of Muslim Religious Holidays," and "My Favorite Teacher" (finding it necessary to exclude myself from the eligible list when I discovered that Pakistani boys are as prone to polish apples as American boys). In short, I kept them writing as hard as possible.

I learned a good deal about my students from these themes, and a good deal about Pakistan, also. But, on the whole, the results were not encouraging. Few boys accepted my invitation to write more than the minimal amount—in part because they were simply bewildered at being asked to do any work outside the college classroom. Perhaps my most successful expedient (I often thought of Mr. Parkhill, Hyman Kaplan's hapless teacher) was to sit down with one boy and go over his work while his fellows created deathless prose. At first, they insisted on rising respectfully when I came to their desks, but, after a time, they became accustomed to the phenomenon of an instructor who would sit down with them. Insofar as I can judge, they responded warmly to this kind of individual attention. Like all boys, they were eager to perform, though they might not have had much to perform with, and so from time to time I followed the convention and had students "read out" their papers, but I could get around to more boys during the period by following the method of individual conference at the desk.

Taken as a whole, the level of competence in English was naturally very low. Inevitably, the boys tried to write English in Urdu idiom. The first year boys were practically illiterate; the second year boys were not much better; the third and fourth year boys were better, of course, but, in the course of a whole year, I encountered about five boys who conceivably might make the grade in standard freshman English at an American college or university—assuming that they would have the benefit of at least one previous semester in a course in English for foreign students such as is taught at Wayne State University. Let it be clear that this judgment applies only to my students' command of English; it is not to be confused with a judgment of their intelligence. I am also aware that, if called upon to study Urdu (or French or German) from the fourth grade on and then expected to do a major part of their college work in that second language, American students, too, would perform miserably. I am further aware that our own students in the United States do not know English as well as they should after twelve years of elementary and high school. The point is that, in both cases, it is quite possible to do better.

Typical Examinations

In this context of curriculum, instruction, and competence, let us take a look at the examinations which these Pakistani boys had to face in English. As I have said, the college had absolutely no control over the intermediate and degree examinations administered by the university at the end of the second and fourth years. The college did give "house" or "promotion" examinations at the end of the first and third years to determine whether the students should remain in college and move on to the next class. Furthermore, it gave "December Tests," which were the rough equivalent of mid-year examinations. All of these were modeled on the university examinations.

On one such test, the first year boys were asked to do the following:

1. Explain with reference to context two out of four passages of poetry to be selected from two Scots ballads, Keats' *La Belle Dame Sans Merci*, and *Sohrab and Rustum*.
2. Write a summary of *The Merchant of Venice*, *King Lear*, or *Twelfth Night*.
3. State the misfortune of Silas Marner.
4. Summarize a story from *Sherlock Holmes*.
5. Correct some faulty sentences.
6. Write an essay.

On the surface this may sound all right, but consider these points: ballads are fine in their simplicity, power, and universality, but these students had trouble enough with basic English without confusing them with Scots idiom. Keats, I think, was completely out of their world of reference. *Sohrab*, as close as they ever came to the Muslim world in English, may have been intelligible on the level of bare story, but still it was difficult in vocabulary. *They had not read any of the Shakespeare plays; they had perhaps read some summaries.* I doubt that many, if any, had read *Silas Marner* or any of the Sherlock Holmes stories completely. The sentences were fair enough, and the essay was approximately what I expected.

How did they pass such an examination? Simply by repeating, parrot-like, what their instructors had dictated in class and learning by rote what they found in the bazaar "notes," prepared for each required work in the curriculum by Pakistani teachers desperately in need of money.

Or take the third year Promotion Examination. Among other questions, these:

1. Write an essay on the main features of one of the following poets: Matthew Arnold, John Milton, Algernon Swinburne, William Morris.
2. Give a critical appreciation of one of the following poems: *The Forsaken Merman* by Arnold; *The Garden of Proserpine* by Swinburne; *Thoughts in a Garden* by Marvell; *L'Allegro* by Milton. Or: [hold your hats!] Write a note on the Pre-Raphaelites.

I will give one more item from this examination. The students were asked to discuss two of four given statements on *Twelfth Night*, which *was* studied in class. One of the choices read: *"Twelfth Night* aims at the ludicrous rather than the ridiculous. It makes us laugh at the follies of mankind, not despise them." I will wager my weight in rupees that not one single bright boy in that whole class had any idea whatsoever of the meaning of "ridiculous" and "ludicrous," let alone the distinction between them.

Such questions would be hard enough for sophomores and juniors in American institutions to write really meaningful answers to; for students who do not know English very well to begin with, they are impossible—without the aid of a good memory and those convenient bazaar canned answers.

In my sardonic moods, I particularly admire the question on the Pre-Raphaelites.

The high peak of this genteel, mid-Victorian academic comedy, which assumed that Pakistani students came from Eton, Harrow, and Arnold's Rugby instead of from villages and government high schools, was a question on English Paper B of the third year Promotion Examination. The students were asked to "Summarize the following passage, equal to one-third of the original length, and suggest a suitable title." The passage turned out to be from Bret Harte's *The Outcasts of Poker Flat,* which was not, of course, identified on the examination. Identification was impossible, for *the students had never read the story, nor had they been exposed to it in any way.*

I did not set this examination, but, as part of my job, I read all the papers submitted and I read them with mingled mirth, compassion, and professional anger. I quote one paragraph from the problem passage as it appeared on the examination paper:

> When night crept up again through the gorges the ready [sic] notes of the accordion rose and fell in fitful spasms and long-drawn gasps by the flickering campfire. But music failed to fill entirely the aching void left by insufficient food, and a new diversion was proposed by Piney—story-telling. Neither Mr. Oakhurst nor his female companions caring to relate their personal experiences, this plan would have failed, too, but for the Innocent. Some months before he had chanced upon a stray copy of Mr. Pope's ingenious translation of the Iliad. He now proposed to narrate the principal incidents of the poem—having thoroughly mastered the argument and fairly forgotten the words—in the current vernacular of Sandy Bar. And so for the rest of that night the Homeric demigods again walked the earth. Trojan Cully and wily Greek wrestled in the winds, and the great pines in the cannon [sic] seemed to bow to the wrath of the son of Peleus. Mr. Oakhurst listened with quiet satisfaction. Most especially was he interested in the fate of "Ashheels," as the Innocent persisted in denominating the 'swift-footed Achilles.'

Those poor boys! They were ignorant of "Mr. Pope and his ingenious translation"; "Trojan Cully" and "wily Greek" were Greek to them; Sandy Bar was evidently a person, perhaps an American; "Homeric demigods"—who, in the name of Allah, were they?

And those words! "Spasms"—surely misspelled; "diversion"; "argument," which ought to mean a dispute, but does not; "vernacular"; and "denominating." All of them were beyond reasonable expectation.

But there was one phrase in the passage which all of them joyfully understood—or thought they did: "The great pines in the cannon."

The chances for misinterpretation of this apparently simple assignment were endless, and our boys made the most of them. I wonder to this day what prompted the examiners to choose this esoteric passage. My guess is that Pope and Homer made it eminently Victorian enough to be a proper question.

What did I do as reader? I was eminently charitable—more charitable than my Pakistani colleagues would have approved, had they known.

The system of class instruction, the total emphasis on examination results, and the type of examinations given lead inevitably to a basic intellectual dishonesty which has, I suggest, very bad effects on the educated Pakistani's control of English, on education as a whole, and, perhaps, on Pakistani character.

It should be clear now that the Pakistani boy learns his English almost in a cultural vacuum, without much, if any, relationship to what he knows best. If he were asked to clothe his own concepts and values in English or to read English versions of them, I think he would learn English faster and more accurately. In his desperation at his failure to understand a foreign climate of opinion and an alien frame of reference with its silent assumptions, it is quite natural that the Pakistani student should seek and find crutches.

This tendency is emphasized by the classroom routine. The lecturer comes in dressed in his academic robe, English fashion; the boys rise; the roll is called—each boy has a roll number, and, in the first year classes, the process seems endless; the period is only forty minutes. At first the lecturer in English was expected to give a complete play-by-play account of the text he dealt with, if it was only a story, novel, or play. If it was poetry, he went over it line by line. Then the lecturer dictated critical notes to the students. They took these down, and, now and then, they read them back. Most of the first and second year boys did not have textbooks, and, if they had them, they rarely brought them to the lecture. Class discussion—the give-and-take of questions to the teacher and the expression of critical value judgments by the students on the matters in hand—was rare. For most of the boys, attendance was simply a matter of getting credit for another lecture toward the grand total which would permit them to take the university examinations.

A Novel Technique

But it does not have to be that way!

I found this out in the third and fourth year classes, which were much smaller than the first and second year groups. After considerable

85

urging, most of the juniors and seniors brought their texts to class and they responded to the opportunity given them of active participation in the day's work.

When the senior class came to the *Mayor of Casterbridge*, I told them that I would give them the detailed summary of the book which they had come to expect, but that I, in turn, expected them to read the book, to prove to me in papers that they had done so, and, above all, to bring the book to class. All this was new doctrine, but they responded well. With something of the sense of performing a treasonous act, I kept my word, and I read out a carefully prepared running account of Hardy's novel; it was much sought after, and I compounded my treason by permitting it to circulate. It was a kind of calculated risk, but, on the whole, it worked. After giving the summary and going over certain passages in a few class sessions, I found that the boys were beginning to talk about Henchard, Farfrae, Lucetta, and Elizabeth-Jane as if they were old acquaintances. Some of them produced essays on these characters which were far more detailed and understanding than the canned answers in the bazaar notes, and, at the end of the time allotted to this work, we were having fairly mature discussions of such topics as whether truth is stranger than fiction, whether good fiction is truer than truth, and whether Hardy had relied too much on the long arm of coincidence. Now I suspect that a few of those boys actually read the whole novel.

Likewise with John Drinkwater's *Abraham Lincoln*, a play which F. D. generously permitted me to teach although, normally, he taught it himself. This play was of great interest to my seniors and to me. We read it together in class, and this time I did not have to give them a summary, nor did they ask for one. Moreover, we had come to know each other comparatively well by this time, and they did not hesitate to raise questions in class.

Abraham Lincoln is a revered personage to the Pakistanis. I have already shown that, in the debate on dictatorship and democracy, his definition was almost invariably cited.[9] Their image of him is, however, primarily that of the Great Emancipator, and they had some difficulty in understanding his dedication to the principle that the Union should come first and the issue of slavery second. They were, understandably, a little disappointed in their hero when they discovered this in Drinkwater. As always, I tried to be absolutely honest with them, and I think that, in the end, they understood that the preservation of the Union inexorably meant the end of slavery, even if the Emancipation Proclamation had not been issued as a war measure.

Lectures on America

In class discussions, it was inevitable that the issue of the Negro in the United States should arise. I would have been both surprised and disappointed in my students if they had not raised it. The Pakistanis and the Indians are extremely color- and race-conscious, not necessarily from a "liberal" point of view, as will be pointed out later.[10] I knew these matters were always in their minds. One boy put the question bluntly in this way: "If Lincoln freed the slaves, why are they not free today?"

It was a fair question, and I answered it as honestly and as fully as I could. Granting that discrimination did exist and that the Negro in our country, particularly in the South, did not wholly enjoy the rights and privileges guaranteed by our constitution, I held that, since the Civil War, the Negro had made remarkable progress from slavery towards his proper status as a full-fledged citizen. Moreover, I pointed out that our Supreme Court had, just three months before, unanimously declared the unconstitutionality of segregation in the public schools, another great step forward. I said further that I did not expect this decision to take effect overnight, but that, in their lifetime, if not in mine, a great majority of American Negroes would be exercising their full rights as American citizens. The case would be harder to argue in Pakistan since the events at Little Rock.

However, the testimony I gave, drawn from personal experience in Detroit, was more telling. I live in an interracial and interdenominational neighborhood. I showed my students pictures of my house and told them about my neighbors: two Irish Catholics—a restaurant-bar owner and the proprietor of a service station; two Jews—the owner of a printing plant and the top executive in an office equipment sales organization; a white Protestant—the owner of a home equipment specialty sales agency, whose son attended my university; and a considerable number of Negroes whose children attended our public schools and my university, including a civil engineer whose wife was a teacher, several auto workers, the prosperous proprietor of a chain of shoe stores, and the principal of a public school. All of these, I pointed out, lived on the same street in the same kind of big comfortable house, and all of them drove better automobiles than I did. Why this last point? Because my boys were particularly interested in cars, and they specifically asked about car ownership.

This state of affairs, I said, came about partly because of the economic status and security achieved by the mass production workers of Detroit through their unions, a status which, I said (and fervently believe), makes the lowliest worker in Michigan far better off than many middle-class Pakistanis. In Detroit, the sons and daughters of what the Pakistanis would call "peons" go to college— or have an opportunity to go—as a matter of course. They may have to work their way through, but they go.

Then I described the political aspects of my home milieu: in recent years the state of Michigan has passed an FEPC law; the voters of the Thirteenth Congressional District elected a Negro to Congress, and white votes were decisive in the outcome; the voters of Detroit likewise overwhelmingly elected a Negro to the Circuit Court bench, and he could not have been elected without white votes. I added that I was proud to have taken an active part in both of these campaigns. I also mentioned, in passing, that I had served two terms on the executive board of the Detroit Chapter of the NAACP.

Quite aside from these evidences of voter maturity, I said that the combination of economic and political power was probably the major force in bringing the Negro his just due; that this power arose out of the practical operations of our economic and political system; and that the Negro was using it within the framework of our democratic system.

And finally I pointed to my own university which has a population of Negro students comparable in ratio to the size of the metropolitan area's Negro population. The salient fact here is that this group is so much a part of the total university community that it rarely occurs to any of us to think of its members as anything but university students. In fact, even to make the point falsifies the matter-of-factness of their routine acceptance, perhaps the only true equality after all.

Having said all this, I was not yet content. In these class discussions, I had observed again a tinge of that "holier-than-thou" attitude in my students which exasperated me above all else. In this context of give and take, I met it head on by first saying that another nation's sins did not justify our failure to achieve our own stated ideals, but that the students might consider the fact that slavery still exists in the Islamic world, notably in Arabia. I added that, for all practical purposes, insofar as I could see, under the feudal zamindar system of land tenure dating from the Mutiny days of 1857, there were more slaves in Pakistan today than in the United States in 1861. At this point, three boys practically jumped out of their seats to shout the Pakistani equivalent of "Amen." This was an unexpected development which comforted me considerably. After this spontaneous outburst from the jury, the defense rested.

In this and similar discussions, such as those which followed the two lectures I was asked to give on the War for Independence and the Civil War, I tried to act on the principle that intellectual honesty and scholarly objectivity were higher values than propaganda for my country. Without playing down the idealism of Washington and Jefferson or the willingness of hundreds of thousands of common men to fight and die for a cause in the years 1861–65, I sought to show that history is far more complex than a simple struggle between good and evil men. After a year abroad, I am more than ever convinced that the capacity for thinking critically about the meaning of history in all its complex interrelationships is a pressing need both in Pakistan and in the United States. The support accorded to the Union cause by the English textile workers during our Civil War and the parallel support of the English Labor Party and thousands of other liberal Englishmen for Indo-Pakistani independence will illustrate what I mean.

The capacity for reviewing one's own history critically may be simply a product of national maturity. For example, I doubt that the case for our own colonial Tories received much of a hearing in our history before the twentieth century. Although it is much too early to expect the young nation of Pakistan to discuss dispassionately its relations with India since 1947, it is surely a desideratum. To some extent, national policy in respect to another nation rests on one nation's sense of the meaning of the other nation's history. Sputnik has forced upon us that kind of revaluation of the meaning of Russian history as a necessary step toward deciding what our policy ought to be in the future. It is a painful process, but there are some indications that we are facing up to the need for it. India and Pakistan must go through a similar process during which the stereotypes and the wishful thinking characteristic of a revolutionary period must be replaced by a more deeply realistic and adequate understanding of what they are and what other nations are.

As yet, neither Indians nor Pakistanis know themselves very well —that is why Nehru's book, *The Discovery of India* seems to me to be very significant—and they do not know each other very well. Furthermore, they do not know their neighboring nations very well, and they certainly do not know the Western world well. In short, they strike me as being very parochial nations indeed, nations locked up in the closed rooms of their own cultures and their own view of history as a simple black and white struggle against the imperialistic West.

The question arises: are we any better by these same criteria? In any statistical sense, it would be hard to demonstrate that masses of Americans know more about the subcontinent than Indo-Pakistanis know about the United States, but in respect to our own history, we are far more critical and knowledgeable, if not in popular understanding, at least in the range and depth of our printed materials. I cite two examples: the flood of books and articles on our Civil War, examining its every aspect from every point of view, as contrasted with the Indo-Pakistani treatment of the Mutiny of 1857; and the spate of critical biography of Franklin D. Roosevelt, as contrasted with the amount of writing and the attitudes expressed in that writing about Jinnah in Pakistan and Ghandi in India.

The United States has been parochial in the twentieth century, and we have paid for it, but, it seems to me that, in any large academic community in this country, there is some interest in and knowledge of the art, culture, and history of Indo-Pakistan. Assuredly, there is not enough. We should systematically offer opportunity for the mastery of the most important languages of the subcontinent. Americans have not yet learned that the knowledge of another man's language is a recognition of his dignity and worth. The utilitarian reasons for such language study are, to my mind, of less consequence.

These ideas stem out of my attempt to demonstrate at Abbottabad that the concept of truth in history was a higher consideration than the opportunity to make some obvious propagandistic hay. It was an effort to encourage some honest critical thinking where not much of it had been done. It may have been quixotic. I can imagine what a trained party-liner would have done in that setting. Yet I have some reason to believe that certain faculty members respected my intentions whereas, weary of political slogans as they were, they would have been polite but unconvinced in the face of the naked "message" to the effect that our Revolution was nothing but a noble struggle against a barbarous oppressor and our Civil War nothing but a noble crusade against slavery.

Indeed, this temperate and objective approach to my own country's history probably gave substance to another proposition which I regularly advanced to my colleagues in conversation: that I considered myself not as an American professor, but as a professor who happened to be an American. They approved of this view, and I commend it to future lecturers abroad, hoping that it is not presumptuous to do so. We are far more likely to win respect for our nation if we consider ourselves as members of an international community of scholars dedicated to learning and truth than if we think of ourselves as "Americans First."

In demonstrating a readiness to act in terms of this principle, I found that, when I did give five lectures on *The American Achievement in Literature: 1900–1956* at Abbottabad and at the University of Peshawar, they were received as a professor's lectures, not as American propaganda.

A brief word about these lectures. It was my understanding when I left for Pakistan that I was to be a lecturer in English and American literature. When I got to Abbottabad, I found that American literature was not in the sacred curriculum. I told Dr. Khan that I wanted no special favors, that I was perfectly willing to do precisely what my colleagues did, but that I would like to have a chance to lecture on the letters of my country. With his characteristic generous cooperation, Dr. Khan immediately arranged to give me five consecutive Sunday morning periods (preceding the tutorial group meetings), at which times the entire college—faculty, students, and some invited visitors—assembled to hear me. Furthermore, at Dr. Khan's suggestion, the United States Educational Foundation later reproduced these lectures for distribution throughout Pakistan. After my return home, the USIS again reproduced them for distribution to all bi-national centers. I record these facts simply to make clear that, by virtue of having an understanding principal, I was given a chance to fulfill my mission. Other Fulbrighters have been less fortunate.

I appear to have strayed from the point at issue: the need for an educational system which encourages independent, critical, disciplined thinking. In my opinion, the Pakistani system, notably in the area of the humanities, does not do this. Factors which militate against this end have already been defined: the curriculum itself, the examination system, and reliance on rote learning and canned answers. Another powerful deterrent of intellectual initiative on the part of the student is the failure to foster a desire to read outside the curriculum, with the resultant neglect of library resources. But perhaps the greatest obstacle to intellectual growth is the impersonal relationship between student and lecturer. Questions are not encouraged. The need for vital questioning is unrecognized.

Desperate Pedagogical Inventions

These generalities may be illustrated by one practical point: no demands were made on the students between the college and university examinations. Aside from the routine experiments in the sciences, just one of my colleagues gave a test of his own during my year of residence, as far as I could find out. He was Manzur, the physicist. I discovered that he had made an arrangement with the principal whereby those who did not show up were fined a couple of rupees, not a small penalty. Encouraged by this break in the accepted pattern, I announced a test for my first and second year students. It was a simple test of vocabulary and identification of the characters we had met in our required reading. Every item on the examination had been patiently discussed and defined in class; in fact, following the example of my colleagues, I had insisted that my students take down notes, which I dictated very slowly.

This test created a sensation in the college—something I learned later. Although I did not set up a system of fines for non-appearance, most of the boys showed up. As advertised, I wrote eight items on the board, to be handled in forty minutes, the standard college period. Then there was a dead silence. One of the braver boys raised his hand and asked, "Do we do one out of eight?" And he was serious. I said they were to do all eight, and they set earnestly to work. The results were not good, but they were good enough to indicate that these boys could have answered for themselves, had they been required to do so regularly.

On a similar kind of examination given to the second year boys, I was driven to elementary expedients. I started a competition between the arts classes and the science classes, both of which were to do the same work. Pakistani boys like competition, and in some degree the device was successful. The boys took this novel enterprise with reasonable seriousness; that is, most of them showed up, and busily copied what their more knowledgeable neighbors wrote. It was impossible to prevent this practice because they were packed together at their long wooden benches like bleacherites at a World Series sell-out. The science boys did markedly better than the arts boys.

On another occasion, trying hard to break through the pattern of passivity, I assigned a theme to be written in class in which they were to demonstrate that they were in fact real students at Abbottabad Government College; that is, they were to justify their presence on the campus. Of all my desperate pedagogical devices (excepting the relatively long essays which some of my senior and junior boys did for me), this one worked best. At first the boys were startled. Then, as I hoped, they began to ask questions. One boy got to the heart of the matter quickly. What did I mean by a "real student"? I answered that a real student was one who did more than was required of him because he wanted to, one who loved learning for its own sake, one who recognized his moral and intellectual obligations to his own family, to his nation, and, above all, to his own intelligence. We talked about these matters for a few periods before the writing of the theme. I confess that I was pretty heavily moralistic in these discussions, but I did not say anything I did not believe. Furthermore, Pakistani boys (and their elders) have a bias toward the moralistic, at least in their public attitudes. And so, after much talk to the effect that it was not enough to wear the college uniform, to pay one's tuition, to attend lectures, to obey the college regulations, and merely to pass examinations, the boys came to class one day and wrote their papers.

A fair number met my challenge. The best paper in the lot was written by a grave, handsome young man from faraway Hunza. He began by asking himself why he had left his beautiful valley and his beloved family to go to a distant place where he knew no one and nobody understood him. It was a moving depiction of a state of loneliness. Then he answered himself by saying that he sought knowledge because he realized how much he and his people needed it. I read this essay to the class, and they agreed that its author was a "real student." They respected this boy, partly because he came from an important Hunza family.

Not the least encouraging aspect of this experiment was the presence of a sense of humor in some of the papers. Humor was usually expressed in cruel and elementary forms, in the universal manner of adolescents motivated by the wolf-pack mentality. This time, however, a few of the boys achieved irony. They took the superficial definition accepted in their own student society and challenged anybody to demonstrate they were not "students." After all, they held, we do everything "required" of us—why not? In so arguing, they revealed that something had sunk in. Although this order of argument was a simple reversal of my preachments, their use of the ironic mode was in itself proof that some thinking had occurred. A further proof was that the class recognized this kind of irony when such papers were read, and they responded with laughter.

A Debate on Coeducation

Another of my desperate devices did not achieve such happy results, but it was illuminating. In an attempt to develop some vital

93

class participation, I once announced to my second year boys that we were going to have a debate and that, after the debate, every boy would be required to write a paper on the subject of the argument. The class was to choose the topic. I suggested several: One Unit for West Pakistan, separate and joint electorates, the Baghdad Pact, and similar subjects. Then I asked for suggestions from the floor. One boy, the son of an army colonel, an earnest student, proposed, of all things, coeducation! The class voted, almost unanimously, for this topic! Why the exclamation points? Because not one single boy in the whole class had ever had any experience with coeducation and they knew nothing whatever about it—a fact which did not prevent their having decided opinions on the matter. The colonel's son bravely undertook to defend coeducation, but, paradoxically, nobody in the class could be prevailed upon to oppose it formally. Thereupon we decided that the colonel's boy would prepare an essay in which he would discuss both pros and cons, after which the class would discuss the points he had made. He did so, and he did it pretty well.

Then all hell broke loose. Another bright boy in the class (the brother of the young freshman who led the field in the university examinations) spearheaded the attack. His case was grounded on two fundamental principles: that coeducation was contrary of the principles of Islam and that it had produced unspeakable immorality in the Western world, specifically, the terrible phenomenon of prostitution. He documented this aspect of his case with a letter from a Pakistani friend studying abroad, in which the whores of Naples were described with fascinated horror.

At this point two things were clear: that the choice of subject had been dictated by a prurient, explosive obsession with sex, and that most of the boys were waiting to hear what I had to say.

I had assumed the role of moderator and had ruled myself out of the discussion, but I told them that, if they really wanted to hear my views, they could so vote, and I would oblige them. Thereupon, the whole class joined battle in a caricature of a parliamentary session, controlled (in theory) by *Robert's Rules of Order*. The main point at issue was completely obscured by technical and hair-splitting motions and countermotions, quite in the spirit of the leader of the opposition in the preliminary fights before the two college debates. I let the travesty go on for a time, and, while it lasted, it seemed to be an exact microcosm of the political behavior I had observed in their elders—once in a meeting of the membership of the

Abbottabad Club in which learned judges acted like schoolboys, and again in press reports of the conduct of the West Pakistan assembly. At last, I took hold. I suggested the parallel with their own parliamentary bodies, and expressed the hope that, in the future, they would use *Robert's* as a means rather than as an end in itself. The "House" finally decided to do what it had wanted from the beginning: it resolved to request me to speak on the proposition of the debate.

I did not waste much time on the prostitution matter,[11] merely pointing out that it was a world-wide, age-old phenomenon, hardly restricted to the Western world. However, I could not resist citing a recent press story in the *Pakistan Times* which had chronicled the legal petition to the city fathers from the professional ladies of Rawalpindi who pleaded for a continuance of their traditional rights in that municipality. I also pointed out that Pakistan already had a measure of coeducation in its universities. But my chief argument was that, without coeducation, Pakistan was denying almost 50 per cent of its human resources, its women, the opportunity of making their greatest possible contribution to the welfare of the state. That is, Pakistan did not attempt to educate women as it did men, and the relatively few who had access to education (excepting a handful in the colleges and universities) had "separate" but not "equal" opportunities—a condition which we know something about in the United States.

The Morality of Survival

At any rate, the time allotted for debate and discussion ended, and approximately one-half of the class handed in their papers a week later. These papers presented a different kind of moral issue; about half of them had obviously been drawn from the same source. After I had read and corrected the first batch (quite a job), I gave another moral lecture. The class, I said, had debated coeducation almost solely on the basis of sexual morality, but this is not the only aspect of morality. There are also the matters of financial morality and intellectual morality. What, for instance, does the Prophet think about theft? The boys told me: He did not approve of it. Very well, then, what is the difference between stealing a man's rupees and stealing his ideas? For myself, I would not trust a man who did either. The boys seemed to be impressed—they were always impressed by moral homilies—and so I delivered the same spiel to the other section of this class just before they handed in their papers. They were also impressed. They applauded loudly, but they handed in their papers nonetheless, and some fifteen of those were practically identical.

What does this signify? Certainly plagiarism is not rare in American educational institutions, but I rather doubt that some thirty out of sixty students in a given class would hand in almost identical papers, if only out of prudential considerations, and it is not claiming too much to say that plagiarism is not condoned by our public morality. This moral blind spot is the product of a number of factors at work in Pakistani education, and now I come back to the possible consequences on Pakistani character of the curriculum, the classroom mode, and the examination system.

To summarize briefly. I have held that the English curriculum is not meaningful in itself for the Pakistani, nor is it made meaningful in its lecture context because the lecturer's responsibility ends with the class period; that the student is not required to think for himself nor to show that he can think for himself nor to give any accounting of his intellectual activity between examinations; that the examinations themselves are the ends rather than means of achieving education; and, finally, that the results of the examination either make or break the student's career.

In this tissue of circumstances, not so much an immorality as a different kind of morality evolves: it is moral to pass by any means; it is immoral to fail. But the greatest immorality of all is the system which imposes on the student the need for summarizing summaries, and then compounds the crime by accepting second- or third-hand canned answers.

I have been speaking of an intellectually immoral principle at work. There are other more specific kinds of practical immorality at work too in the educational system. Much of this stems out of the same state of mind that produced the endemic political corruption which plagued Pakistan. For one thing, as my colleagues told me, there is the perennial danger of corruption in the examination itself.

The atmosphere of the examinations at Abbottabad was heavy with suspicion. Once my department head asked me to prepare some questions for a "house" examination on material I was teaching. I did so and took them out to the college next day. He was not on campus. I left the questions with the chief clerk. My department head was very unhappy about this because, as he made clear, he simply did not trust the head clerk to keep them secret.

I remember discussing with my colleagues the American system, whereby the professor himself has charge of the course, determines the curriculum, sets the examinations, and gives the grades. This system sounded fine to them, and yet they seemed to have certain reservations, which, largely because of Pakistani politeness, they did not disclose. Finally, with the help of my wife, the light dawned. The question in their minds was: how can we in the United States trust the professors to be honest? It is a good question, and it speaks volumes about the psychic atmosphere which either generates or is generated by the national mores.

It is this fundamental atmosphere of distrust, I think, which (among other reasons) tends to prevent any decentralization of Pakistani higher education, with the result that affiliated colleges of universities have very little autonomy and the lecturers in those colleges have little power to assess the work of their students. The tragedy is that, without power or responsibility, neither the administrators of the colleges nor the lecturers seem to have any initiative in respect to their programs. Most American faculties are concerned in one way or another with educational policy in their institutions; my Pakistani colleagues could not be involved in any vital sense. As a result, they were not much interested in the larger aspects of their professional obligations. They were servants of the system—that is all.

In this total situation, the almost innocent amorality of my students becomes understandable. The fundamental point is that plagiarism and beating the system in one way or another are not really wrong in their minds. Yes, they might be caught and punished for cheating on examinations, for they are heavily proctored, but I do not think that the culprits incur any social obloquy. I am reminded of one typical German judgment on Hitler: he was not wrong; he failed.

I come down from these lofty peaks of moral superiority to the level of low comedy in the classroom. In my first weeks at Abbottabad, I was plagued with a parade of young men who interrupted my lectures with notes solemnly attesting to the fact that Hamid's brother, or Abdul's, or Husain's had come to visit him, and would I excuse the student from the hour—once he had been safely marked present in the roll book. For a while I went along with this gag which invariably stirred up smothered laughter in the class while I remained poker-faced. Then, after making sure that I was not in danger of violating the sacred family tie which binds Muslims together, I cheerfully expressed pleasure at these visitations, expressed a desire to meet the visiting brother, and invited him (presumably standing outside in anxious affectionate waiting) to hear the rest of the lecture. Of course, Junior's brother, if there was one, had no desire to hear an extra lecture, and the boys gave up on this gambit. The laughter which greeted this countertactic was not smothered.

A variant of this strategy in the game of getting a lecture scored to one's credit without attendance was the easy device of answering the roll call by proxy. It was difficult to cope with this in a large class, particularly because I was not much interested in playing cops and robbers with the students. However, one of the student proctors (each class had two), in his professional zeal, finally told me that I was being imposed upon by this practice. I suspected that he wanted to see how I would handle the situation. I found an easy formula: by a system of random sampling or spot checking, I would suddenly ask roll number sixty-two or eighty-five to stand up. Often sixty-two or eighty-five was not there to stand up, and his proxy did not dare to. Another expedient was to call on suspect roll numbers to recite unexpectedly. After a week or so of this, the proctor expressed himself as satisfied, but I am sure that there were a great many ghosts recorded in my roll book.

A more sensational episode in this perennial war of the jailers and the jailed occurred when it became apparent that a number of lads in the back of the room were sneaking out after the roll call. This kind of childishness both amused and annoyed me, and so, one day, I put on a fine dramatic performance.

Scene I: Professor gives another of those popular moral homilies. I was accustomed to deal with young gentlemen, not with children. I was not a policeman, and I resented the need of becoming one as a degradation of my noble profession. The boys who skipped class were only penalizing themselves and their revered fathers and mothers, who had scrimped and saved to send their ungrateful sons to college. What kind of impression of Pakistani students did they want me to take back to the United States? Patriotism and all the moral forces of Islam demanded that they come to class and stay there. I wanted to work at my job as professor, but, since the delinquents did not want to work at their jobs as students, I had had enough. If the rest of the class wanted me to try to prepare them for the examinations (a shrewd touch), they had better bring the criminals back into line.

Scene II: Professor stalks out of the classroom in a state of fine simulated rage.

This playlet had two consequences: the first, not unexpected, was that the boys thereafter stayed in the classroom, even with the back doors open; the second, wholly unexpected, was that a number of my faculty colleagues sought me out and apologized for the students.

To conclude this discourse on education, I must add that the criticisms herein set forth of the curriculum and education systems in Pakistan are supported by Pakistani educators as well. This fact, gratifying to me, was demonstrated very clearly at a professional conference, held in Peshawar in December 1956, in which I was privileged to take part. It appears that, as usual, the workers in the vineyard not only know what the score is, but that they also have pretty sound ideas about how to improve it for the home team—the workers in this case being the teachers themselves. I had further evidence of this in Dacca at a similar conference, held in early February of 1957, in which I also participated.

Indeed, I later discovered that nearly every conclusion I had arrived at as a result of my own personal experience had already been trenchantly stated by the Planning Board of the Government of Pakistan in Chapter 26, "Education and Training," of *The First Five Year Plan: 1955–60 (Draft)*. Here is what the Board had to say.

151356

The Examination system is generally recognized as one of the unsatisfactory features of higher education and the major institutional barrier to higher learning. It is a formidable obstacle in the path of curriculum revision. Accompanied as they have to be by prescribed syllabi and text books, the centrally prepared external examinations stifle teacher and college initiative and experimentation. The slow and cumbersome process which is required to revise syllabi and change text books forces teaching to lag behind the current state of knowledge and inhibits the introduction of new knowledge and new ideas by the teacher. The teacher himself has little or no incentive to keep himself or his students up-to-date. Exclusive reliance upon the examination system also has adverse effects on the teaching and learning process. The teacher is judged by the number of his students who pass an examination which is prepared by someone else, and not on his success in inspiring their understanding and independent thought. The student's diligence and the excellence and creativeness of his work are not the subject of judgment or guidance by the individual teacher, by the college—or indeed by any one. It is small wonder that about three-fourths of the degree candidates fail to pass their examinations. Reading for two years without discipline in preparation for a single examination does not encourage habits of industry and thought. On the contrary, the system develops pressure from the students for procedural changes—more time, simpler examinations, lower passing grades, etc.—all resulting in lower standards and discipline.[12]

Furthermore, I found in the same document, paragraph 160 (b), a point of view about the teaching of English which in part, at least, supports the conclusions I expressed to Principal Rustomji's group. Is it a contradiction then to state that the voices which speak out for reform of curriculum and examination systems are lonely ones? Not necessarily so. The planners are, perhaps, the most enlightened group in Pakistan, and the professional educators who come to the conferences are also likely to be relatively advanced in their thinking. However, I think that most educational personnel in Pakistan tend to be fixed in their grooves, and the Pakistani bureaucracy, like all bureaucracies, moves at a molasses pace. If the recommendations of *The First Five Year Plan* in all fields should be carried out, Pakistan would take a long stride forward, but I saw little evidence of any practical or realistic efforts to do so on the operating level, excepting possibly in the industrial area. Insofar as land reform and education are concerned, the vested interests, aided by habit, inertia, and apathy, were still too powerful to permit much change.

At the University of Peshawar

The intellectual climate of the University of Peshawar was quite different from that of Abbottabad Government College. We spent ten days at the University towards the end of February 1957. The weather was fine—sometimes almost too hot; the hospitality was equally warm; and the student-faculty response to our visit was gratifying. Altogether it was a rich, invigorating, and satisfying experience.

The University of Peshawar was established in 1950. It has twenty-five departments of study, and, as stated earlier, it is also the controlling agent for some nine affiliated colleges of which Abbottabad is one (there may be more now). It is located about five miles from Peshawar city on its own generous campus within easy sight of the entrance to the Khyber Pass and the brooding mountains which are the northwestern rampart of Pakistan. All of the University's buildings are in a uniform style of architecture, including the faculty housing, an integral part of the campus plan, characteristically arranged according to academic rank. As a whole, the University is a small town in its own right, and it is an attractive place even in its raw newness. When the landscaping is completed, it will be lovely. It is justifiably the pride of the Northwest Frontier Province. (The people of West Pakistan do not think in terms of One Unit, and I doubt that they will for a long time to come.)

100

This pride did not rest on buildings alone. The University showed promise of intellectual stature as well. Its chief executive, the vice-chancellor, was Dr. Siddiqi, a mathematical physicist, well known in his field. Some two months earlier, he had impressed me with the caliber of his mind in his opening address to the conference of educators in Peshawar. This impression of a tough and disciplined intellect was confirmed by a conversation held in his office. Dr. Siddiqi had very clear ideas as to what his university should be, he knew what he was up against, and he was moving toward the attainment of his ideal by means of careful policies.

Our own academic host at the University was the head of the English Department, Dr. Mazher Ali Khan. Born in what is today India, he had been trained at Cambridge in England, and, like so many of his compatriots, he had cast his lot with the new nation of Pakistan. In early middle age and unmarried, he lived in a faculty house, had an impressive library, was a gentleman, a scholar, and a charming host. The only other member of the English Department, a man a little younger than Dr. Mazher and also trained in England, had a ready wit and a shrewd gift for the penetrating question.

Under the auspices of the English Department, I gave eight lectures at Peshawar. My audience was composed of graduate students who were candidates for the M.A., other interested students, the English staff, and visitors from other faculties of the University, including the head of the Medical College, economists, and lawyers.

What made this audience unique in my Pakistani experience was the presence of girl students, comprising about one-third of those who regularly attended. They came to the lecture room in their *burqas*, and they were separated from the males by a curtain which ran from my lectern to the back of the room. Yet, it is pleasant to relate, the girls were not shy, and, at the end of the lectures, they asked questions with eager curiosity. After the strict purdah of Abbottabad, it was refreshing to see them and good to hear them talk spiritedly about literature and ideas.

Any American facing a Pakistani or Indian audience is on trial in more ways than one. The American professor is particularly on a spot because American scholarship is, to put it frankly, suspect on the the subcontinent. Part of this attitude stems from the traditional English condescension towards American intellectual enterprise, a condescension which, I believe, is not so marked now as it was in the nineteenth and early twentieth centuries—that is, at the time when the English teachers of the current generation of mature Indians and

101

Pakistanis were being educated and conditioned to passing on this condescension to their pupils.

In this situation, I sensed a challenge and I took an opportunity. Therefore, I chose to begin my series with three lectures on Swift, Dryden, and Pope rather than with the five lectures on American Literature which I had prepared back in Abbottabad. There were obvious advantages in this choice. The three figures were English; they were "classic"; they were in the syllabus; and students were to be examined on them for their degrees.

As an introduction, I said that, because Pakistani students of literature were handicapped by inadequate libraries and by the un-availability of learned journals, I would, insofar as possible, attempt to summarize for them the most important contributions of modern scholarship to the critical study of those three great writers.

In the process, it was easy to demonstrate, without overstatement or artificial emphasis, that American scholars had done impressive work in these and related fields. I am sure that our English colleagues would agree. It was not necessary to wave the Star-Spangled Banner over the ramparts of scholarship, and I did not do so. I let the facts speak for themselves.

This approach was effective, I think. At the end of the first lecture on Swift, Dr. Khan himself was kind enough to express the warmest approval, and he urged me to take more time for the next two lectures. At first I demurred on humanitarian grounds, but, since he insisted and I am no exception to the principle that professors enjoy talking to captive audiences, I yielded. The result was that the following lectures on Dryden and Pope, with question periods, ran two hours each.

What pleased me most about this experience was that the audience was curious—intellectually curious. Of course, the students were interested in what I had to say because the information might be of value in the examinations, but they were also interested in scholarship and, especially, in the fact of American scholarship, something they had had little chance to know about before. Above all, I was delighted with the probing curiosity of the girl students. They asked more questions—and more searching questions—than did the male students. This phenomenon is a happy augury for the future of Pakistani women. All they need is a chance.

After having established my academic qualifications, so to speak, I proceeded to give five lectures on modern American literature. By this time, it seemed to me that my audience was disposed to listen somewhat more respectfully than it might have without my Restoration and Augustan prelude. Again the questions were eager, and again many of them came from the distaff side of the curtain. Pakistanis know very little about American literature (they have heard of Whitman and Emerson) and less about contemporary American literature. Conversely, of course, we know very little about Islamic literature and less about contemporary Urdu and Bengali literature.

One other small but significant incident developed out of the lectures on American literature. At the end of one session, a girl, certainly the most articulate of her group if not the brightest, asked where she might get access to the writers I had discussed. It so happened that, in a room adjoining the lecture room, Dr. Khan had established a sort of auxiliary library for his students—a happy arrangement inasmuch as the main university library was some distance away. Furthermore, these books were more readily available to students than the books in the Abbottabad library. I had earlier noticed, much to my pleasure, that this subsidiary collection contained a fair number of American classics and standard anthologies, gifts of the Asia Foundation and the USIS. Apparently the young lady had not been aware of their presence; she seemed surprised when I pointed them out to her.

The significance of this event lies in two things: the failure of students, both Pakistani and American, to exploit the resources available to them on their own initiative; and the universal psychological phenomenon of the failure to *see* what has not been made important to us.

The cosmopolitan flavor of the University's life was another pleasant aspect of our Peshawar experience. My two colleagues in English were, as I have noted, sophisticated men. One of the lecturers in economics was a Canadian who, with his wife and children, was an integral part of the University community, not merely a guest for a year. He worked hard at his teaching and his scholarship, and it was plain that he was liked and respected by his Pakistani colleagues. He attended the lecture series regularly. He was, of course, quite at home with Swift, Dryden, and Pope, but a good deal of what I had to say about modern American literature was new to him, and he responded to it with challenging questions and shrewd comment. Another person who attended regularly out of a combination of courtesy and professional interest was the principal of the Frontier College for Women, Miss Harbottle. She was an unusual person. She had elected a career in the Pakistani educational service, and she was dedicated to her job. Perfectly at home with her Pakistani associates, she was as far away as one could get from the Kipling memsahib psychology. Born and bred in Britain, possessed of a solid English university training, and very English in some ways, she was profoundly anti-colonial in her values and her outlook. It was her personal rejection of racist doctrines which had brought her back to Pakistan after a tour of duty in Africa, which she had found distasteful.

At a dinner party given in our honor by Miss Harbottle, we also met, among the Pakistani guests, two non-Pakistani young men who were teaching in local colleges. One of these, like Miss Harbottle, had cast his lot with Pakistan and was making his life career there. He was a man whose honesty and integrity in conducting a polling place had elicited favorable comment from my Abbottabad faculty friends who knew him by reputation.[13] The other young man was an American teaching in Peshawar under the auspices of the Asia Foundation. Both of them were thoroughly enjoying their assignments.

Another couple in what might be called the international set was composed of an architect of Hungarian origin, working for the Pakistani government, and his wife, who taught French at the University. The architect was an able professional with wide interests in art and music, and his wife was a charming, cultured woman. The evening we spent in their home was noteworthy for the range of the guest list and the scope of the conversation. It happened, for instance, that, like many eggheads on this side of the water, the architect was devoted to Adlai Stevenson, a devotion which he volunteered with great fervency and enthusiasm.

There was also in Peshawar a sizable ICA (International Cooperation Administration) contingent of Americans. During our ten-day stay, we lived with a Kansas girl who was a specialist in home economics assigned to the local Village AID Institute. She made us feel very much at home. However, my busy schedule of lectures prevented us from getting any more than a superficial knowledge of the operations of the ICA program in Peshawar. On the social side, we were warmly and hospitably received by the American colony; on the program side, it seemed that the ICA team working with the University were not quite as much in the full current of the University's life as the other people discussed above.

There is, I think, one compelling reason for this state of affairs, which is not wholly the fault of the ICA personnel. As I was given to understand the situation, the basic policy governing ICA operations in Peshawar was that ICA personnel should serve in advisory capacities, not in executive or administrative capacities. There is a limit to how much advice can be given and taken effectively. The obligation to give advice without the power to put it into practice produces a situation which is frustrating to one side and exasperating to the other.

Fulbrighters (except those who have specific research assignments) work as organic members of the teaching faculty. For reasons which I do not know, there were no Fulbrighters officially assigned to the Peshawar campus in the academic year of 1956–57. However, Fulbrighters had served the University in preceding years in various fields, and the unsolicited reports on their work from University people were uniformly favorable.

Fulbrighters in Pakistan did not have many of the privileges enjoyed by their ICA fellow citizens. The Fulbrighters were paid in rupees, not in dollars. They did not have access to motor vehicles as all ICA personnel do as a matter of course; their stipends were not comparable to ICA salaries; and they did not have commissary privileges which permit ICA personnel to buy staple United States canned goods, liquor and cigarettes at relatively cheap prices. ICA people have semidiplomatic status; Fulbrighters are pretty much on their own, except for the usual services rendered to American citizens abroad by our consular and embassy personnel and except for the hospitality accorded on a personal basis by resident Americans to transient Americans.

Still, the Fulbrighters had some advantages by virtue of their somewhat detached position. Within the limits of professional standards, sense of mission, and the great responsibility of being cultural ambassadors at large, they were free to speak their minds. These limitations are formidable enough, but they are to a considerable extent self-imposed; they constitute approximately the same kind of implicit standards which govern the American professor at home. Overseas, the Fulbrighters do not have to follow any "line" other than the line they set for themselves through their own awareness of their total purposes as citizens and professors. Above all, the Fulbrighters are free to teach—even within the confines of the prescribed curriculum there is a measure of freedom, for teaching and lecturing are highly personal enterprises—and they are free to lecture according to their learning and their lights. In their holiday periods, they are free to go where they choose and to do what they choose. In short, Fulbright professors are not bureaucrats; at least, they don't have to be bureaucrats.

These are no small advantages, and they were impressed upon me by the Peshawar experience, which was the most satisfying period in the year. The personal and official hospitality of Dr. Mazher and his faculty colleagues; the intellectual curiosity of the students; the opportunity to lecture in my special eighteenth-century field and in American literature to advanced students and to faculty members of the University community; and the invigorating atmosphere of the University and its people—all of these made it so. Yet, more important than the personal pleasure derived from this halcyon ten days was the feeling that the University of Peshawar was on its way to being what a university should be.

This is not to say that Abbottabad Government College and what it represents in Pakistani education is less important; on the contrary, if anything, it is more important. What happens at Abbottabad and the other affiliated colleges of the universities will obviously determine the quality of the work done at the highest level.

Chapter Five

Social Life in Abbottabad

The Club

The club in Abbottabad was the center of the town's social life for the army officers, the lawyers, the judges, the gazetted officers, and the small contingent of foreigners who turned up in the area for a variety of interesting reasons. The club members were the dominant group in the community, and they constituted a cross section of the dominant social classes in Pakistan. For most of the town's inhabitants and for the visitors from the surrounding villages, the bazaar was the club.

In its present state, the Abbottabad Club was built just before partition in 1947. It was dedicated by a British general on an occasion suitably commemorated by an inscription on a prominent stone block. A rambling, one-floor structure with a very large screened porch, it is set in well kept grounds, and it commands a view of the valley and the distant snow-topped mountains, a view which familiarity cannot stale.

107

Among the club's amenities were two tennis courts (groomed daily) and a small swimming pool. It also had squash courts in an outlying building, but they were not in use. Army men played squash at Kakul, the big base which included the Pakistan Military Academy.

Inside the club there were card rooms, a large ballroom, and a bar which was by far the most popular spot in the whole building. One wing was taken up by living quarters for six men, assigned by the British War Office to teach "signals" to the Pakistani Army. All of them were a credit to their country and to the human race. They were civilians working on a contract basis, not officers, and they wore mufti. They had their own bearer and cook. After we left, these Englishmen rented their own house on Mansehra Road.

A smaller building adjacent to the club provided quarters for the club office, presided over by a permanent secretary, and for the club library which had interesting things in it but which was rarely used because it was too cold to be comfortable, no matter how warm it was outside.

The club steward was an efficient Portuguese from Goa, and he had a brother who did similar work in the Government House in Dacca, East Pakistan. Evidently the Goan Portuguese have made a specialty of this vocation on the subcontinent, as the Greeks are supposed to have an affinity for the restaurant business in the United States.

The club was quiet until four o'clock in the afternoon. Then, after tea, the devoted tennis disciples would appear—among them, a judge, a leading advocate of the local bar, a high forestry official, the cantonment executive officer, a lieutenant colonel from the Pakistan Army Medical Corps who had served a tour of duty in Texas, other assorted officers, representatives of the Public Works Department, and the Deputy Commissioner, the most powerful of the civilian officials. On weekends, the German technicians from Siemens who ran the telephone plant at nearby Haripur would turn up for a game, and the Englishmen, who usually worked too late on weekdays to play, would also be on the courts.

In Chapter VIII, I deal with sports in Pakistan, but here I will discuss the club tennis as a social phenomenon. As at most small clubs, the players would alternate; doubles was the common game. One did not play singles if people were waiting. There were other unspoken conventions. The good players always waited for the first court; the forester, as the senior member, usually decided who would play with whom; the club professional, called the "marker," generally played with the weakest player in order to balance the competition; and it was tacitly assumed that the last set of the afternoon would be played by the four best players present, including the marker. If anybody wanted to work out with the marker, he came early. The game was always played fiercely with much good-natured comment in English and Urdu from the players on the court and the kibitzers on the porch. The best players were a lawyer, who had won his "colors" (we would say his varsity letter) at the University of the Punjab, and the medical colonel, who had been in Texas. As a matter of plain fact, the latter looked like a Texan, especially since he always wore shorts and a baseball cap, and he played like a Texan—or a Californian. When these two played each other or when one of them played the marker, first-rate tennis resulted. In fact, the quality of tennis was rather better than run-of-the-mine club tennis in the United States.

All of this may sound very much like tennis at any club in the United States, but there were two important aspects of the game which made the sport at the Abbottabad Club quite different from American club tennis. These were the presence of the marker and the ball boys, and the general absence of women. Although a number of army wives were not in purdah, I never saw one of them on the courts, or in the swimming pool either. Pakistani women play tennis in Lahore and Karachi, but not in Abbottabad. The only women I saw play, and these not often, were Western women—the wife of the English captain who was in charge of the Pakistan Army Music School, the wife of a German technician, the guest of a European doctor practicing in Abbottabad, and my wife.

It is true that American clubs do have tennis pros, but, I think, not very many small clubs comparable to this one can afford such a luxury, nor can our small clubs afford to have a staff of six ball boys daily for two courts. In these days, it is hard enough to get ball boys for tournaments. The Abbottabad club had both ball boys and pro, and the pro was unique in my experience.

His name was Mir Abdullah. He was reputed to be at least sixty years old, and he may have been older. I was told that he once had been the All-Indian professional champion, and I believe it. He was still, very probably, the best all-around player in Pakistan. He could adjust his game effortlessly to the veriest tyro, make a mediocre one play over his head, and, when he chose, give lessons in tactics to the best players during the process of beating them. He had every stroke in the game under absolute control, and, despite his age, his reflexes were amazingly sharp, a fact which was most evident in his volleying and overhead. Of medium height, he was greyhound lean and whipcord tough; he could play all afternoon, seemingly without tiring.

Mir Abdullah was much liked and respected by the club members because he was a lovable man. They called him "Kaka," an affectionate term of address approximating the word "uncle."

Nevertheless, there was a great social gap between Kaka and the members. In the United States our pros are today the chosen favorites of our society. They are the kings of their clubhouses. It is not so in Pakistan. There the old English attitude towards professionals still prevails. Kaka's office was not in the clubhouse. He had a chair under a clump of trees near the courts. When it rained, he was permitted to take shelter on the porch, but he always stood apart. After a set of doubles in which he was a participant, he remained some yards away from the other players until it was decided who would go on next. Whenever a sahib (European or Pakistani) appeared, he stood up and saluted respectfully and he always said "sir." No comment was ever made on this state of affairs by either the marker or any member. Apparently it was taken for granted on both sides as right and proper. The attitude of the college boys to their own marker was much the same; he was regarded as a social inferior, a servant.

The ball boys ranged in age from about nine or ten to fourteen. They were dressed in their school uniform of butternut gray. They came directly to the courts after school, and they served as groundskeepers and maintenance men before play started. Then, three to a court, they kept track of the balls. This group was under the marker's control, and he exercised a benevolent but very firm grip on his young charges. At times, when they did not perform their duties properly, the marker did not hesitate to smash a tennis ball at the culprit; he rarely missed. The boys never seemed to resent this form of punishment. Being a ball boy at the club was regarded locally as a prize job for youngsters.

One ritual performed by the marker never failed to move me. Between four and four-thirty on every tennis afternoon, he would quietly excuse himself, go to his out-door office at the edge of a stone pool of water under his trees, put on his turban, take off his shoes, and say his prayers in the direction of Mecca—to the southwest. He had made his own mosque, a lovely one. Often the ball boys would join him in these devotions. The marker was, as Ali would say, "a pukka Muslim."

The other Pakistanis at the club were not generally so pious in public, but I have seen two members also take time out from their game in order to say their prayers. One was a judge. The other was a well-to-do local tycoon who had made a good deal of money in the taxi business; he was an MLA (Member of the Legislative Assembly), representing the local constituency. Their bearers would lay out prayer rugs next to the courts, and these gentlemen of exalted social status would don a turban or cover their heads with scarves, and then recite the time-honored prayers.

Tennis at the Abbottabad club was tennis, but it was something else, too: a revelation of the way of life of the upper-bracket Pakistanis and of their attitudes toward servants. The ball boys were never seen as persons; they were simply there to serve a purpose. When I greeted them as boys rather than as ball boys, they were startled, but, when they realized what I was up to, their faces would break out in the most enchanting grins. They particularly enjoyed having Memsahib take their pictures.

Another sidelight: two of the tennis regulars, the forester and the MLA, came to the club in their own cars with at least two servants each, one to drive and one to take care of assorted paraphernalia. A few Americans have chauffeurs, but how many ever appear at a tennis club with two retainers?

Although hostile to Britain as a symbol of a bitter past, this group was not hostile openly to individual Englishmen, nor to British goods, nor to British mores. On the whole, the Englishmen at the club got on very well with their Pakistani hosts. Even during the Suez crisis, when all of Pakistan was ardently on the Egyptian side, the arguments in the club bar were kept within the bounds of oral contention. Below the surface, there was a latent antagonism to the British which was at times expressed to me by Pakistani officers, but it did not become overt, at least not in the form of physical violence.

Pakistan has a flourishing sports goods industry, but the tennis *aficionados* did not favor Pakistani rackets; they much preferred English or Australian equipment. They wore English cricket sweaters, English-type scarves tied ascot-fashion around the neck, and I noted one Harris tweed jacket from Simpson's in London, regularly worn to the courts by the forester. Tennis manners and club manners were also quite English.

Pakistan has tried to get an effective *Buy Pakistan* campaign underway, but it has not succeeded because there seems to be, unfortunately, a widespread distrust of the quality of consumer goods

111

produced by Pakistan's infant industries along with the continuing snob appeal of possessing and wearing imported goods. We have had the latter phenomenon in the United States, and in some degree we still have it. However, Pakistani resentment of Britain's past colonial role and suspicion of her present policies, coupled with an obvious respect for British craftsmanship and social and cultural standards, highlighted that fundamental ambivalence which is so strongly fixed in the national psychology of both India and Pakistan.

But let us return to the pattern of club life. While the tennis battles raged on the courts, another battle raged around the bridge table in the card room, and both battles had their kibitzers. The Pakistanis like to gamble. They will bet on anything, and the stakes in the bridge games were pretty high. When the tennis was over for the day, everyone (except me) adjourned to the bar. Islam prohibits the consumption of alcohol, but many upper-class Muslims in Pakistan drink as a matter of course; most of the army officers and gazetted officers in Abbottabad did. Their drinking was moderate, however, perhaps because the price of liquor was a natural economic sanction. These bar sessions lasted until 8:30 or 9:00 P.M. at which time, I presume, the married men went home to dinner. Pakistanis tend to eat dinner much later then we do.

At first I was puzzled by the duration of these week-day gatherings in the bar. My impression was that the group was composed entirely of lonely bachelors who, denied the company of women, sought solace and companionship in a man's world. This naive assumption turned out to be wrong. The judges, the senior barristers and advocates, and the senior government officials were all married. During the year, two of the younger members of the group got married—the cantonment executive officer and the advocate who was the club tennis champion. But marriage did not seem to make much difference. They still spent the hours from 4:00 to 8:30 at the club— when they did not go to the movies. It is possible that they did not want to go home; a similar reluctance to embrace domesticity is not unknown in American club circles and in our bars and taverns. As for the bachelors, except for the movies, they had nowhere else to go.

For the primary reason of respect for my mission, I did not spend much time in the bar with the boys. A secondary consideration was that the club, though quite plush by Pakistani standards, did not have showers or standard toilet facilities; after my game, I would return promptly to the hotel, a half-block away, for that hot bath which Ali and the *bhisti* would have ready for me. Another compel-

English Majors at the University of Peshawar. This picture, without *burqas*, was a favor to Mrs. Linck.

An Army Wife and Her Younger Sister (right) in Characteristic Costume: Palace Hotel, Abbottabad; post office at the right.

"Passing Out" at PMA: graduation day, Pakistan Military Academy, Kakul. Pakistan ladies drinking tea under their *burqas*.

ling reason for a fast return to the hotel was the fact that we very often had guests before dinner, which, according to Pakistani social custom, is a "proper" time to call.

Week nights at the club, then, were quiet. The Saturday night parties held at regular intervals were more lively, though not wildly festive. These parties had the advantage of an army band, furnished by courtesy of the station commander, but, notwithstanding their earnestness and willingness, Pakistani musicians simply are not attuned to the beat of Western popular music (the "Oklahoma" score took a terrible beating), nor are Pakistani dancers who try to cope with Western dance rhythms. Not that there was much dancing. The normal ratio of men to women was about ten to one.

The women were the relatively emancipated wives of the army officers and the wives of the German technicians. However, the Pakistani ladies did not dance—they were not that emancipated. The German ladies did, and they were much in demand as partners. But such affairs are not much fun for European women. They have to work too hard; their Pakistani partners are enthusiastic, but awkward, and the surrounding ring of staring faces becomes embarrassing. The result is that most European women who have had experience at such affairs prefer the quieter pleasures of social conversation. And so the band plays on, one or two intrepid couples dance, the ladies drink soft drinks, the men drink harder drinks, everybody stares at the people on the floor as if they were performers, and, as usual, the boys in the bar get drunk. It is wise to leave these parties early. Both Hindus and Muslims have a low tolerance for alcohol, and, under the influence, they get exuberant, as who does not? Saturday night is Saturday night all over the world.

And on Sunday morning from time to time there was a band concert and Tombola, the equivalent of Bingo.

These Saturday night parties were hybrid evenings, with their mixture of standard Western ways modified by Pakistani mores. The most interesting party we attended at the club was the celebration of Pakistan's Republic Day on March 23, 1957. For this gala event, my wife wore a Banaras sari which scored a great hit with our Pakistani friends and induced enthusiastic requests for repeat performances at later functions. But what made the evening memorable, aside from the general air of festivity akin to the atmosphere of our own Fourth of July, was that, in addition to the usual Western-type military dance band, there was a Pakistani orchestra and a band of singers. This made for quite a different kind of entertainment. The audience was very much at home with the Urdu and Punjabi music. The professionals sang; a young army M.D. sang by popular request; the audience also sang; and a number of Pakistani officers danced solo. These dances were in a much older tradition than the Western fox trot and waltz. We liked this kind of evening much better than the semi-Western kind.

At these affairs and others—the reception for the outgoing Deputy Commissioner, the reception for the incoming Deputy Commissioner, the reception for an outgoing judge, a reception for an incoming judge—I was always conscious of the absence of my faculty colleagues, with the sole exception of Dr. Khan. As I have observed before, they were not eligible for club membership and they could not afford to join, anyway. For sport, they played badminton on the college grounds and they could have played tennis on the college courts (though only Arif, strangely enough, took advantage of this opportunity). Their club was a chemist's shop (drug store) in the bazaar run by the young man whose wife was trying for an English M.A. at the University of Peshawar.

Psychic Tensions

All these observations may make the club life sound routine, commonplace, conventional, bourgeois, if you like—basically much like comparable club situations in England or in the United States. Up to a point, it was all of these, but underneath the surface one became aware of disturbing tensions, of psychic stresses and strains. The frequenters of the club lived ritualized lives, and the ritual was in part an artificial, unnatural attempt to conform to English patterns and in part an almost automatic conditioned conformity to Muslim patterns. But these rigid patterns of behavior have not resulted in any sense of psychic security any more than our own rigid middle-class rituals have produced any real psychological security in the United States, if we accept the validity of Riesman's *The Lonely Crowd*.

We observed a terrible underlying insecurity in sensitive Pakistanis, an insecurity compounded by grim economic and political factors: Kashmir, ineffective government, inflation, the struggle to maintain a decent standard of living, and, in too many cases outside the club circle, the struggle merely to exist. Sputnik and other developments since Sputnik have made the United States uneasy, but we have resources. The Pakistanis have more cause for uneasiness, and very few resources. Worst of all, there was growing in the land the devastating suspicion that Pakistan itself might be a failure—that the attempt to found a political state on Islam might be a failure. This was, naturally, very hard to take.

This tension, this uneasiness, manifested itself in different ways. The febrile intensity of the tennis, squash, and badminton indicated a desire to escape. These sports were just as much an escape mechanism as drugs or alcohol or addiction to golf in the United States. At times on the court and in the bar, there would occur sudden outbursts of hysterical laughter, a kind of high-pitched maniacal chortling which seemed to be a much stronger response than the stimulus warranted. Other Westerners have noted this phenomenon and have commented on it to us. It was the memory of these disconcerting outbursts which made my wife and me come to attention when, in July 1958, a TV news analyst, who had had several interviews with Nasser, stressed the fact that the Egyptian leader giggled continually. The unpredictable explosions of nervous laughter happened again and again when we entertained guests at the hotel. In their intensity and shock power, the explosions constitute a disturbing behavioral pattern, one which may merit the attention of social psychologists as, indeed, the whole subject of Pakistani upper-class social behavior needs to be objectively examined—preferably by scholarly Pakistanis.

More specific evidence of frustration and repression was brought forcibly to our attention. One Pakistani career official, secure in his position, respected by his fellows, reasonably well off financially, shocked us one day at the club with sentiments which suddenly erupted from him. He was ashamed of being a Pakistani. If he went abroad, he would try to conceal his nationality. There was no hope for Pakistan because of the corruption in its government. The United States should not give Pakistan one cent of aid until a decent government had been established. These things were said neither in confidence nor *sotto voce*. He said them loudly enough to be heard by everybody in the room.

Then there was his colleague, a younger man, well established in his service, recently promoted, and regarded as a comer. Like his senior, he had nothing to fear from political upheaval, short of total chaos or revolution, because his position was under civil service. He, too, was a popular man in his circle, smiling, gracious, polite, and seemingly self-assured. We thought of him as doing very well in his own country. But one day the mask dropped, and, with a dreadful,

115

disconcerting earnestness, he said: "Get me out of this place—I'll do anything, but help me get away."

Admittedly, these glimpses into troubled psyches may be regarded as isolated instances, as special cases. I may be reading too much into them, but, in the light of all that I have seen and heard, I judge them to be significant. I think that they illustrate what Professor Wilfred Cantwell Smith has called "the failure of Pakistan to command the constructive fidelity of its own dominant class." Professor Smith continues in this vein:

> Demoralization reached such a pitch that many of the intelligentsia gave serious thought to emigrating. This illumines not merely the discouraging condition of their environment. At the same time it betokens the alarming irresponsibility within their own spirits. Similarly, the complaints against the 'failure of leadership' were many, petulant, and bitter; and although the public welfare was, as we have seen, indeed threatened by the behaviour that widely elicited complaints, yet it was jeopardized no less by the inclination of others to complain rather than to strive.[1]

This summary, I think, applies not only to the two officials just discussed but also to my faculty colleagues.

The Abbottabad Club, then, was important as microcosm and symbol. Its pattern provided insights into the values and attitudes of the people who control Pakistan, people of power and position. This basic pattern is, moreover, quite similar to the one we found in similar clubs in Peshawar and Dacca. But the club is, of course only one social milieu—by definition, highly restricted. In the course of the year, however, we met many other Pakistanis in other social circumstances. Let us see what we learned from them.

Host and Hostess

As expected, we entertained a large number of Pakistani guests at the hotel; faculty colleagues and, much less often, a few of their wives; students; lawyers and doctors; officers and their wives; local business men; the lady principal of a cantonment school; the colonel's lady who, at the behest of her husband, was trying to learn English under my wife's tutelage; the young lady who sought my help in preparing for her M.A. examination in English at the University of Peshawar—her husband consenting; young professors from the Pakistan Military Academy; a lady doctor, the sister of a young army officer who was also a friend of ours; the sophisticated upper

116

class young man, formerly with the BBC in London, who returned to his country under family pressure to be properly married; the scion of the powerful Afridi tribe, a lumber merchant, also highly sophisticated, who, wearing cashmere sweater and foulard scarf, turned up regularly at the hotel in a sports car, looking very much like an illustration from a *New Yorker* advertisement; two Anglo-Indian army nurses; and a bus driver on the Abbottabad-Peshawar run who had been happy to have us as his charges one day. It was a rare day on which we did not have Pakistani callers for tea.

Over a period of nine months, we also entertained and were entertained by a number of non-Pakistanis in Abbottabad. I shall summarize this aspect of our life briefly because my fundamental concern is, of course, with the Pakistanis and their way of life. Still, the mere enumeration of the members of the foreign colony will throw some light on what is going on in Pakistan. Here they are: a Japanese couple who were fellow guests at the hotel—he was a forestry consultant for the Pakistan government under UN auspices; the British captain who headed the Pakistan Army Music School— in the middle of our stay his wife returned to England with their two children; the English and Dutch fathers of the Mill Hill order who operated Burn Hall school; the three Swedes from Bofors working as technical consultants at a nearby defense installation; the Italian engineer who had a contract with an American firm doing work for the Pakistan government (he lived at the Palace Hotel with his wife and child); the Italian's boss, an American engineer, formerly a major in the Air Force, who arrived late in our year and who, with characteristic energy, set about making a home for his beautiful Icelandic bride, an erstwhile air line hostess; a trickle of American ICA officials, among them village AID personnel, a sheep specialist from Ohio (with a large family of engaging blond kids), and an able forester from Oregon; the six Englishmen who lived at the club; occasional visitors from the German Siemens contingent at Haripur; and seasonal Britishers from Karachi and Lahore who came to the hills for a holiday. At times, life in Abbottabad was distinctly international in flavor.

Like ourselves, these foreigners came and went. Excepting the Burn Hall fathers, we were all transients.

In the Pakistani community itself, we had these experiences as guests: dinners with Dr. Khan; high tea and ceremonial lunches with faculty colleagues; tea at local restaurants with students; dinner with the Anglo-Pakistani nurses in their comfortable army billets;

117

an all-day trip to a neighboring village as guests of the head of the English department; tea with the repatriated BBC staffer, his sister, and friends; tea and dinner with the young local barrister who had been admitted to the English bar from one of the Inns of Court in London; a few small parties with a young army couple with whom we became particularly good friends; a dinner in the Frontier Force Officers Mess; two variety shows put on by the cadets of the Pakistan Military Academy; PMA's graduation—called "Passing Out" in Pakistan; a reception given by the local MLA for a departing Deputy Commissioner; a reception given by the station commander for a high-ranking Pakistani general, just returned from the United States; a couple of marriage receptions in the marriage season, April and May; the farewell dinner given in our honor by the faculty of the college; dinner with the young chemist and his wife, the M. A. candidate; and a party with the family of an embattled Kashmiri matriarch.

This record of social intercourse with Pakistanis and non-Pakistanis as both host and guest represents a fairly wide range of people, but in reprospect we see that almost all of our relationships were with the educated community; we did not really meet the man in the street or the mainstay of Pakistan, the peasant, except second hand through Ali, our bearer. The people we knew ran Pakistan in the sense that they controlled its public and business affairs on the operating level from day to day, even though they seemed to have a sense of impotence about the formulation and carrying out of high policy. But the real essence of Pakistan's life, the way of life of the majority, was centered in the village. The failure to know the village and the peasant was not altogether our fault. Our mission was in the realm of education and related cultural areas, and we simply did not have time to explore that mysterious and all-important village world; that is a job for the anthropologist, the sociologist, and the economist.[2] There is another reason for this omission. Although nearly every Pakistani seemed to have a strong tie with some village, not many of those we met seemed to have any real concern for what happened in the village.

As in the United States, there was much talk on high levels about the farmer and his lot, but I think that there was also a tendency among the people we met not to want to discuss either the village or its problems; with the exception noted above, there was no great desire to invite the stranger to visit one of them.

But, granting that there was a large area of Pakistan's social life which we did not know, we learned much from the world we moved in, which was typical and representative of the upper strata.

I will begin with our guests. My faculty colleagues came often and stayed late. We were glad to have them, and they enjoyed the tea and cigarettes. But, strangely, in conversation there was not much interest expressed in the United States. We were prepared for and hoped for a great many questions about our country. We got some, but not many. Conversely, we were curious about Pakistan. There was not much shop talk. American university people tend to talk shop a good deal. I like to talk my own shop and the other man's shop as well, but not so our Pakistani friends. They were, moreover, not much interested in the materials I had taken along (graciously donated to me by the Detroit Institute of Arts) in the hope of being able to show that Detroit is involved in something other than the making of automobiles. Nor did they look hard at the pictures we had of our home and neighborhood back in the United States—items which one might suppose would be of special appeal.

This somewhat disconcerting lack of curiosity about our home country may be due in part to the pervasive failure of Pakistan's educational system to encourage intellectual curiosity, a failure which might also account for the disinclination to talk profesional business. The lack of interest in the visual arts may be due to traditional religious hostility to anything savoring of idols and idolatry. Islamic culture is historically strong in architecture and design, but not so strong pictorially, excepting seventeenth-century Mogul court painting, especially miniatures. Our guests (with exceptions to be dealt with later) did not talk much about Pakistani politics, and it was not because they were afraid to. Rather, they seemed not to care much, and they seldom could tell me as much as I wanted to know. Kashmir and India would kindle a flame every now and then, but most of what was said seemed to be the result of conditioned intellectual reflexes—deeply felt clichés, but clichés, nonetheless. Altogether, conversation was a little difficult because the initiative was usually left to us.

Another powerful element in this social situation was the presence of my wife. Muslim men in the Frontier Province are not yet wholly accustomed to the presence of women in social gatherings. It was interesting to observe our guests' reactions to the Western woman who was at ease in male company, had a mind of her own, and did not hesitate to participate freely in the conversation. I think that they

119

liked this novel experience, and I suggest (with due caution) that it did them good. It both intrigued and bothered them. Her presence was, in effect, a challenge to their taken-for-granted notions about the relations of the sexes. It was almost surely one of the reasons why the conversation tended to be a little formal, a little stiff, and superficial. And if conversation is not easy, communication is difficult.

Conversation is not necessarily communication, but it may lead to communication, assuming good will and a friendly atmosphere. The fuller the talk, the better the chance for real understanding. These conditions obtained, I believe, but it would be mere wishful thinking to assume that a genuine meeting of minds occurred during our year in Pakistan. One measure of that failure is the inner knowledge of what we ourselves did not say—by which standard the amount left unsaid by the others can be at least partially realized. Basic understanding is difficult to attain; it must be worked for and worked at. It takes knowledge, wisdom, patience, determination, and time. One year is not enough. Perhaps the best we can do with such a differing culture is clearly to understand not only the differences but the reasons for those differences. That is something; in fact, it is a good deal. It is worth working for, even if the effort may at first appear to be singularly one-sided.

These observations on the difficulties of communication apply also to our conversations with students—only more so. The prime fact about these students was their eagerness to come and their delight at being invited. Life in Abbottabad was dull, and a visit to the American professor and his wife was something different. It was also, I fear, taken as a mark of status in a highly status-conscious society. But, with due allowance for boredom and prestige, there remained a core of genuine gratitude in their reactions, which was touching. They were embarrassed by the presence of a foreign woman —and fascinated. They were also under a severe handicap in respect to the English language. They had a great many questions to ask— more than their elders, I suspect—but they did not have the words in which to ask them, and there is a limit to my own clairvoyance. I think too that they had questions in their minds which remained unspoken, unphrased, unformulated because they had to know the answers to them first in order to ask them, or, at least, they had to know the conditions, the conceptual framework, in which the questions would be relevant. However, those queries which they did manage to articulate were not (as I thought they might be) largely about Hollywood or motor cars. They were about religion in America,

American social life, and American schools. At the conclusion of these trying visits, I presented them with copies of a publicity brochure describing Wayne Sate University. I found that these were highly prized.

Of the professional men who were our guests I remember most vividly a doctor, the product of one of the best medical schools in Pakistan. He came one night with a forester who had been trained at Michigan State University. Both men had sons in the Abbottabad college. The doctor's son was the defender of Adolf Hitler in the debate on dictatorship and democracy which I have already described.[3] The doctor was the bitterest man we met in Pakistan. His freedom of speech in the presence of his fellow townsmen (we had other guests that evening) is one of the reasons I have said that Pakistanis who happen to feel strongly about conditions have no reservation or hesitation in expressing them. The government used its police powers from time to time on the political opposition—as in the case of the Karachi *Mirror*—but, for all its faults, Pakistan was not a police state, or, at least, not yet.[4]

The doctor's principal diatribes were directed against political influence on his alma mater whereby, as he told the story, candidates for medical degrees who had pull were given priority in admissions, examinations, and degrees. Such conditions would have been unthinkable in his day, he said. From this specific iniquity, he launched into a blanket attack on the whole system of government in Pakistan. When I attempted to argue that there was hope in the younger generation, as witness his own son's intelligence and industry at the college, he would have none of it. His son was getting a very bad education, and there was little hope for him either.

It was not the first nor the last time that I found myself in the position of defending Pakistan and its future to Pakistanis, but the doctor's vehemence left little to be said in rebuttal from an outsider, and no rebuttal came from our other Pakistani guests who listened but did not contradict him. Though extreme in his views, he was not, I judge, atypical. As a footnote to this account, we met him not long afterward at a local movie house. He said he had come because he was low in spirits and had to do something. A small thing to note? I am not so sure. Psychically, Pakistan had a pervasive atmosphere of melancholy.

An American newspaperman stationed in New Delhi on a long-term assignment made the same point to us about the apparent gravity of the Indian people, and he made it before we had said

121

anything at all about this phenomenon in Pakistan. It was interesting to observe, in contrast, that, on the way home to the United States, an atmosphere of gravity, an outward absence of gaiety and humor, did not prevail in Ceylon, Singapore, Bangkok, Hong Kong, Japan or Hawaii. The Japanese, who might be thought of as an exception in this group of peoples, are serious, but not sad.

The Women

Of the ladies who came to our suite, the colonel's wife, devoted to her family, was of the older generation. She was learning English simply because her husband wanted her to, and she was never at ease in the alien environment of our hotel home. She still had a semi-purdah point of view about meeting men not in her immediate family, and, out of consideration for her sensibilities, I tried to stay away from the rooms at lesson time. However, it could not be done all the time, and I met her twice. She was embarrassed, though I was able to ease the situation by saying nice things about her son, one of my best students and a very fine boy. He was the lad who proposed coeducation as the subject for debate in the second year English class.

The wife of the druggist (or chemist) was a good deal younger. Newly married, she gave evidence of the tension between the old values of the purdah system and the new values of Pakistan's more advanced women. She was an educated girl, and she very much wanted to get that Master's degree at the University of Peshawar. It was to her husband's credit that he permitted her to try. She came to her tutoring sessions with me in her *burqa* accompanied by her servant, who was all of eleven or twelve years old. My wife, of course, was invariably present. It would have been unthinkable for us to be alone. Indeed, it was a high compliment that I should have been given the privilege of assisting her in the first place. As a student, she was typical of what I had come to expect. Not at all stupid, she was averse to hard digging, and she was content to reel off the standard platitudes and clichés which had served other successful candidates in the past. I was not able to create in her any fiery intellectual curiosity about the wider world of letters, but I was able to improve her writing a little. The mere fact that she wanted that degree for no other reason than to have it was recommendation enough for me. She did not intend to teach; she was destined to be a wife and to bear children.

As a person, she was quite appealing in her young matronliness. She came just as much to talk with my wife as to be tutored in literature, and, in the course of the long woman-to-woman talks (my wife reported), the ambivalence spoken of earlier came to the surface.

On the one hand, she was rebelling against the village and its ways, rebelling against the traditional position assigned to women in the Frontier society. She wanted a larger and richer way of life of which the Master's degree was the symbol. Yet, whenever the purdah system or its implications seemed to come under criticism, she would argue for the old pattern. She did not not quite know where she stood, and many more Pakistani young ladies in this transition age (if it is, in fact, a transition age) will go through similar stages. In her case, I predict that the village will triumph in the end.

Five other women who were our guests at one time or another were in rather sharp contrast with most Abbottabad women in that they were the Pakistani equivalent of career girls. One was the sister of a faculty colleague; she taught civics and political science at the local girl's college. She came to us to take a proficiency examination in English (which I administered) as part of an application for an overseas study grant. One was the lady doctor, the sister of a young army officer, who was the most self-sufficient and integrated woman we met locally. One was the principal of the cantonment school who also wanted to take a proficiency examination in English for the purpose of a scholarship abroad; she stayed in town and married the cantonment executive officer, a tale I will come to later. The last two, nurses in a nearby army hospital, were members of that tragic community, the Anglo-Indians or Anglo-Pakistanis.

These five women struck us as being healthy-minded, probably because they had jobs and worked hard at them. They seemed to have a gratifying sense of mission, something that too many Pakistanis lack. And yet (at which point our Muslim friends would say, "I told you so") every one of them would probably have preferred husbands and babies, in which respect they were precisely like their American sisters. The lady doctor, who particularly impressed us as an example of what is possible for Pakistani women to accomplish on their own, was cheerfully honest about this: she loved her profession, and she was good at it, but she wanted to be married. She said so in the presence of her smiling brother who, presumably, should have been doing something about it. But marriage for such a woman is not easy, nor is it easy for educated men in Pakistan either. They are too sensitive, too modern to marry just anybody

123

who happens to fulfill the traditional specifications. As the tennis-playing judge at the club said over and over on this point, "The desirable are not available, and the available are not desirable."

The Anglo-Pakistanis

As for the two nurses, one unmarried, one widowed, they lived lonely lives. They served society and served it well; they had a fair standard of living—their army quarters were quite attractive; and they were fine, decent women. But there was something sad in their lot because they were suspended between two worlds socially, the Pakistani world and the English world. John Masters' novel, *Bhowani Junction*, has a good deal of Hollywood melodrama in it, but there is much truth in his depiction of the Anglo-Indian psychology. These are the people of mixed parentage. When they speak of home, they mean England. They have never been there, and chances are that they will never get there. On shopping trips to the bazaar, they carry unbrellas to guard their complexions against the sun, professing amazement at the English and American women who do not fear tanned faces. They will go to any lengths to establish clear distinctions between themselves and the "natives" (that term regarded universally in Indo-Pakistan as insulting) even to the extent of denying any knowledge of Urdu or Punjabi which they have known from childhood. And, saddest of all, these are the people whom certain Britishers (to use the Pakistani term of reference) make fun of for these very attempts to be British.

It is a sardonic situation, and the reactions it evokes are complex: pity for those who must pretend; anger because the pretensions themselves are the age-old attempt to establish superiority on a false basis; and anger at those who, safely superior by the standards underlying the pretense, enjoy the pleasures of complacent laughter.

What makes the plight of the "Anglos" tragic is that they do not want to be completely identified with the national community; they are not wholly accepted by the community they want to belong to; and their own is not big enough to live in comfortably. We saw what the Anglo-Pakistanis wanted to be, and we heard what some Englishmen thought of the aspiration, but, strangely enough, we did not hear any comment from the Pakistanis themselves. What did they think? I am not sure, but I can guess. One "Anglo" in Abbottabad seemed to have made his peace with life. A retired police officer, he was also the lay rector of the local Anglican Church, St. Luke's. It was a pretty little church, directly across from the Palace Hotel, with its gardens and grounds scrupulously cared for. Its interior walls were lined with memorial tablets to long-dead British officers of Ghurka regiments and their families. Reading these evoked the nineteenth-century world of Rudyard Kipling with its hill stations, its subalterns, and Mrs. Hauksbee. The rector did not have a very large congregation, and it was gradually dwindling into nothingness. His chief parishioner, the popular and respected brigadier who was the last British officer to be head of the Pakistani Military Academy, departed for Scotland, retirement, salmon fishing, and civic enterprises. The British sergeant-major for PMA, a very impressive character on parade, who was granted a commission and left for another assignment, will probably not be replaced by another of his unique type. The British captain in charge of the Pakistani Army Music School will go, too, and soon there will not be six Englishmen in town teaching signals to the Pakistan army. The officer's wife, who used to play the organ on Sunday, also departed. It will not be long before the church will have to close because there will not be enough local Pakistani Anglicans to keep the congregation alive. Then the church and its grounds will, no doubt, revert to the Pakistan Government, and an era, already closed for all practical purposes, will lose its last British symbol. It is surprising that the church and the congregation should have survived for as long as ten years after Pakistani independence. I wonder what will happen to it? Surely, it will not become a mosque.

As I remember the church and its rector or vicar, another remaining symbol of the British Raj comes to mind. It is a full-dress photograph of Lord Birdwood, hanging in an honored place in the impressive Victorian officers' mess of the Frontier Force Regiment just a block down the road from the church and the hotel. Lord Birdwood was a former commanding officer of the regiment. When I first saw the picture, I turned in surprise to our host, a staff captain from PMA. He smiled, shrugged his shoulders, and said, "We'll get around to it—there's no hurry." This is to say that the Regiment is still proud of its traditions, and, now that the substance of independence has been gained, it is in no great haste to remove the evidence that those traditions were established in the days when the British ruled and the Pakistanis resented that rule. Indeed, such mementos of the past are to be found all over India and Pakistan. One might suppose that all of them—pictures, plaques, statues and similar reminders of past deeds—would have gone up in one great holocaust in

1947. But they did not. Though they will gradually disappear, their continuing presence in 1957 can be read as a kind of tribute to both the rulers and the ruled.

The PMA Professors, the BBC Repatriate, the Afridi

I believe that the academicians from PMA, on the whole, were intellectually superior to my colleagues at the Government College. They had had much more advanced study. Under the direction of an able dean of academic studies (with whom I once had a rewarding conversation), the academy had a quite good program of work in the humanities, in addition to military training—all in the spirit of achieving the Sandhurst ideal of the officer-gentleman. One of our young guests, a professor of history, in himself exemplified the strength of the program. He was a scholarly person and equally at home in polite conversation. He was reported by our staff-captain friend as an inspiring lecturer on the glorious deeds of Muslim heroes, and he seemed to have more sense of direction and more psychological assurance than most of my co-workers—perhaps because he was better paid and had more social status than they did. I take it that the dedication to duty and career, the peace of mind, and the general competence of the young Pakistani officers we met were the product of their particular educational system of which the professor was an effective agent.

The repatriate BBC announcer, the scion of a local wealthy family of landowners, was an urbane man whose voice and diction qualified him for BBC broadcasts in English as well as for Urdu. The quiet elegance of his manners and his Bond Street clothes marked him as belonging in the Carlton Grill rather than in Abbottabad. He had been very happy in London and in his job with BBC. Clearly, he had not wanted to return home. Why did he? For two reasons: the strong power of the Pakistani family tie and the economic sanctions which, he implied, might be enforced on him. What would he do in Pakistan? In the first place, he would be married to some suitable girl of his family's choice. What then? It was hard to say. He talked vaguely about working for Radio Pakistan, but with no great conviction or interest. He will probably continue to be a gentleman of leisure for the rest of his life. He will marry, he will superintend the family lands and monies, and his routine will be pretty much what it was when we knew him: aimless motor trips, the movies, billiards with his friends, tea, talk, and home to sleep. Despite all his gifts and intelligence, it is unlikely that he will ever be as much of a functioning human being as he was in England. There is plenty of work to be done in Pakistan, but such personable, educated, and bright members of the privileged class do not seem to have the taste for it. *Noblesse oblige* is not a dynamic concept in Pakistan, insofar as I could see. He had worked in England, and he enjoyed it, but back home another point of view seemed to obtain. If this conjecture sounds like an unduly dark picture of an empty future, it is nonetheless what the repatriate himself suggested by his words and attitude.

The Afridi had something of the same psychology although he had never been out of Pakistan. His English was impeccable, a fact attributable to his family environment rather than to formal schooling, for he had not finished college. He had an incisive and acute intelligence (a family characteristic) combined with a mordant wit. I am sure that he was a good business man. He ran a lumber yard at Havelian, a few miles away, the nearest rail point to Abbottabad, but he did not have to work very hard at it. Unmarried and apparently not wanting to be married, his life appeared from the outside to be as aimless and empty as the ex-announcer's. He liked to drink and to talk, and he did both with skill and grace. We had perceived these same qualities in his younger brother, a Burn Hall graduate (renowned as a polo player), who went on to study law at the University of Peshawar.

These two young men came from one of the best known tribes and families on the Frontier. The head of the family had been a high officer in one of the UN organizations. It was a challenge to the imagination to look at this Afridi in his tweed jacket, foulard scarf, and cashmere sweater, to think of his sports car in the hotel parking lot—and then to remember that, in April 1930, his fellow tribesmen had broken into Peshawar! A parallel case would be a successful raid on Tuscon or Albuquerque by the Apaches or Navahos during the administration of Herbert Hoover.[5]

I asked our friend about this recent history. Yes, his people had raided Peshawar. He was proud of it. There was a glint in his eye and an ironic smile on his face when he spoke of it. One got the impression that it might happen again: the veneer peeled off; that Western exterior faded; the nation of Pakistan disappeared; and the Pathan tribesman emerged, sharply drawn. At that moment, the Afridi had ceased to be a businessman at odds with his workaday world; he was one with his own people, part of a tradition to which he responded powerfully and emotionally; at that moment, he "belonged."

127

I have seen this phenomenon on two other occasions. The first was at the Abbottabad Club in conversation with a young captain who later asked for and got an assignment with a Pakistan army unit whose special duty was to keep the peace in tribal areas, a mission not unlike that which led to the death of General George Custer and his command. It is dangerous duty, I am told, exciting and better paid than standard army service and, for these reasons, it is much sought after by career officers. This captain, handsome in his dinner jacket, had a salty wit and was much liked by his fellows. Upon finding that I was really interested, he began to talk about his own people, tribal neighbors of the Afridis. The same thing happened: the eyes flashed, the officer-gentleman faded, the dinner jacket disappeared, and the Pathan leaped out. He was a good soldier, he would do his duty, but his heart belonged to the people he was to police, not to Pakistan.

The second incident took place in the Malakand Agency on the way to the autonomous state of Swat. My wife and I were going there as guests of the Wali of Swat. We went with one of the Wali's sons, a student at Lower Burn Hall in my wife's class, and two of his cousins. The Wali's chauffeur delivered the two cousins to their father, a man in young middle age. He had served with the Pakistan army in which he held a commission and he had spent some time in England. Like so many of his type, he was much like an English army officer in mufti, as regards speech, manners, and dress. Hollywood could have used him in such a role just as he was. Naturally, we had to have tea (served by pistol-packing retainers) before going on to Saidu Sharif, the Swat capital, and we had to have a tour of the new house he was building. At tea, I asked him about the administration of the Malakand Agency—how did it operate in respect to the sovereignty of the Pakistan Government? The same thing happened: the eyes kindled; an ironic smile appeared; the English in him disappeared; and (in his case) the tribal chieftain emerged.

Yes, he was the head man in the district. He had a simple agreement with the Pakistan government, especially with the political agent under whom the army units operated. On the roads, the tribesmen promised not to carry weapons; in return, the representatives of the sovereign state of Pakistan promised not to leave the roads without permission from the tribal chiefs, of whom our cultivated, civilized, and sophisticated host was one. It was clearly implied that, if Pakistani officials or troops did leave the roads without prior agreement, they were fair game.

It is this fundamental loyalty to the tribe on the Frontier which

produces political difficulties for the government. It is all very well
that Pakistan should be the Islamic Republic of Pakistan; the tribesmen are fanatical Muslims. But locally the tribe is more important
than the nation; the tribe commands the basic allegiance.

The Pukhtunistan Stunt

For this reason, what the Pakistan government calls "The Pukhtunistan Stunt" (in a government publication, published in April
1956, of which I have a copy) is a perennial source of trouble. It is
the idea that the tribal belt on both sides of the Afghan-Pakistan
border, from the remote northern borders down to the Arabian Sea,
should be an autonomous country on the grounds that the tribesmen
in this area have a common denominator of language and culture quite
separate and distinct from both nations. From the official Pakistani
point of view, this stunt was largely an Afghan propaganda campaign,
kept alive by Kabul for highly suspect reasons. The issue is one of the
reasons why relations between the two countries have been uneasy.
A startling fact to recall is that Afghanistan was the only country to
oppose Pakistani's admission to the United Nations in 1947. Recently,
however, Afghan-Pakistan relations have improved, as demonstrated
by the signing of a pact in June 1958, guaranteeing reciprocal transit
rights across each other's territories. This was reported in the *New
York Times* of July 13, 1958.

To the outsider with no ax to grind, the Pukhtunistan scheme appears to be grandiose and illusory. The tribes, it is true, tend to
think of themselves as neither Afghans nor Pakistanis. They do not
seem to have any consciousness of national identity at all. They are
perfectly willing and able to fight each other, and they do. The history
of the Frontier is largely a history of local blood feuds, plus occasional
ganging together to oppose the British invader or for such occasions as
the foray against Kashmir. Furthermore, the tribes are clever about
playing off Pakistan against Afghanistan for their own benefit. Frontier peace is largely kept by subsidies. Under these circumstances, the
idea that the tribes could establish a going government of their own
is chimerical.

Nevertheless, the psychology of which I have given three instances
makes the *idea* of autonomy an attractive one. Its potency accounts
for much of the uneasy ferment in the politics of the old Northwest
Frontier Province which works against the concept of national unity.
I fear that the Stunt will trouble Pakistan for some time to come and

that it will be a long time before the tribes are wholly integrated into the national state.

More specifically, the Afridi, the captain, and the tribal chief illustrate the difficulties of a young nation in creating and maintaining the idea of national citizenship—of being a Pakistani rather than something else. Comparable situations would be the states of mind of England's feudal knights and barons before the advent of Tudor nationalism (the captain, for example, was a Pakistani Hotspur); of the Highland Scot clans up to and after the end of the Jacobite hopes in 1745; of the American colonists during and after the Revolution; of the unreconstructed Southerners after our Civil War; and of our contemporary extreme states-rights advocates, nullifiers, and secessionists like Faubus and Strom Thurmond.

The bus driver? He had taken personal responsibility for our safety and comfort on the trip to Peshawar. He was good at his job. After all, bus drivers are government workers, and he had a certain pride in his official position. He had insisted that we have tea with him at a rest stop, and we had taken his picture. He came to the hotel twice on the pretext of getting a copy of the photo (Ali, the bearer, did not approve of these visits), but he just wanted to pay a social call and to offer his services in case we wanted anything from the Peshawar bazaar. We remember him vividly because he typified the invariable courtesy we received from Pakistani government workers everywhere we went. We remember him also because he was an attractive human being, a true Pathan, sturdy, blue-eyed, and black-haired.

We are Guests

Much of what has been said about our guests at the hotel and their significance holds true equally for our experience as guests in various local milieus. However, there are some qualitatively different things to be noted arising out af the fundamental fact that, as guests rather than as hosts, we were on Pakistani home grounds. Our hotel suite itself no doubt created a special kind of atmosphere.

I will begin with the physical circumstances of the Pakistani middle class home. Here it must be understood that I am not concerned with furniture and household equipment on a comparative basis. The average middle class American home has many things which the Pakistani home does not have, the most important of which are bathrooms, flush toilets, some kind of central heating, and gas or electric stoves. But these are not of essential importance. What is more important is the kind of total atmosphere created in a home by the use of those artifacts which the given culture takes for granted. By this criterion, the Japanese, for example, no matter how poor they may be financially, do very well esthetically. By this same criterion, the Pakistanis do not fare so well.

In general (insofar as we were privileged to see it) the Pakistani home interior seems to derive from the nineteenth-century Victorian tradition. It is strongly reminiscent of the American middle class parlors at the turn of the century, those sacrosanct rooms which were never opened except on state occasions. The furniture was substantial and heavy; arm chairs had doilies on their arms; the color key was invariably dark and somber; there were few pictures on the walls— those in evidence being of traditional English subjects (calendar art) plus an occasional calendar from a local merchant; very few books were in sight; lamps were heavy and ornate; naked light bulbs would glare down at the assembly; and the walls, though white-washed, were dull with a film of dust. The total effect was usually one of somber formality.

Of course, in Pakistan, there are reasons for some of this effect. Paint is expensive and white-wash is not a very effective substitute because it flakes, powders, and streaks. Glass also is expensive and that is one reason why windows are small—to keep out heat in summer and to keep heat in during cold weather.

The rooms are small, too—both absolutely and relatively; that is, a fairly large house will have a considerable number of little rooms rather than a few big ones. Moreover, the fireplaces in these rooms are small because wood and coals (as stated before) are high in price.

But having said all this, something remains unsaid. In essence, the air and atmosphere of a country's domestic architecture stem from the mind and spirit of the people who live in the houses. The Pakistani middle class culture is a formal one; it is rigidly mannered. This rigidity is manifest in the very arrangement of chairs at a party: they are lined up against the walls in strict military array. The idea of conversation groups is, apparently, a foreign one. Once you are in a chair, there you remain. It is only by chance that you will have an opportunity to change conversational partners; you are condemned to a dialogue for the rest of the evening. Dinner will provide a break; it is served either formally at a table or buffet style. But after dinner, once you are seated again in the living room, you are stuck for the rest of the evening. Then, at last, the ranking guest will make a move, and the other guests will follow quickly. As a rule, we found that Pakistani dinner parties end earlier than our own.

Another feature of Pakistani living rooms illustrates the parallel with our turn-of-the-century parlor and "fumed oak" atmosphere. This is the omnipresence of photographs thickly arranged on the fireplace mantels. The Pakistanis are camera conscious (an international characteristic, I would say), and they delight in what they call "snaps." A typical gallery will consist of a formal photo portrait of Father or of some other distinguished male member of the family; a tinted formal wedding portrait, with the two principals looking very grave and dedicated; and numerous group photos of school and college clubs and classes. One might conclude that a sure way of winning friends abroad is to take plenty of pictures and to send copies of them to the subjects. The American with his camera is, justifiably, a standard target for international cartoons, but, in our experience, the Indians and Pakistanis are no less fanatical in their enthusiasm for this hobby. Abbottabad has a surprising number of camera shops and commercial photographers, considering its size.

Although purdah is dominant on the Frontier, its protocol did not apply to us in full measure for two reasons: for one, we were in a somewhat special position as a husband-and-wife team who were regarded as guests of the whole community; for another, the people we knew best were among the most sophisticated in town, and, being familiar with Western ways, they tended to modify standard practice.

To illustrate, Dr. Khan's begum was in strict purdah, but he always thoughtfully managed to have another lady or two present when he entertained us in order to make things easier for my wife. His social task was lightened for him by the fact that the senior army officers and their wives tended not to observe strict purdah. One of his dinners was graced by the presence of the new station commander's wife, a lady notable for both a quiet dignity and an ease of manner, probably the result of having been a full partner in her husband's busy military life. This lady and her husband are not to be confused with the former station commander and his wife referred to above.[6] The "old" ranking officer was the colonel whose son was one of my best students and whose wife was trying to learn English from my wife. The "new" ranking officer was a brigadier general, and therefore he automatically took over the position of station commander from the colonel. The general had been around, and, in the process, both he and his wife (who knew English well) had acquired considerable social grace.

132

Another female guest of Dr. Khan was a charming younger army wife who had been born in Singapore and who was clearly at home in male company. The Lady Principal of the local girl's college, who had spent some time in the United States, was also recruited for social duty on this occasion. Still, the ladies were out-numbered four to one. At these two dinners, my wife paid her respects to Begum Khan in the women's quarters backstage, so to speak.

Twice, however, at faculty parties, my wife was the only woman present. She visited briefly with the wives of my colleagues in the purdah quarters (reporting that the women were always eager to see her and to talk with her), but I was not allowed that privilege; the women did not appear before the guests. A modification of this pattern in other faculty social settings—for high tea and state luncheons—permitted the ladies of the household to be in the company of the foreign professor and his wife, but with no other males outside the family circle in attendance.

Indeed, during our stay in Abbottabad, excluding the military circle and the weddings, we were guests at just two affairs which could be regarded as family gatherings in the American sense. One of these was a dinner party given by the young chemist and his wife, the M.A. candidate. There the party was fairly well balanced between male and female. The other guests were all relatives, including a student at the college and a lively young lawyer.

The second family affair is a story in itself, and it requires some background. The head of this family, Mrs. Hafiz, was a formidable matriarch of Kashmiri stock—and very proud of it. Her husband, a well educated man, had died not long before, leaving her with seven children—two married daughters, one daughter of marriageable age, two very young girls, and two young boys. I do not know how she managed to carry this heavy load, but she did. She had arranged good matches for her daughters (their education and good looks certainly helped), and she was educating the others.

Mrs. Hafiz was the only woman we met on the Frontier who deliberately challenged the local mores. The army women, after all, were in a separate community. She did not respect purdah, did not wear the *burqa*, and did not hesitate to march grandly through the bazaar, challenging anybody to make something of it. Yet she maintained a solid position in the community for both herself and her family. She enjoyed life, had a deep vein of humor, and was passionately devoted to her family. Above all, she had an elemental force of character which would make her a personage in any land or in any society. She combined the strong qualities of Eleanor Roosevelt and Carrie Chapman Catt with a dash of the Wife of Bath.

It was not surprising, therefore, that Mrs. Hafiz and her family had become intimate friends of my Fulbright predecessor at Abbottabad, and she called on us early in our stay. In the course of our conversations (much freer and easier than most), when she was asked her opinion of purdah, she answered very simply: "The men keep it up for their own convenience." She was equally scornful of the men who had to have purdah to satisfy their own selfish ends (as she saw it) and of the women who put up with it.

When we then asked her how she was able to defy local custom, she shrugged her shoulders and smiled—as if to say, "Who is to stop me? Let them try!" Insofar as I know, nobody tried. Yet she was not ostracized, nor were the members of her family, for she compelled respect. Mrs. Hafiz was awe-inspiring.

And so, in due course, after a number of teas and conversations at the hotel, we were invited to the Hafiz home. This was quite different from the other parties we had attended. The whole family was present, men and women together. Among the guests were the Bitter Medical Doctor, a forestry official, and other local professional men, all with their women.

It was not only the presence of women, equalling the men in number, that gave this party its distinctive flavor; it was the gaiety and humor of the atmosphere. The little girls danced charmingly; the married daughters sang beautifully; and Mother Hafiz beamed and made salty comments on the whole proceeding. Even the Bitter Doctor had a good time.

On the Frontier, Mrs. Hafiz was a special case. Yet there was nothing neurotic, fanatic, or feverish in her makeup. She was the epitome of health, both physically and mentally. She was not rebelling against former male domination in her home. It was evident that she had had a rich married life in full partnership with her husband, a man of enlightened views, whose memory was still warmly alive in his wife and his children. He had been a sportsman, and Mrs. Hafiz, in conspiracy with my wife, knitted a tennis sweater for my birthday, modelled on an English one her husband had worn in the good old days.

What gave Mrs. Hafiz her power and assurance was her education, her happy marriage, her Kashmiri background (evidently something of a social asset in Pakistan), and, of course, her unique personal qualities. It is not without significance to note that she was

134

active in the All-Pakistan Women's Association, too, that organization which is one of the hopes of Pakistan.

Pakistani Weddings

The gaiety which was usually absent from Pakistani social life was in evidence, as might be expected, at weddings. May was the time for nuptials on the Frontier—after Ramazan (so spelled in Pakistan), the great Muslim month-long fast, and the Id festival (sometimes spelled Eid and so pronounced), which corresponds to our Easter in some respects. These weddings are highly complicated and ceremonial affairs. Although we did not experience the complete cycle in any one case, we did get some insight into the ceremony through attendance at functions which were part of two weddings—I on the male side and my wife on the female side.

The most impressive of these was the biggest wedding of the year, a real society event. Everybody who mattered was there. It was that night on which Ali, our bearer, refused to hire a tonga because the driver was attempting to charge too much, and therefore we walked to the party in full evening dress. On arrival, my wife was taken to the women's quarters and I was ushered into the courtyard reserved for the male guests. I found that status distinctions were being observed as usual, for one of my students (the Bitter Doctor's son), watching for me, quickly came forward and led me to an inner circle of seats. There I found myself talking to a courtly old gentleman from Dacca, East Pakistan. Had he come all that distance for the wedding? He had. Moreover, later in the evening, I met several other guests who had come from Karachi (about a thousand miles away), expressly to do honor to their kin. Nothing much seemed to happen at this reception. The high point was the reading of a poem celebrating the marriage, copies of which, handsomely printed, were passed out to the guests as souvenirs of the occasion. It was noted with great approval that the father of the bride had written this epithalamium.

After the collation (once more my helpful student ushered me to the head of the line in order to make sure I was fed), I waited a decent interval, and called for my wife. From her, I learned that things were somewhat different on the distaff side.

According to custom, the bride sits in a prominent seat all dressed up in her wedding finery, with her eyes cast down, looking very sad and miserable. It appears that this demeanor is customary whether she is sad or happy. The bride, I was told, does not participate in the

135

festivities. She sits, and the guests come up to her, examine her finery, assess the value of her jewelry, and freely comment on the style and quality of the ensemble. The bride says nothing; she might as well be a store-window display figure.

However, the rest of the ladies are not thus inhibited. The more gifted ones, by popular request, sing and dance for the amusement of the company, and, in this setting, they are gay and happy.

Other People, Other Functions

Of the people we knew in Abbottabad, the younger army officers and their wives came closest to the American pattern. Typical of this group were two couples, the male halves of which were an engineering officer and an intelligence officer. We had met the engineer and his wife at the hotel before they moved into an army house, and, through them, we later met the second couple. Both men were career soldiers, competent, dedicated, hard working. Both of them had married cousins, more or less removed—arranged marriages, of course. The intelligence man, a sharp character, confessed that he had stolen a peek at his bride before marriage, and the engineer had seen his future wife at family gatherings. Both marriages seemed to be working out well. These young people visited back and forth in the manner of army officers at any American post. They went on picnics, to the movies, and to the club parties; they worried about promotions and assignments in typical army manner; and they called on us. Their wives were not in purdah, and they did not wear the *burqa*, albeit they always wore the *dupatta*, or shawl, as a standard part of the female costume.

Both girls were attractive and intelligent. The engineer's wife was a rarity among Pakistani women in that she had a college degree and was unwilling merely to vegetate. She tried to keep herself alive mentally, and she had unusual maturity and good sense for her years. It was possible to have a conversation with her. When we left, she took over the teaching post at Lower Burn Hall vacated by my wife.

These four young people, educated, good-looking, happy in their work and in their marriages, exemplify the point that the army is one of the most progressive and influential social institutions in Pakistan. The qualities of social ease and grace in army circles as against the formal and stiff qualities of other Abbottabad social groups were dramatically emphasized for us at a reception held for a Pakistani major general who had just returned from the United States to take over an important staff job at army headquarters.

It was a large party at the "old" station commander's house. A good many army wives were there, not in purdah and not in *burqas*. As often happens all over the world, the men quickly congregated in the sunroom to talk army shop. It suddenly occurred to me that the general and I were the only males in a roomful of some twenty-five women. Under these circumstances, most Pakistani men would have been embarrassed, or annoyed, or arrogant. Not the general. Perfectly at home, he made the rounds with a witty and graceful remark for every lady present. It was a fine drawing room performance.

The general told us that, in a big New York hotel, a total stranger, observing that he was alone, invited him to have a drink with his wife and friends, entertained him at dinner, and wound up the evening by taking him to see *My Fair Lady*—and this at a time when tickets for this show were almost impossible to get!

It gives me pleasure, by the way, to report that incidents of this kind were regularly reported to us by Pakistanis who had returned from the United States. Whatever doubts our allies may have about our national policies, there is (in our experience, at least) no doubt about the spontaneous hospitality of individual American citizens outside of official channels. This capacity for friendship is a national asset, and more Americans should be given opportunities for demonstrating it to foreign guests.

In the social life of Abbottabad, the semiannual variety show, put on by the cadets of the Pakistan Military Academy, was an important event. It was part of the graduation ceremonies which culminated in the "Passing Out" Parade, an impressive spectacle attended by the highest Pakistani officials, representatives of the diplomatic corps, and military attaches from many nations. Through accident of timing, we were privileged to see two parades and two variety shows.

As for the parades, they were marked by precise drilling on the part of the cadets, by extremely colorful massed pipe bands in kilts (a British legacy to the Pakistani army which will not die), by the awesome sight of a British Guards regimental sergeant-major in action, and by a spectacular exhibition of horsemanship by the PMA adjutant in command.

However, the variety shows were more revealing than the parades of the pull-and-haul of Western mores vs. national cultural traditions in the education and psychology of the cadets. A typical program was composed of a satirical skit on the Academy, an English one-act play, an Urdu one-act play, a quartette rendering "Walking My Baby Back Home," a few Urdu songs, an impressive Muslim Frontier dance solo, and a macabre depiction of a drinking party, which featured a boogie-woogie piano player and some enthusiastic but literally off-beat improvised jazz strutting. This last item was something like an all-male Saroyan skit in a 'Frisco dive without dialogue and in a somber key. There was a quality of frenetic desperation about it which indicated that the boys were desperately trying to have the time of their lives.

The satirical skit was a good one—a credit to both the boys and the academy. It showed that the stiff competition and demanding program of PMA had not killed the cadet sense of humor. The English one-act was "veddy veddy British" in clothes, manners, and accent. It came off as an unintentional parody, but it also revealed (again) the Sandhurst officer-gentleman concept under which the Academy operates, as did the formal manners of the cadet ushers. The Urdu one-act, a play about a writer with domestic difficulties involving a stream of visitors, was delightful. The boys, some of them in female roles, were completely at home, and they acted so well that, though we knew little Urdu, we understood the play without trouble. The "Walking My Baby Back Home" number showed that the cadets had listened religiously to a certain popular American record and that basically their rhythms, their sense of cadence and beat, are not Western and never will be. The Urdu songs were plaintive and appealing. The traditional dance, depicting the daily cycle of the sun, was the best thing in the show to our Western eyes. And the drinking party number pointed up once more that American jazz and popular music are our most successful cultural exports. The reasons why a group of Pakistani young men should put on a wild drinking act may be worth the serious attention of a sociologist. In view of the Islamic prohibition of alcohol, it was a curious spectacle.

A Day in the Village

I have said that most of our experiences were with the top strata of Pakistani society and with the marginal middle class, and that we, therefore, did not really get to know the way of life of most Pakistanis—the villagers and the farmers. There was one exception to this generalization: an all-day trip to Nawashahr, the village home of one of my faculty colleagues, about five miles away from Abbottabad. However, this was a state occasion, and, like all such conducted tours, it cannot be taken for the norm. Still, it gave us some insights worth setting down.

In the first place, there is the obvious point about Pakistani hospitality. Everybody tried to make it a red letter day. Then there was more evidence of the tight clan and family social organization of the village; everyone seemed to be related to my colleague, and we made the rounds of the clan houses. Purdah was strongly observed—suspended momentarily for the benefit of the American couple, but for them alone. No other outside male was present, and I myself heard my colleague brusquely refuse his best faculty friend permission to come along on this expedition.

There is little point in dwelling on the physical aspects of this village. It was like hundreds of others through which we passed in our travels: narrow streets, walled houses with inner courts, smelly open drains, mud-brick walls, cobblestone paving, bustling bazaar, and general air of desperate poverty. These things are normal in Pakistan; after a while, one takes them for granted.

What remains in the mind are certain pictures. There was a huge banyan tree, sheltering a stone pool, patronized by water buffalo and bullocks—a sort of shrine in itself. Not far away, at the site of another spring, was a relatively new white mosque, appealing in its white simplicity. This was a holy place. It was involved with the memory of a *pir* (a famous local holy man), one of those saints which Islam, in theory, should not have but possesses in abundance. The villagers were proud of this mosque. Before 1947, there had been a struggle for its site between the Muslims and the Hindus, and the Muslims won. The local populace, I gathered, had a much stronger feeling for the place than anybody in Abbottabad had for our town's local mosque. On the other side of the village, there was a large Hindu shrine, empty and unused, which, with some adjacent wrecked houses, spoke silently and eloquently for what had happened in the cataclysm of 1947. On the way to this place, we passed one part of the village grammar school. The children, under the direction of a gentle schoolmaster (who was paid less than we paid our servant, Ali) squatted on the ground in the warm sun and worked on their slates. The other part of the school was held indoors in a bare room where the students sat on the floor. This class, a little older, was dominated by a martinet who put on a great show of authority for his unexpected visitors—in the immemorial manner of pedant tyrants the world over. Under these conditions, the children in this school could not fail to touch a person's heartstrings.

All around the village as we saw the sights, we met women who were not in *burqas*, staring at the strangers with frank curiosity and no embarrassment. It has been said that purdah is not for the village or farm women because they can not afford the *burqa* and they are too busy making a living to stay indoors. This is to say that purdah is for the middle or upper classes who can afford it. There may be some truth in this.

And surrounding the town we were aware of the fields. Small in size, checkerboard in pattern, they looked tired and wornout—they were so brown under their thin covering of green.

In some ways, the village was like Abbottabad—in its bazaar with blasting radios and in its houses—but in other respects it had a timeless quality which its more cosmopolitan neighbor did not have—in its fields, its animals, its banyan tree, and its spring. In the fields one thought, "So has it been for a long time; so will it be for a long time to come."

Some Conclusions

As I consider the social life of Abbottabad, I think that the most important aspects are these: the formal manners; the continuing strength of purdah; the intense consciousness of status and position; the ambivalence and tension resulting from the conflict of Western values with traditional Muslim values and social patterns; the struggle for subsistence; and (excluding the army) the absence of a sense of direction and of a sense of mission—call it an absence of meaningful values in life—except that of Islam itself.

For, on the whole, this was not a happy community, and I think its malaise was deeper and more pervasive than the kind of unhappiness which has been and still is the theme of American writers on the town and the village. The underlying discontent and melancholy were more prominent in the educated members of the town than they were in the uneducated and underprivileged, always excluding those of the army group who were "integrated" because they had social status, economic security, and opportunities for steady, though slow, advancement.

Genteel poverty, unavailability of consumer goods, and comparatively low incomes do not wholly account for this unhappiness. As I have tried to show, sadness was characteristic of some people who were, relatively speaking, well off. Furthermore, it must be kept in mind that the social climate created by Islam is, almost by definition, grave, dignified, and solemn. It is not a gay religion, and in some respects it engenders the kind of atmosphere which we know as Puritanism. One should not confuse gravity with the deep unhappiness which I sensed.

Some of the reasons for this endemic state of mind are not far to seek. The tragedy of Kashmir; the ineffectiveness of the political process; the inflationary spiral and the cost of living; resentment of India and its resources, power, and prestige in world affairs; a similar reaction to England, the United States, and the West generally, which produces the ambivalence of hate and reluctant respect—all of these elements are present.

There are other more subtle factors. In a large measure, the Abbottabad community is part of a closed society, not an open one. It is closed or restricted in its economic, professional, and social opportunities. It is literally closed in the sense that travel in Pakistan is arduous and relatively expensive; travel outside Pakistan is, in effect, prohibited by currency and passport regulations and by plain considerations of expense. In the physical sense then, where can one go and what can one do? Occasional trips to Rawalpindi, Lahore, and Peshawar—that nearly exhausts the possibilities. The fluidity of the American populace in its automobiles comes to mind in this context as a unique and tremendously significant symbol of social mobility.

In Pakistan, as only a chosen few could travel, so could only a few become doctors and lawyers. As for business, a chosen few entrepreneurs could make millions of rupees in Karachi, but there are no corporations in Pakistan which make a practice of sending recruiting agents to the colleges and universities, and the way of the small merchant in the bazaar is a tough one, as the lot of the little businessman is in the United States. As for farming, a man might inherit part of his father's lands—and that would be that. As for marriage, a chosen few might be fortunate in getting congenial mates, but not through their own choice.

In sum, it seemed to me that most of the people we knew acted as if they were locked up in a closed room. They all "wanted out" in one way or another. Some of the younger ones literally "wanted out" of the country; I have received letters beseeching my aid in this enterprise. But most of them will never get out, and therefore they are fundamentally unhappy.

There is another important factor to consider. At the time we were in Pakistan, the nation was some ten years old. It came into existence through an explosion of enthusiasm for the Islamic state, which surprised even Jinnah. In 1957, the élan was gone. The state seemed to rest on dead center. Leadership was lacking. Apparently, it was not enough simply to create the new state—to declare that it was to be founded on Islam and henceforth would be a Muslim Utopia, free of Hindus and Englishmen. The very conduct of ostensibly devout Muslim politicians since the death of Jinnah and Liaquat has been a matter of grave disappointment to the people whom I knew. How can this be? How can good Muslims be corrupt?

Up to this point, I think that few Pakistanis would challenge what has been said in this paragraph. Now I speculate a little. I suggest that an awful thought now plagues some of my friends, a thought that possibly Islam itself may not be the total answer. Yet it must be for many, because it is now all they have, and for this reason they are all the more fervent in its defense.

In short, the psychology we observed as host and hostess, and as guests, corroborates by personal examples what Professor W. C. Smith generalizes thus:

> The tragedy of the failure to find adequate content for the [Islamic state] ideal has lain in part in the vast disenchantment with the whole social enterprise in the country. Many in coming gradually to the persuasion that Pakistan cannot after all be an Islamic state have in fact been coming to the desperate conclusion that their new nation is not worth while.[7]

We saw evidence of the disenchantment in 1956–57. However, the dynamism of the current Ayub military regime may have restored the national morale.[8]

Chapter Six

The Great Debate

East vs West

When we started out for Pakistan, we were determined, insofar as was possible, not to judge what we found there by our American standards. We wanted to meet Pakistani culture on its own terms in order to enrich ourselves. Specifically, we wished to avoid that subtle subconscious process of making comparisons, the result of which is almost invariably, "We do this better," and, ultimately "We *are* better." Comparisons are odorous, as Dogberry so wisely remarked, but, as we found out, they are nonetheless inevitable. For such comparisons were literally forced on us by some of our Pakistani friends in discussions of the relative merits of Western and Muslim society in respect to purdah, the role of women in society, the family, coeducation, marriage, and divorce. In formal social affairs these subjects were not touched on, but they often came up in informal gatherings.

In these discussions we observed an ambivalence in our friends. On the one hand, there seemed to be a strongly felt need to affirm, by

143

direct statement or polite implication, that their religious and social systems were the best of all possible creations; on the other, there was a reluctant, perhaps half-conscious, recognition of the stultifying social effects of the rigid segregation of women from the blood stream of national life and a deep concern over the failure of traditional ethical sanctions in respect to public morality in education, in politics, and in public administration.

The result of these friendly debates on ourselves was an interesting reaction. At home we cheerfully exercise the birthright of every American in leveling the sharpest criticism at our own failures; abroad, in the face of implied assumptions of superiority, we found ourselves psychologically much more aware of the fundamental worth of American institutions and cultural patterns and much more disposed to defend their values with emotional warmth and conviction. It is the old familiar story: the American knows his own land better abroad than he does at home.

Still I do not like the kind of polarization into which we were driven in Pakistan. It certainly does not make for a realistic comprehension of relative values or of the true state of affairs on either side. Ideally, it should be possible for an American to express his country's positive values and to assess its shortcomings objectively in conversation with foreign friends. Conversely, it should be possible to understand sympathetically the same pattern of explication from a Pakistani. The trouble is that an analysis of American failures is likely to be taken as the whole picture; in the minds of the beholders, the warts are substituted for the face. On the other hand, some Pakistanis feel that any criticism of the social consequences of Islam is treason to the faith, or, excluding the faith from their minds for the moment, they will go to the other extreme of nihilistic pessimism in respect to secular affairs. In part, these reactions stem from the fact that Pakistan is a young country having difficulty in finding its way, and, in part, from the fact that we have just begun to conduct an international dialogue with the Muslim world. With time and patience on both sides, it may be possible to achieve a state of intercommunication in which thoughtful discussion will not be confused with unilateral defense of two mutually exclusive perfect societies.

Some Specific Illustrations

In discussions with our Muslim friends of social institutions, we were somewhat at a disadvantage because of the American propen-

Mrs. Linck's Students at Lower Burn Hall School, Abbottabad, "The Eton of Pakistan."

Palace Hotel Servants on Our Departure Day: Ali from Nathia Gali, our personal servant, is second from the right. The others are: cook, gardener, water carrier, dishwasher, room bearer, and sweeper.

"Passing Out" at PMA: Pakistani ladies with a high ranking officer. The absence of the *burqa* in public is noteworthy.

sity for statistics. We keep careful records of crimes, births (legitimate and illegitimate), juvenile delinquency, marriages, divorces, desertions, and the like. Furthermore, we analyze these records and their implications endlessly. The figures and the analyses are summarized in our press and made public to the world in *Time, Newsweek, Life, Reader's Digest* (all of which are well known in Pakistan), and similar mass media. Of course, Pakistan collects some statistics in these areas, but its vital statistics are not yet adequate, for it can not afford an elaborate statistical apparatus.

The consequences of this situation in discussion are obvious. The Pakistanis know all about our high divorce rate, but what about their own? Divorce is, in theory, simple under Islam, but it is also regarded as a family disgrace. Moreover, divorce is not the business of the state; it is a private affair, nobody's concern but the families involved, and it is better to conceal divorce than to reveal it. Furthermore, as I understand the situation after conversation with my lawyer friends in Abbottabad, the nation does not require a civil marriage license, although a copy of the marriage settlement is usually recorded legally to protect the bride's economic interests, a matter in which APWA, the women's organization, is much interested.[1] Under these circumstances, then, nobody really knows how many people are married in Pakistan, nor how many are divorced. And in debate such ignorance is useful.

There are, of course, other forms of divorce besides legal or religious modes. A man may simply desert his wife and family and disappear into the big city jungle. We got the impression that this happens frequently in Pakistan in all levels of society—with no legal consequences to the runaway. Or a couple may simply agree to separate without any legal or religious formalities. In these cases of divorce, desertion, or separation, the family of the woman absorbs the burden; the family is the great shock absorber of Pakistani society. The state is none the wiser; as yet, it is not officially concerned. Therefore, I suspect that there are many more "broken families" in Pakistan than would at first appear. I suspect, too, that this is the case with illegitimacy. Muslim morality is fierce on this head, but what are the figures?

One aspect of the social system which all Muslims of our acquaintance were reluctant to discuss was the matter of plural wives. There are differences of opinion about fundamental Islamic doctrine on this point. The general notion is that one man may have four wives at the same time. However, in Islamic theory, he must be prepared to support them equally and to accord them equal treatment in all respects. It is this injunction which, very likely, prompted one of my students to ask me in class one day whether a man could love more than one woman at the same time. I answered that in the sexual relationship, a man obviously could, but that in any deeper or more meaningful sense, I did not think so.

It is evident that the boy was perfectly serious in his query. I believe that his concern may be indicative of the latent, subsurface doubts in the minds of many Pakistanis about the merits of polygyny.

When, in the course of the Great Debate, we asked our Muslim friends how many cases of plural wives they knew of, the answers were invariably evasive. One answer was: "Only some members of the older generation have as many as four wives." Still, the incidence of plural marriage is, I think, not known. Perhaps it can not be known. One is given to believe that it is small. However, when people gossip in Pakistan (as people do all over the world), the story is somewhat different. Then one hears references to the city wife and to the village wife. This kind of arrangement is, naturally, very convenient for the Pakistani businessman, officer in the armed services, or top-grade civil servant whose work takes him into cosmopolitan circles in which the village lady, confined to purdah, generally not educated, and ignorant of English, would be at a definite social disadvantage.

Yet, no matter how Westernized Pakistani men may become, and no matter how much time they may spend in the big city or abroad, most of them still have strong organic ties with their home places, their villages. Therefore, the pattern of the country wife and the city wife is a good solution for the problem of living domestically in two worlds discrete—for those who can afford it.

Furthermore, as more and more Pakistani men—many of them handsome by any standard—go to Europe or the United States for graduate work, advanced training in government service, or military missions, they bring back Western wives. Some of these girls have been understandably dismayed to find that their husbands already have wives on the home grounds. It follows that any young lady from Europe or America who may be considering marriage with an attractive and romantic Pakistani would do well to find out what his matrimonial status is and to find out, too, just what kind of domestic and social life she would be expected to lead. It is difficult for Western women to adjust to Pakistani life and for Pakistani men to adjust to the ways of Western women, but it is possible for such marriages to be successful if both parties fully realize what they are up against.

146

In the absence of dependable data, the case in respect to plural wives may be summarized thus: the sheer power of economics tends to make for monogamy because relatively few Pakistani men can support more than one wife, but there are probably a great many more cases of plural wives than is generally admitted. Since the foreign male, on the Frontier, at least, rarely sees his host's womenfolk, he is not likely to know whether his host has one wife or more.

Arranged Marriages

Of course, marriages in Pakistan are generally arranged between families. A number of the people we met in Abbottabad were married to their cousins, and apparently quite happy. It is probably for this reason that everybody in Pakistan seemed to be related to everybody else, and this tissue of family relationships is very important in the advancement of young Pakistanis in the professions, in the civil service, and in the armed forces.

The pattern of arranged marriages seems to be completely accepted, even by the Westernized young men in Abbottabad. For example, there was the likable sportsman-lawyer, a graduate of Punjab University, reputed by gossip to have a mistress in town— how he got away with this, I don't know. He married a cousin who stayed in their nearby village while he spent most of his time in town playing tennis at the club. There was another barrister, practicing law in town, who had been admitted to the English bar from Lincoln's Inn Fields in London. He was one of the most cultivated and Westernized of our friends; yet he was quietly waiting for his family seniors to complete the arrangements for his nuptials, wondering what was holding them up, but expressing no curiosity about the appearance of his bride-to-be. And then there was the ex-BBC broadcaster, an urbane type if there ever was one, who had delayed his return to Pakistan for years before yielding to family entreaties and implied economic threats; he was evidently resigned to his marital fate, soon to be arranged.

In this environment, social sanctions growing out of local mores are very strong. During our stay in Abbottabad, the sensational social event of the year was the love marriage between the cantonment executive officer and the assistant principal of the Cantonment Middle School. From the outsider's point of view, it looked like an ideal match. Both persons were well bred, well educated, and physically attractive. But the marriage was almost a scandal. It was reported to us that the male's family was desolate; they felt dis-

147

graced because the young lady, a stranger in town, had necessarily lived alone, and the local gossips had tried to make something out of the situation, without foundation, I am sure. But the two did get married and were accepted, as we saw, at social functions. However, this kind of marriage was unique in our Abbottabad experience.

There is a footnote to this story. The bride quit her job at the school. At first, it was said that she was forced to resign because of governmental policy. Later on, it developed that the husband, who had challenged the ways of the town by marrying the woman of his choice, had insisted on her resigning. After all, woman's place is in the home, is it not?

The issues involved in this running debate between Islam and the West may be further illustrated by a summary of my conversation with an able professor of agricultural chemistry from the University of Peshawar, who had recently returned from Canada where he had taken a Ph.D. at a well known university. We were walking home from a stag dinner given by his former student, the barrister from Lincoln's Inn, who was, incidentally, a graduate of Abbottabad Government College. It had been a good evening. The conversation was easy and varied. We talked about his pleasant experiences in the United States and Canada, and about mine in Pakistan. We discussed academic affairs on both sides of the world and education in general. I did not get such talk very often in Abbottabad, and it was refreshing.

Then, as we strolled along the deserted streets of the town in the coolness of the night, he raised the question of divorce in the United States. He said that we were both educated men, we understood each other, we could talk openly and frankly. I agreed, and he began. His first point was that the high divorce rate in the United States was certainly a cruel thing for wives and children. I assented, but I pointed out that divorce in the United States for the great mass of Americans is not as easy as it is thought to be abroad; that arrangements for the maintenance of divorced wives and children, though often inadequate, are made and carried out under the law; and that, despite the bad consequences of broken homes, the converse consequences of rearing children in a domestic atmosphere poisoned by hostility between parents ought to be taken into account.

He agreed politely, though patently not convinced that there are really any effective limitations on divorce in our country. Then, in rejoinder, he said something like this—the words may not be exactly quoted, but their substance is accurate: "Suppose, as a married man,

148

you meet another woman—you can't live without her—she drives you crazy—you must have her: wouldn't it be better to marry her, too, rather than to carry on an affair with her?"

This somewhat startling defense of plural marriages came unexpectedly, even in the context of the divorce discussion. Up to this point, polygyny had not been in my mind at all, and there had been nothing to indicate that it was on his. I replied that I did not see much absolute moral difference between a man who married four wives, one after another, and a man who is married to four wives at the same time; that is, there seems to be little difference between simultaneous polygyny and serial polygyny—or serial monogamy, if you wish. At any rate, it was a very interesting question, and it revealed a very interesting attitude. By mutual consent, we went on to other matters.

He defended purdah as the proper base for family life; his Canadian experience had not changed his mind. Then I asked him what, as an educated and cultured man, he thought about the education of women. He was in favor of education for women; as a matter of fact, he sent his daughter to a convent school. But, in his opinion, women should primarily serve the family function: the state of Pakistan's economy would not permit women to take men's jobs; there were not enough jobs to go around as things were. This view was widely held in Pakistan.

Aside from the obvious bases for this attitude resulting from the traditional notions about the position of women in Islam, what the professor had in mind was that the posts available in the civil services and in the educational system are limited and competition is bitter. Pakistan does not have a rapidly expanding industrial economy, and the need for women in clerical posts (a need which, in our own country, gives women an opportunity for jobs on the secondary and tertiary levels of executive rank) is not yet pressing. Rather, such clerical jobs in the large cities of Pakistan are handled by men and jealously guarded.

The economic fear of feminine competition in the powerful state bureaucracies is one of the complementary modern reasons for the maintenance of the old-line policies governing the education of women. In the United States, we went through this phase in the Thirties when the depression put a premium on jobs. Then there was a radical change in our views respecting women in business, industry, and education during World War II when we had to exploit our total potential work force. After 1945, there was a considerable carry-over of the emancipation into the peace-time period. However, we still have a powerful, though covert, hangover of this Pakistani attitude toward women at work, an attitude which obviously becomes stronger whenever a recession occurs.

But this attitude towards women in the United States is recessive; it is not dominant as it is in Pakistan; and my evening with the professor, fresh from his years in Canada, underlined this fact. I think no single conversation I had was more revealing of the cultural chasm which yawns between the American and the Pakistani—no matter how much they may have in common.

The professor may be taken as a reasonably typical example of the educated older generation in the Northwest Frontier Province, the bastion of Islamic fundamentalism in Pakistan. In retrospect, it is interesting to compare his views with those of a member of what might be called the mature younger generation—that is, of the generation which has come to full maturity since 1947. The person I have in mind was the manager of the local branch of the National Bank of Pakistan. He was, I judge, in his early thirties. He came from a good Lahore family, a fact of genuine importance in Pakistan. He held a degree from the University of the Punjab, and he proposed to make a career for himself in the bank, which, as far as personnel practices were concerned, was run on principles analogous to those of the British Civil Service. Since our departure from Abbottabad, I have learned that he has been transferred to another branch bank in a larger city.

The manager was a hard-working and competent public servant. Intellectually curious and well educated, he observed what was going on both in Pakistan and in the world with keen interest and clear understanding. Indeed, in the breadth and depth of his concerns, he was unusual among our acquaintances. Though a thoroughly patriotic Pakistani in an unostentatious way, he had a refreshing capacity for intellectual detachment and objectivity which made conversation with him a valuable experience. Though he had never been outside Pakistan, he was in no way narrowly nationalistic or chauvinistic. In the exercise of his intelligence, he was truly a man of the world. Furthermore, he was personally charming by virtue of a deep innate courtesy which transcended mere politeness. With his personal qualities and his official position (he was rated among the gazetted officers), he had an important place in local society.

The manager lived at our hotel (in itself a mark of distinction in Abbottabad), and by the end of the year we three were the senior

150

guests of the establishment—at times practically the only guests. We, therefore, came to know him pretty well. I think he was significant not only for what he had to say but also for the example provided by his own way of life.

In respect to Pakistani society (with the issues of the Great Debate always running beneath the conversation) he was willing to accept the concept of three middle classes: upper-middle, middle-middle, and lower-middle. He believed that the institution of purdah was weakening in the two top brackets, particularly in cities like Lahore and Karachi. He once told us that 95 per cent of Pakistani women were not in purdah and that purdah will disappear in twenty-five to fifty years.

The Peshawar professor would not have agreed with the bank manager, and, as much as we liked and respected our fellow inmate, I have grave doubts about the validity of these opinions. As far as I know, there is no statistical evidence on these moot points. To establish the truth of the matter would require a systematic survey of Pakistan's social system. What interests me about the manager's assertions is the reason which prompted him to make them. In contrast to the professor and his convictions about the worth of purdah, the manager seemed to be indulging in some wishful thinking. Certainly, 95 per cent of the women around Abbottabad and Peshawar were not out of purdah, and I doubt that so high a percentage of women in the other big cities are either.

On this point, I am reminded of the remarks made by a British observer in Karachi. He said that there was a tendency on the part of Pakistani women in the highest economic brackets to move out of purdah, but there was an equal or greater tendency on the part of families moving into the middle class brackets to go into purdah. I think that there is substance in this view because, in our observation, purdah is a sign of status. While it continues to be so, I see little hope of the fulfillment of the manager's optimistic prediction.

Moreover, on the related question of plural marriages, the manager told us emphatically that a very strong social taboo against having more than one wife had developed in the upper levels of Pakistani society in the last twenty-five years and that this taboo was growing stronger year by year. He may be right, but, in the absence of documentation, I suspect that the number of plural marriages is currently higher than would please him. The real point is that the manager, in his heart, does not really approve of either purdah or plural marriage, though he never said as much flatly.

Whatever the real state of affairs is now and whatever the incidence of change, the consequences of purdah, modified purdah, or the purdah point of view are very clear in Pakistan's society. The manager himself is a good case in point. He was a gentleman, he was unmarried, and he obviously would have welcomed the companionship of women. In Abbottabad, his life was restricted to work at the bank and social activities at the Abbottabad Club. For him, these consisted of badminton, a little tennis, much gin rummy and bridge at high stakes, some social drinking with his friends of an evening in the club bar, and long conversations at tea and dinner about politics, economics, and literature—all with male friends. He had no chance to talk with any respectable women except with army wives at club parties and the wives of his European friends. He was essentially a lonely young man, and he was condemned to this loneliness until he decided to marry, but he did not want to get married because he had hopes of going abroad for advanced work in banking and also (I suspect) because just any nice girl wouldn't do. Nor could he "date," in the Western sense, any respectable women.

We asked him whether he would be any better off in Lahore when it came to social relations with women. The answer was, to some extent, yes. He could go and visit with his female cousins in the presence of his aunts and uncles; he might occasionally take one of his relatives to a movie with an older relative; and he might go on family outings and picnics in mixed company. But he could not take the daughter of his father's best friend to the movies, to a dance, or to any other social gathering. In sum, he could not "date" a well brought up Muslim girl in Lahore either.

The manager was only one of a good many young Muslim gentlemen we met in Abbottabad who lived lonely lives because of the social separation of the sexes. These gentlemen are among Pakistan's finest: the dashing young surgeon-sportsman serving his tour of army duty; the young-middle-aged staff captain at the PMA who will not marry until he gets a crack at foreign duty; the numerous young career officers at the army base; the research specialist at the Forest Institute, a Ph.D. from the University of California; and the five or six eligible young bachelors on the college faculty. All of them have been living lop-sided lives for too long.

Two Worlds Discrete

But the influence of purdah does not cease when these men marry. I have already commented on the group who gathered nightly at the

club. I had assumed that all of them were unmarried. It turned out
that most of them were married and were the fathers of many children. But they did not act like married men, and they did not talk
like mature married men. They acted and talked like lonely bachelors who were grown-up children—with the significant exception
that they did not appear in conversation to be obsessed with sex.

My guess is that these men at the club did not want to go home
because home was dull. The conversation of their wives was so
repetitive and banal that the men had to find release in one way or
another. But the rigid exclusion of one-half of their lives from the
other made both halves the poorer.

At this point I can hear the thoughtful reader saying to himself,
"Well, what is so different about all that? There are plenty of American clubs and taverns which exist on the bar bills paid by tired
businessmen between 5:00 and 8:00 because these men do not want to
go home, they find their wives dull, they laugh inanely, and they have
an obsession for dirty stories to boot."

But there are some essential differences. In any gathering of
American males, the females are unquestionably present in spirit.
Not many minutes will pass without some reference to home, mother,
the children, or to the "little woman." Many of these remarks will be
"kidding," but not necessarily uncomplimentary, and it is a rare
occasion on which some member of the club, in or out of his cups,
does not produce a picture of Junior or Junior Miss. In fact, the wife
and the family are very much there—for better or worse. In Muslim
male society, the wife and the family are very much *not* there.

As for the charges that the American male is dominated by his
women, there are grounds for this judgment, and one extreme is no
better than the other. But our social system is not organized to insure female dominance as the Islamic system insures male dominance. The balance in the United States is certainly nearer to fifty-
fifty, and, if a man is henpecked, it is largely his own fault. As it
appears to me, the Pakistani mode of living in two worlds discrete
tends to force both men and women to live in half-worlds. By and
large, the women have no concern for the affairs of the nation, the
province, or the town; conversely, the men have little or no interest
in the domestic economy except for the bills.

In sum, other than the All-Pakistan Women's Association, there
are no social mechanisms whereby the dynamic moral and intellectual forces of womanhood may be harnessed in the service of the
nation. This fact of exclusion from the main stream of national life

153

relieves Pakistan's women of social responsibility, save for the functioning of their own households. Probably many of them like it that way, but, fortunately, an increasing number do not. A great many men like it that way too. It is a man-centered world, and they run it pretty much to suit themselves.

When you ask who perpetuates this way of life, some outspoken women will answer: the men. When you ask the men, they will answer, "My wife will not come out of purdah—even if I order her to." One man said that his wife would kill herself rather than to break the pattern.

The Leisure of the Begums

Added to the crippling effects of purdah in the middle classes are the debilitating effects of an excess of leisure with not many constructive ways of using it. This leisure results from a cheap and plentiful supply of servants. Even lower-middle class Muslim families have bearers and cooks: for example, my lecturer-colleagues trying to live on salaries of some three hundred rupees per month (about $60.00), a sum which nevertheless put them in the middle, if not in the upper-middle class. How their servants lived is beyond my comprehension. The result of the servant system is that middle class Muslim ladies do very little household work. They may supervise the cooking, they may prepare special dishes from time to time, and they may occupy themselves with embroidery, but they do not have to clean house, wash or iron clothes, mend socks, or take care of the gardens. The assorted *malis, dhobis, dherzis,* cooks, and bearers perform these tasks.

The American middle class housewife, who sadly recalls the days when it was possible to have a hired girl on a full-time basis, might think of this situation as Utopian—especially since, in Pakistan, full-time babysitters (with a real fondness for children) are cheap. But I rather doubt that the American housewife would like to spend her days as her Pakistani counterparts do.

Pakistani women of the middle and upper class eat heavily, and their diet is dominated by starches, sweets, and ghee (that clarified butter which is a basic staple). They drink tea with large amounts of milk and sugar in it; they go from one purdah party to another; they gossip about their clothes, their children, and other women; and they grow fat and misshapen at an early age.

So do American women? Of course, but it is the rare woman in any economic class who does not have some interest outside her home, some kind of outside contact with the larger society.

These observations on Pakistani middle-class women are not merely an outsider's opinions. They are a fair summary of the bitter comments we heard from young Pakistani men who were sharply critical of the change in physical appearance of their women folk— once slim and pretty women, but somehow, between twenty-five and thirty-five, transformed into overweight matrons.

A contributing factor to this characteristic obesity is the comparative absence of post-natal care in Pakistani medical practice; many women could not afford it even if it were available. The effect of this deficiency on the figures of Pakistani mothers is sad.

As a result, many Pakistani women are old at thirty. The comparative youth of Western women—slim, well groomed, and active in community affairs and sports—is a constant wonder to them. Of course, Western women are scorned for being unwomanly, and very likely immoral, but, underlying this attitude, some respect and some envy may be present.

The final charge made by Pakistani men against middle- and upper-class begums is that they are lazy, but when these same men were asked what they were doing to provide their women with a basis for a more active and richer life, the answers were evasive. The system is to blame, but nobody seems to have any sense of responsibility for changing the system. Would they take their wives out of purdah once they were married? Probably not. The social sanctions outside the big cities are still too powerful; yet, they say the purdah system will disappear in the course of time. Like segregation in our South? I wonder.

Of course, it is impossible to determine what goes on behind the walls of the family compounds. The bank manager asserted that Pakistani women exercise a very powerful influence on family affairs. Granting that this is so, we may ask upon what knowledge this influence is based. Relatively few Pakistani women have any knowledge of sanitation, diet, first aid, disease, or education. A great many of them are illiterate and uneducated. These women can and do give their husbands and children much love and affection. I have seen moving tributes to home and mother in themes written by my students, and love in the family circle is surely more important than material matters. But love is not enough. Wisdom and understanding of a changing world are also needed. No student of the world's culture will underrate the efficacy of traditional knowledge, but a folk tradition is not in itself an adequate basis for rearing strong and healthy children, for mediating between old cultural values and the hard imperatives which face young Pakistanis in their struggle to create and maintain a viable nation.

Where the institution of purdah, with its concomitants of servant-operated households and the tradition of genteel leisure for ladies, is now dominant, I am sceptical of any major change for this generation. But the forces tending towards that major change should be taken into account. Though many women are perfectly content to be absolved from any function or duty outside the family, there are signs of unrest in the younger wives who are not satisfied with the routine of child-bearing, tea parties, and gossip. The reader will recall the chemist's wife seeking an M.A. degree, the army engineer's wife who replaced my wife at Lower Burn Hall, the brigadier general's wife who was her husband's constant companion and full partner, and the intrepid Kashmiri matriarch who defied purdah. In addition to these, other local ladies in Abbottabad worked for APWA, which, if not yet a major force in bringing Pakistan's women into the main stream of national life, is certainly the most promising base for such an eventuality.

The All-Pakistan Women's Association

APWA was fortunate in having as two of its leaders Fatima Jinnah, the sister of Pakistan's great national founder, and Begum Liaquat Ali Khan, the wife of the martyred prime minister, who is second only to Jinnah in the national pantheon. They are both able, energetic, and formidable ladies. Their work in Pakistan is comparable to what was done in the United States in the late nineteenth century by a pioneering group of American feminists, the fruit of which was universal suffrage and the emancipation of American women. The male opposition to Carrie Chapman Catt and her embattled band is analogous to what APWA faces today in Pakistan. However, comparatively speaking, the two redoubtable Pakistani women commanded more influence than their American counterparts because they inherited great prestige from two national heroes; they have ability in their own right; and they exploit both advantages to the full. Perhaps the most significant aspect of their work is that they have made APWA socially acceptable—in which respect APWA is comparable to our Junior League.

Nevertheless, APWA faces far greater obstacles than American women did in the nineteenth century because, no matter how much the latter were discriminated against in the law of the land, they were much freer, much more a part of total society than Pakistani women are today.

Let us take a look at APWA in action. Its governing body met at the Metropole Hotel in Karachi for a three-day meeting, November 27–29, 1957. Begum Iskander Mirza, the president's wife (a very handsome woman) inaugurated the session. The proceedings were given full coverage in the Karachi press. In her opening remarks, Begum Mirza, after paying tribute to the work of the organization, made the following important points, among others, as reported on November 27 on the first page of the Karachi *Dawn*, one of the most influential dailies in the nation.

> In the context of education and social welfare, Begum Mirza said that, while in the urban areas the Association had done a substantial work, a great deal of groundwork remained to be done in rural areas in these spheres as well as in health service.
>
> She expressed the hope that the Governing Body would also discuss ways and means of carrying the message of APWA to the masses of womanhood in the country, thus overcoming the suspicion that the Association is a body representative only of educated and well-to-do women.
>
> As a national organisation, the APWA should enjoy the support of all sections of women in both the Wings. Thus alone, she said, will it be able to speak with an effective voice and influence public opinion in favour of causes which it held dear.

In those statements, Begum Mirza laid her finger on both the strengths and weaknesses of APWA.

After this address, a member "read out" a speech prepared for the occasion by the absent Begum Liaquat Ali Khan, referred to as the founder-president of APWA. She was then serving as Pakistan's ambassador to the Netherlands. In this presidential address (as covered in *Dawn*, November 27, page 3), Begum Khan laid down a program for the consideration of APWA which speaks volumes about conditions in Pakistan (numbers added):

> 1. ... to embark on a practical programme of educating public opinion for voting so that APWA can act as an honest and influential guide to its less fortunate sisters and brothers and also as a check upon the more educated and fortunate....
>
> 2. Reasonable and adequate opportunities for women to make an all-round educational, economic, social, professional and cultural development;

and legal and practical measures to provide the highest possible security to women in the matter of laws and domestic security.

3. A wider and more active programme for the proper protection and development of the rights and interests of children, especially the orphans and the handicapped.

4. Provision for prompt and stringent disciplinary measures against those who practiced nepotism, jobbery, corruption, intimidation, wastage of public funds, black-marketing, harassment of women, etc., which should be regarded as treasonable offences.

5. A separate Central Ministry of Social Welfare to be formed; social welfare to be introduced as a subject in educational institutions; provision of adequately paid and recognised professional opportunities for work; and extension of short-term courses in Service Training.

6. Complete overhaul of the whole educational system and formation of a separate Central Education Ministry; extension of compulsory free primary education; provision for better training facilities for teachers; encouragement of teaching profession by providing adequate salaries, allowances, scholarships for special study and travel grants, and by raising the status of the profession; introduction of science (including Home Science for girls) teaching at all levels and open to both boys and girls; and better provision for the education of normal and handicapped adults.

7. More maternity and child welfare clinics, centres and hospitals, especially in rural areas; encouragement of the nursing profession by providing better training facilities, adequate salaries and allowances, and by raising the status of the profession.

8. A more honest, active, speedy, better planned and supervised programme of refugee rehabilitation and claims settlement.

9. Extension of the Village AID Programme and wider development of the cottage industries.

10. Immediate and active measures for stabilizing the cost of living (with special reference to daily food, clothing, housing and transport needs) at a level which will bring the greatest relief to the middle and lower income workers.

11. An active and nationwide program to be started for housebuilding.

12. A firm and graded ban on extravagance with regard to food, clothing, private building projects, etc.

13. An All-Pakistan Agricultural Development Board on the lines of the P.I.D.C. [Pakistan Industrial Development Commission] to be set up.

14. Better safeguarding of small industries; and greater scope and encouragement for employment of women and deserving refugees with better safety and security measures for them.

15. The setting up of local self-governing bodies and measures on a more secure, adequate and better organized basis; and encouragement of women in these bodies.

16. Proper supervision of all foreign aid and relief supplies.

Because of my particular professional concerns and my experiences in the realm of education, I was pleased with two other points made by Begum Khan: she urged that APWA should concentrate its next year's work on (1) the establishment of mobile libraries in as many areas as possible; and (2) the translation into Urdu and Bengali of short stories, plays, and songs for children, and encouragement of those who are able to write for children. She also said that short, interesting stories of the lives of Pakistan's great men were a crying need.[2]

At its concluding session (reported in *Dawn*, November 29, page 4), APWA took two positions which struck home with me in respect to certain discussions I had had with students about delinquency in the United States and in regard to other discussions about the institution of marriage in Islam.

As to the first, APWA expressed its concern about "goondaism," a term which can in general be defined as any form of antisocial behavior and, specifically, as rowdyism or gangsterism. Often it seems to be applied more narrowly to the molestation of women in public, and, as a consistent reading of the daily press shows, there are real grounds for concern. APWA called upon the government to take strict action against those responsible for such incidents. This is to say that Pakistan's delinquency problem in respect to the public behavior of its youth is quite like our own.

As to the second point, APWA, through its Secretary for Women's Rights, is working for the implementation of the Family Law Commission. One worker is quoted as follows: "Begum Faridi felt that a model *nikah-namah* [marriage contract] should be drawn up. In Islam, marriage is a contract, not a sacrament, so women should know what should go into a *nikah-namah*. The Karachi Branch is working on a model *nikah-namah*. . . ."

APWA also pointed out that there was not a single woman on the Family Laws Commission and that this omission offends "the fundamental rights granted to women under the Constitution."

Miss Fatima Jinnah was not reported as present during this three-day session during which, it is obvious, Begum Liaquat Ali Khan's influence was powerful. But Miss Jinnah gave a speech to the students of the Islamia College for Girls in Lahore on the opening day of the Karachi APWA meeting, a speech which got full coverage in *Dawn*, November 28, page 5. It was a good speech. In it, she stressed the importance of home making and the danger of women becoming third-rate copies of any alien culture or way of life. Then she added these remarks:

If you delve into your social, cultural and intellectual history you will find sources of inspiration which will spur you to creative thinking and purposeful activity.

It does not mean that you should shut yourself from the bracing influence of new forms of knowledge and new intellectual trends. Far from it. What I mean is that you should have a due sense or appreciation and even a sense of pride in your cultural heritage because it was really the product of your special genius and on its basis you should build your new life, taking advantage of all the good things that modern knowledge and science have to offer....

I would like to stress the necessity of giving a somewhat practical bias to your education. While it is all very well to enlighten your minds and familiarize yourself with ideas and theories, it is also important to learn to do things with your own hands. There is dignity in labour and it is a soul satisfying pursuit to do and make things which would turn one's home into a heaven of rest and happiness.

What Pakistan needs above all, it seems to me, is some practical idealism in action, and it is for this reason that I have devoted this much attention to the views of its most powerful women and to APWA. This organization was just about the only one operating in social-political problem areas whose motives and programs were not suspect for one reason or another. In my opinion, Pakistan would do well to listen to its women.

In terms of the Great Debate, the theme of this chapter, I believe that the program put forth by APWA illuminates on the one hand what both the nation and its women are up against; on the other, it indicates the great potential which is now denied to Pakistan by the failure of both its political and social systems to give its women the opportunity of exercising full citizenship. It appears, in short, that Pakistan's most enlightened and influential women want for themselves a way of life closer to that of their Western sisters than the pattern which they have been forced to follow for centuries.[3]

This conclusion is reinforced by the testimony given by another Pakistani begum, Zeb-Un-Nissa Hamidullah, in a little book entitled *Sixty Days in America*. Begum Hamidullah came to the United States under the Foreign Leader Exchange Program of our State Department. The book is made up of a series of daily columns which she wrote for *The Times of Karachi*. One chapter (XII) is called "Pakistani Begums in U.S." In it Begum Hamidullah has this to say:

Strange though it may appear, coming to America has made good cooks of our Pakistani Begums. What's more, it's made them most energetic. So much so, that the majority of them are doing the jobs of ayahs, bearers, cooks, drivers and cleaners combined and at the same time managing to look more attractive and self-assured than they did in Pakistan.

Quite an achievement, this, you'll agree. And maybe agree with me too when I state, not without a little legitimate pride, that our Begums are as good or as bad as any in the world, and *if* in Pakistan they tend at times to become slothful, self-centered and intellectually sleepy, it's not so much they themselves who are to blame as our whole way of life....

It's an education in itself for our Begums to come here, and I do wish more and more of my sex had the opportunity to do so. For, once having come to America and living here for a considerable period of time, no Pakistani Begum can ever be quite the same. Her whole outlook will have widened and her horizon become much wider than the narrow four walls of the home. What's more important, she will have learnt, by watching the average American housewife, that it is possible to be a good wife and mother while at the same time being a good citizen. For she will have seen how eager an interest the American woman takes in the affairs of her district and State and how she has her say in almost all matters of local importance.[4]

However, women like Miss Jinnah and Begums Mirza, Liaquat Ali Khan, and Hamidullah are exceptional, and APWA is not yet a powerful force in Pakistan. Its numbers are few and, despite its promise for the future, its influence is small. I think we can get a better gauge of true Pakistani sentiments in respect to the outer world and its values by reverting, for the moment, to the younger generation which I taught for one college year—sentiments which are likely to hold true for a long time to come.

The True Believers

One morning a few days before we left Abbottabad to return home, two young students called upon us at the hotel. They were second year boys, just completing their promotion examinations for entrance into the third year. They were among the better students. One of them had taken a leading and creditable part in that hilarious debate on coeducation described above; his companion was the secretary of a tutorial group.

These young men brought gifts—a book and a group photo of their tutorial group function, at which I had been a guest. The debater gave me the book because, as he put it, he had observed in my lectures a continuing curiosity about Islam. It was a generous gesture because the book had been presented to him as first prize in a student competition. Grateful to him for his thoughtfulness, I sat down and read it as soon as I could find time.

The book is called *Towards Understanding Islam*. It was written by Sayyid Abul Ala Maududi; translated into English by Dr. Abul Ghani, ex-director of Public Instructions, Afghanistan; and published in Lahore, 1940. My copy is of the fifth edition, 1954, an indication of its popularity.

This work explained a number of attitudes I had encountered in class, in personal discussions, in public debate, in student papers, and in speeches by political figures as reported in the Pakistan press. I think it may be regarded as a fair sample of what is taught in Islamiat, the course in religion taught in Pakistan's educational system.

I will quote and discuss some of its doctrines. In so doing, I hope that it will be absolutely clear that I am not in the slightest degree concerned with making a critique of Islam as a faith. I am primarily concerned with the attitudes reflected therein towards Islamic society and the non-Islamic world, the ways in which the author and his readers look at their own society and at non-Islamic society. Furthermore, I will select those statements which, I think, are most interesting or relevant to the Great Debate. I will make no attempt to give any consistent summary of the book as a whole. Everybody who is concerned with Pakistan should know something about the basic principles of Islam, but I do not conceive it to be my function to deal with that very important matter in this context. For one thing, it is beyond my competence, and, for another, *Towards Understanding Islam* is admittedly an unpretentious introduction, a "first approach to the study of Islam," as the "Foreword" states. Its worth lies in the fact that it is directed to Muslims, not to Westerners, and that the points of view expressed in it reveal clearly what the West must take into account in our efforts to establish real communication with dyed-in-the-wool Muslims. For an able, sympathetic, summary statement of the essence of Islam, put in the perspective of history for the benefit of the Western student, the reader should see Professor W. C. Smith's first chapter in *Islam in Modern History*.

Let us see what we find in *Towards Understanding Islam*. First, it is important to keep in mind that Islam is an Arabic word meaning submission. "The religion of Islam is so called because it is submission and obedience to Allah (God)." The Muslim is one who submits to the will of God. The one who does not submit to the will of God is a *kafir*, an unbeliever—literally a concealer in that he conceals by his disbelief what is inherent in his nature (pp. 2–6). Now for the key quotations, which I have arranged under suitable headings.

On Science and Arts:

> The man who knows God with all his attributes knows the beginning as well as the end of true knowledge.... Through science he will endeavor to know the laws of Nature, dig out the hidden treasures of the earth and discover and direct to his service all the hitherto unknown forces created in his own self and in the world at large.... At every stage of his enquiry his God-consciousness will save him from making wrong use of science and scientific method. He will not conceive himself claiming to be the master of all these objects, boasting to be the conqueror of nature, and determining that through the help of science he would subvert the world, subdue the weak, and establish his superiority by plunder and bloodshed. Such an attitude of revolt and defiance can only be taken by a *kafir* scientist. A Muslim scientist, on the other hand, the deeper his insight into the matters scientific, the stronger and surer will be his faith in God, and the deeper will be his sense of gratitude to him....
>
> Similarly in History, Economics, Politics, Law and other branches of Arts and Science, a Muslim will never lag behind a *kafir* in the fields of enquiry and struggle, but their angles of view, and consequently their *modus operandi* will be widely different. The Muslim will study every branch of knowledge in its right perspective, will strive for the right object and will arrive at perfectly sound conclusions. (pp. 14–16)

On the Character of the Muslim:

> If you understand the true character of the Muslim, you will be convinced that he cannot live in humiliation or abasement of subjugation. He will always be dominant, ruling and governing, for no earthly power can subdue the qualities that Islam inculcates in its adherent. (p. 19)

On the Prophet:

> But if you go a little deeper into the matter, you will notice that a person who denies to have faith in the true Prophet cannot at all find anyway, straight or not, to reach God. (p. 42)
>
> One who turns away from the Prophet of God is surely a *kafir*, be he a believer in God or a disbeliever. (p. 43)
>
> For these reasons it is incumbent on all men in the world [to] follow Muhammad alone. To become a true Muslim it is necessary to have faith in Muhammad from three standpoints:
>
> 1. He is a true Prophet of God.
> 2. His teachings are absolutely complete, free from any defect or error.
> 3. He is the last Prophet of God. After him no prophet will appear among any people till the Day of Judgement, nor is any such personage to appear, to believe whom would be an essential condition for a Muslim, or to deny whom would make a man *kafir*. (p. 105)

A brief comment or two on the foregoing. In the statements about science and the arts, we can perceive the Muslim's resentment of Western superiority in science and technology which, in his view, has been perverted to the uses of imperialism. In the quotation on the character of the Muslim, there is likewise, it seems to me, the strong emotional reaction induced by contrasting the position of the Muslim in the modern world with his past glory—a reaction underlying the militant Muslim nationalism which we are just beginning to understand. The Islamic view of the prophet is, of course, elementary information, but it would be wise for the Western world to keep the basic propositions in mind and to reflect upon the psychic implications of these fundamentals as they affect the true believer's reactions to non-Islamic ideas.

On Family Relations:

> Men's relations begin from a family. Let us see what it is. A family consists of husband, wife and their children. The Islamic rules of conduct for the family assign to man the duty of earning and trying to provide the necessities of his wife and children and to protect them, and to woman the duty of managing the household with her husband's earnings, to give to her husband and her children the greatest possible comfort and to bring up her children as best she can. The duty of the children is to obey and respect their parents and, when they are grown up, to serve them. For the satisfactory conduct of this management of the household Islam has adopted two measures. One is that the husband is given the position of governor of the household. . . . The second measure is that the burden of all transactions and doings outside the house having been placed on the shoulders of the husband, the woman has been ordered not to go out of the house except when it is necessary. (pp. 160–61)

It will be noted that there is no mention in this passage of plural wives, *nor, significantly perhaps, is the matter discussed anywhere else in the whole book.* The possible reasons for this omission are intriguing, but I cannot account for them. Observe, too, that this passage contains a strong sanction for the seclusion of women. I quote further on the topic of family relations:

> Marriage connections between two families which freely associate and mix with each other, and which, therefore, know each other's habits and customs, are generally successful, while such a union between strange families often ends in unpleasantness and disagreement of parties. For this reason Islam prefers relations with kindred families to those with

strange families, though it is not forbidden. . . . The Islamic principle is that a man's relatives have the greatest right on him. (p. 163)

I see in these two statements some explanation for the large number of marriages between cousins and for the nepotism which the APWA ladies decried but which is, I believe, regarded as basically moral in Pakistan. One more quotation in this area:

> To preserve the morality of the nation a rule has been formed that those men and women not coming within the prohibited degree of marriage as specified above should not mix freely with each other. The society of women should be separate from that of men. Women should in the main attend to the duties relating to the house. If they have to come out for some necessity, they should not go out adorned. Their bodies should be well covered and their dress plain. They should also cover their faces and hands unless it is necessary to expose them, when they might be exposed, but they should be covered again after the necessity is over. Along with this, men have been prohibited from looking at other women, and if accidentally their eyes fall upon them, they should at once look away from them. To try to see them is wrong, and to try to seek their acquaintance is worse. It is the duty of every man and every woman to look after their personal morality. As God has ordained marriage whereby sensual appetite is gratified, no man should attempt to overstep its limits, not even entertain such a wish in his mind. (p. 166)

Hence the *burqa*, purdah, and the embarrassment of Muslim men in the presence of strange women.

Relations between Muslims and Non-Muslims:

> Muslims have perfect liberty to learn sciences and arts with their practical useful methods from non-Muslim people, but they have been prohibited from imitating the way of living of the latter. One people begin to imitate the mode of living of another people only when the former are conscious of their own abasement, and admit the comparative superiority of the latter to themselves. This is the worst kind of slavery. It is an open declaration by the imitators of their own inferiority and defeat. The final result of such an act is that all culture and civilization of the imitating people dies away. It is for this reason that the Prophet (God's blessings be upon him!) has positively forbidden the Muslims to assume the mode of life of the non-Muslim people. Any man of ordinary intelligence can understand that the power of a nation is not due to their mode of dress or mode of life, but it is due to their knowledge, their discipline, and their energy of action. Therefore, if you wish to gain power, adopt those things which give power to a nation, and not those which bring slavery in their

turn, and which ultimately must lead to your absorption among the people whom you imitate and to the death-knell of your nation.

In dealing with non-Muslim people the Muslims have been instructed not to be intolerant and narrow-minded. They have been prohibited from speaking ill of the religious leaders or saints of other people as well as from saying anything derogatory to their religion. They have also been instructed not to seek dissensions with them. If they observe peace and canciliatory [sic] attitude towards us, we are instructed to keep peaceful and friendly relations with them and to deal with them fairly and justly. Our national nobility demands that we should possess greater human sympathy and politeness than any other people. Bad manners, oppression and narrow-mindedness are against the dignity and constitution of Islam. The Muslim is born in this world naturally to become the best example of humanity, nobility and goodness, and thereby win other people's hearts. (pp. 168–69)

Most of these passages require no comment. However, observe that the tolerance enjoined is based on the assumption of a natural superiority. This sense of over-righteousness is nothing new in the world. The seventeenth-century Presbyterians in England (derisively called the "saints" by their antagonists) had it; our Puritans had it (and there is a strong kinship between Muslims and Puritans); some of our Catholics have it; our fundamentalist Protestant sects have it; Christian missionaries of all faiths have it (consciously or sub-consciously); and the Sikhs and Hindus have it. The difference is that in the United States, in Europe, and in India, the daily consciousness of such an invincible and seamless conviction is, to a considerable extent, tempered by the annoying presence of greater numbers of people who think otherwise.

But in Pakistan, an overwhelming majority of the population are of one faith, and Pakistan is a semitheocratic country in both principle and practice—to the extent that the shibboleths and slogans of Islam control, more or less, both public and private life. One must remember that the nation's name is officially "The Islamic Republic of Pakistan." It is also important to keep in mind the significance of the name "Pakistan" itself. It has been translated in various ways for me: as "Sacred Home"; as "The Land of the Faithful"; and as "The Land of the Pure." It has the unmistakable connotation of "The Land of the Elect," and this odor of sanctity particularly annoys the Indians.

Individual Christians are received according to their merits as human beings; Christian missionaries are tolerated and their work in education and medicine is generally appreciated; and Christian church-goers are respected because they are believers in the Book.

But, behind the façade of friendly social intercourse, I think the tacit, unshakable assumptions of Islamic superiority in religion and culture are still articles of faith.

The strength of this basic attitude is, naturally, in inverse ratio to knowledge of other cultures, as it is in the United States. The old Northwest Frontier Province is a citadel of Islamic fundamentalism, as our southern Appalachian states and their colonies in our northern cities are the strongholds of American fundamentalism. On the Frontier, my students knew very little about the United States, and not much more about Britain or Europe. Moreover, most of them knew very little about India (or Bharat) either. Their fathers and mothers in the villages knew even less, and the less they knew, the more positive they were of the excellence of their own way of life. The students in Lahore and Karachi were more sophisticated and cosmopolitan, but at heart I rather suspect that they too shared this point of view.

I will give two examples of the way in which these convictions were made manifest to us in Abbottabad. Once I set a composition paper for my students: What profession or vocation is your choice, and why? The boys wrote most idealistically about their desire to serve their nation as engineers, civil servants, teachers, doctors, businessmen, and officers in the armed forces. To digress for a moment, I found this idealism refreshing after experiencing the cynicism of their elders. When I once cited these evidences of public spirit to my colleagues as a sign of hope for the future, they shrugged their shoulders and said, "Just wait until they get out of college. They will be corrupted."

But the point is that, in the themes I read, a number of boys also said that they wanted to be missionaries; that is, they wanted to carry the Prophet's message to the rest of the world. Fair enough. But, in several papers, the young men said—or clearly implied—that, if the powers of reason and persuasion should fail to convince the *kafirs* (the unbelievers), they would not hesitate to use the sword.

As an experiment, I once pointed out to a zealot that there were more non-Muslims than Muslims in the world and that there might be some trouble in converting these unbelievers to the True Faith by force, especially since millions of these benighted souls in outer darkness believed that *they* were the possessors of the True Faith. He seemed not to know what I was talking about. The Prophet, in his mind, was right, and people must either believe in him or be forced to believe in him. This attitude is not unknown in our own country, of course.

For my second example, let us consider the pig. The Muslim taboo on this unclean animal is well known; it is comparable to the practices of the most rigidly orthodox Jews (the Muslims and Jews have much in common). In Abbottabad this taboo was carried so far that my wife's students at Lower Burn Hall (all of whom were Muslims save one lone Parsi) even refused to read the dirty word aloud, perhaps because it is also a term of abuse. On one occasion, students asked me (not in class) whether I ate pig. I answered that I did and that more people in the world ate pig than did not. But, I added, in the United States, as a rule, we did not drink dirty or contaminated water; we did not drink dirty or unpasteurized milk; we did not eat sick chickens; we demanded by law that handlers of food pass medical examinations; and our city boards of health regularly inspected restaurants. None of this mattered to them in the least. People who ate pig were, by definition, unclean. Pigs were held to be dirty, but germs were not unclean in the same sense. The germ theory of disease is not really apprehended by many Pakistanis, educated or uneducated, as a useful principle. By a conscious act of the intellect, they may recognize the theory as an academic truth, but it is not yet accepted psychologically as a practical truth to be acted on in daily life. "What you can't see can't hurt you" is likely to be the standard view for a long time to come. In the face of this deep-seated cultural attitude, it does not take much imagination to envision sympathetically the tremendous problems facing Pakistani officials in charge of public health programs.

The West is Materialistic; the East is Spiritual

To conclude this discussion of the Great Debate, I will speak forthrightly about a perennial issue which tends to dominate the dialogue between East and West: spiritual values vs. material values. It is a cliché that the ancient wisdom of the East, whether Hindu, Buddhist, or Muslim, is far superior to the West's concern for material comfort and the superficial worth of an industrial technology. In other words, it is held that the West substitutes faith in gimmicks and gadgets for faith in the more enduring values deriving from God (or gods) and for the contemplation of man in respect to Time and Eternity. The extent to which this charge is true of the United States is demonstrated by the amount of soul-searching now going on here.

However, this "fact" should not be allowed to obscure another "fact": that the cultures of both India and Pakistan, as I saw them, were currently even more materialistic, more predatory, more belly-centered, more possession-centered than our own.

The reasons for this materialism are not far to seek. Millions of people in Indo-Pakistan rarely, if ever, get a square meal, and therefore they have a fixation on food. These same millions are hard put to it to get enough clothes to hide their nakedness; textiles of all kinds are relatively expensive. Fuel is scarce and costly in cold weather; therefore wood, coals, buffalo chips, and camel dung take on the prime value of survival. Mere shelter is a luxury in itself; therefore a home on earth is more important than a heavenly abode. In short, millions of Indians and Pakistanis have to be materialistic all through their waking hours to exist at all. It might be argued that they are "spiritualistic" as a last resort.

Then, if they find that they are really not living in any real sense or are in imminent danger of ceasing to exist tomorrow, the turning to their God (or to their gods) can hardly be regarded as any great triumph for spiritual values. This is not a free choice; it is a choice of desperation. Give these millions a chance for a decent day-to-day existence, and I wager that they will become far more truly spiritual. It may be necessary, under present conditions, to consider a hungry man as the noblest work of God, but a reasonably well fed man could be regarded as an even nobler work.

In our own country, having licked the problem of mere survival, we are now on the verge of seriously exploring the problem of what we are living for, and, as the wonders of space unfold, what we are living in relation to. To put it bluntly, there is in the United States as much or more concern for things not of the flesh than I observed in Indo-Pakistan.

Up to this point, I have been talking about the great proportion of the subcontinent's population which lives at, just over, or just under the subsistence level. Now, in respect to materialism and spirituality, let us consider the state of mind of those who are better off. The middle classes and upper economic classes in both India and Pakistan have inevitably become aware of Western consumer goods. Our salesmen and the movies have seen to that. As might be expected, the Indians and the Pakistanis want these things with an agonizing intensity—the things which we have come to take for granted. Specifically, I have never encountered such a yearning for clothes, cameras, automobiles, fountain pens and automatic pencils, radios, plastic raincoats, automatic cookers, refrigerators, washing machines, and automobiles. These things are wanted, not only for what they can do, but also for the status they confer on their owners—as would be the case in the United States if so many people did not have them. Surely it is not wrong to desire the amenities of life, but a passionate pursuit of a Chevrolet and the great respect accorded to the man who owns one are not exactly consonant with scornful attacks on American materialism, couched in terms of moral superiority.

There are still other forms of materialism. There is the materialism of pride in place and office—of social, economic, or political status. We in the United States know about this very well. The executive rat-race has become a national joke, with vice-presidents as the butt, and the range and depth of the joke indicate our national probing of the worth of the run. Furthermore, the arenas in which these races are run non-stop (business, politics, and the professions) are far more open than they are in either Pakistan or India—and woe to the man in our country who gets too big for his britches. Indeed, American mores demand a playing down of status, not an emphasis on it—not that status is less important or less meaningful to us than it is elsewhere. Status is merely easier to obtain here than it is on the subcontinent.

I find that India and Pakistan are more alike in their social systems than either would be happy to admit. This opinion has been strengthened by a reading of the novel called *The Nature of Passion,* written by R. Prawer Jhabvala,[5] which deals with a Hindu family in New Delhi. The social patterns depicted are quite like those we saw in Abbottabad. Moreover, India has its religious caste system, and Pakistan has a rigid social and economic caste system. Hierarchy and gradation are carefully observed in both countries. The clerk in the business office is subservient to his superior and insolent to the peon (that is the term used) whom he summons grandly with a handbell on his desk to deliver a file to the next desk. My colleagues at Abbottabad rose respectfully every time the principal entered the staff room—no matter what they were doing. It will be remembered that the Abbottabad faculty did not have the status of gazetted officers, a status for which they were fighting when I left. Socially, they were in the position of higher clerks, much inferior to cantonment officials, public works officials, members of the bar, judges, and army officers. But the lecturers nevertheless had peons to order around and demonstrators to do the routine work in the laboratories. Full professors and vice-chancellors of universities were far better off socially, and the gap between such exalted personages and mere lecturers is far wider than the analogous gap between assistant

170

professors and full professors, or department heads and presidents, in American universities and colleges. Distinctions in rank in Pakistan's armed forces on social occasions are observed even more rigidly than in our own, where they are sufficiently well kept. The deputy commissioner, the chief civilian executive in a Pakistan district, has no counterpart in the United States in the powers he commands or in the social status accorded him.

The police are also run on army lines in respect to rigidly observed distinctions of rank, and one of the greatest differences between our societies may be observed by contrasting our attitudes towards the guardians of the law. Americans with nothing to fear in their own conduct think of the police as public servants; Pakistanis, particularly poor ones, with no criminal conduct on their consciences, seem to be afraid of the police. For instance, when we gave our servant, Ali, a good many articles at departure time, he insisted that we give him a letter to the police, itemizing these goods and stipulating that they were gifts from his employers. He was not taking any chances of casual search and seizure.

Furthermore, the National Bank of Pakistan was operated in terms of very strict protocol. In Abbottabad, our friend, the bank manager, had to initial practically every transaction in his inner sanctum, where he was waited on literally hand and foot by peons, and in the Karachi main office the same strict social and business line of command was in evidence.

And so it was in the Pakistan Land Customs Service. Just before we left the country, I was invited to deliver an address to the Customs trainees in their camp, some twenty to twenty-five miles out in the desert from Karachi. It was an extremely interesting experience. The whole function was run off strictly by the numbers, and I still have a program to prove it: official reception, salute, inspection, march-past, pipe band, and all the trimmings.

In the course of my remarks to the Customs cadets (who enjoyed "good advices" as much as my students did), I made the point that public officials in Pakistan could make a great contribution to the stability of their country and its government by treating their countrymen with the same kind of courtesy accorded to foreigners like us. The point is worth developing briefly: we did not have one unpleasant experience with Pakistani officials, and the law demands that foreigners have many contacts with many different government offices. From the time we entered the country at the Karachi airport to the time we left on the Italian motorship *Asia*, our business was politely and, in the main, efficiently transacted. This generalization holds true for customs officials, bank officials, passport officials, the police in Karachi, Abbottabad, and Dacca, the income tax officer in Peshawar who had to grant us clearance for our trip to India, and, above all, for the police captain in Lahore who, on very short notice, managed to get us another kind of police clearance from Abbottabad in order to permit us to catch a plane for New Delhi. In part, this uniform courtesy derived from what these officials seemed to regard as our own privileged status; in part (I would like to think), from our own politeness; and, in part, from their own natural courtesy.

But is it so for the average Pakistani? I fear not, and if the man in the street is pushed around by his own officials, he will distrust, fear, and hate his own government, in Pakistan or anywhere else.

These last paragraphs may appear to be a deviation from the immediate issue of materialism. In fact, they are not. Pride in office, rank, station, and the social position guaranteed by these distinctions are just as materialistic as money, land, or the possession of consumer goods. These jobs are hard to come by, and their prerogatives are jealously guarded. The Pakistanis have many rat-races of their own in every area of national life, and the fear and respect accorded to superiors along with the insolence and contempt accorded to inferiors are as materialistic—as tangible—as money in the bank or two cars in every garage.

Color Consciousness in India and Pakistan

One other aspect of materialism, perhaps the most important, is color consciousness and race consciousness. The United States is justly suffering for its sins in these respects, and it is only fair that the trial balance of morality be kept. Both Indians and Pakistanis are almost neurotic on this score. I had supposed that, on a subcontinent inhabited by millions of dark people, color would be taken for granted, and, as a card-carrying member of the NAACP and as a former executive board member of the Detroit chapter of that much maligned organization, I looked forward with pleasure to a state of affairs in which color as such would be unimportant. What I found was very different.

One of the first questions asked me in Abbottabad by a respected member of the faculty was, "What color are Americans?" I replied that we were of all colors, and he seemed to be pleased and relieved by the answer. Many Pathans were obviously proud of their ruddy skins and blue eyes, and, on occasion, reference was made to absent persons who were described as being "like you"—with the pointed addition of phrases like "blue eyes" and "light skin." My wife's students at Burn Hall, lads from nine to fourteen years of age, used to taunt their darker classmates during recess periods with repetition of the epithet "Blackie, Blackie, Blackie." We were told that photographers habitually had to underdevelop their pictures in order to make their customers appear as light as possible, and we saw the resulting photography in which certain faces were somewhat washed out. In Swat, one Muslim lady, commenting to my wife on the marriage of a Pakistani officer (a man of impressive dignity) to a blonde from Yugoslavia, a World War II marriage, said, "I don't know how they can be happy—she's so light and he's so dark."

I believe that one reason for the hardly-disguised contempt which West Pakistanis have for East Pakistanis is that the Bengalis tend to be darker than the people from the West Wing, and the natural resentment which results from this attitude (along with many other factors) has much to do with the strained relations between the two halves of Pakistan. Pakistani ladies in Abbottabad made a point of staying out of the sun, or, like the Anglo-Pakistani nurses referred to above, ostentatiously carried a sunshade, marveling at the intrepidity of European women who did not take such precautions to protect the skin. And I rather think that part of the tension between the Pathans and the Punjabis (which was the cause of a disturbance at our college before my arrival) is, in a measure, due to the color and race consciousness of the Pathans.

The most disturbing and dismaying single experience we had in Pakistan and India was this pervasive color consciousness. It led me to observe, after some months on the subcontinent, that it might be wise to organize some new chapters of the NAACP overseas.

For the moment, let me illustrate this state of mind from Indian culture. Pakistanis will surely disagree violently with the statement that they are just as color conscious as their neighbors, but I believe it to be true nevertheless, and I also believe that fair-minded Pakistanis will bear me out.

Historically, there appears to be a very strong relationship between color and caste in India. As Chester Bowles summarizes the case in *Ambassador's Report*:

Out of the relations between these conquering Aryans and the darker inhabitants [Dravidians] came caste, which Nehru says "in its origin was

173

based on color." The very Sanskrit word for caste, *varna* means color. Even today some Indians spend as much time trying to lighten their skins as some Americans spend in an attempt to suntan theirs. While Indians are intensely, and rightly, incensed at color discrimination in the West, they, too, have not freed themselves from the same kind of senseless prejudice.[6]

Nor, in my opinion, have the Pakistanis.

The strongest indictment against discrimination founded on color which I found during my year in India and Pakistan came, not from an outsider, but from an Indian lady named Indira Sen. She wrote a column called "The Human Side" on this subject which was published in *Trend*, a monthly magazine for Indian women.[7]

Miss Sen, unmarried and charming in her explicit dislike for the status of spinsterhood, pinned her column to the advent of a niece. She had constituted herself an information bureau, the conveyer of glad tidings. What appalled her was that everybody wanted to know at once about the newborn child's complexion, and I quote her at length with her own dramatic punctuation and italics:

> It could have been as black as a Nubian for all I cared; quite frankly I didn't know. Facetiously and foolishly I asked whether it made any difference if she—not 'it' was as black as ...before I could go any further I was advised to have the child *'bathed in goat's milk, covered with gram flour, massaged with saffron.'* To my horror my attempt at humor recoiled so alarmingly that every foul-smelling, vile-looking, unpublishable ingredient of a high class witch's brew was helpfully recommended!
>
> All in order that my poor little niece would maintain or develop a 'fair' complexion so that one day she might be able to top her list of matrimonial qualifications with the indisputable virtue of 'fairness.'
>
> As I look down on my dark brown fingers hammering out the 'Human Side' to meet the printer's deadline, I perceive the reason for my pitiable maiden state!
>
> And you say *'We have no colour prejudice!'*
>
> Take the Matrimonial Columns filled with the pathetic last-ditch appeals of the unwed. One would presume that members of the Lonely-Hearts clan would abjure colour prejudices in their advertised attempts to find soul-mates. But no!—Mr. or Miss Lonely-Heart (be he or she as dark as they come) invariably yearns for a sallow spouse.
>
> Apparently *caste is no bar*, nor is lack of income or education; status is not of utmost importance when frustration begins to rear its ugly head ... but a *fair* complexion is a *must*. A little laxity in the latter is occasionally admissible because the degree of fairness is not always stipulated! But then again, often it *is....*

174

Miss Sen proceeded to cite a typical matrimonial advertisement, and then, after discussing the categories of "Very Fair" and "Wheat Complexion" in such advertisements, she took up the larger issue:

We Indians were the first to take up cudgels against segregationists. But within the boundaries of our own land there still exists probably as much— if not more—color consciousness than there is anywhere in the world. In America or South Africa, black is *black* and white is *white*. In India which is entirely peopled by coloured races, not only is there black and brown but these are sub-divided *ad infinitum* into countless gradations and shades. The lighter the shade, the greater the distinction.

Some readers will defend Indian colour consciousness on the grounds that it had its birth at the same time when the Hindu religion was born. (The caste system originated in colour, *Varna*; divisions on the basis of occupation and birth came very much later.) This defence is untenable. Tradition, local prejudices, hide-bound convention provide no arguments in the face of logic and commonsense.

If we are to preach tolerance let us begin to practise it first at home.

Instead of washing other people's dirty linen, let's get started with our own.

This cleansing will not be limited to any one province, any one income group, any one social level. Colour consciousness exists in every corner of India. It can be found amongst paupers, it can be found amongst millionaires. And what is most reprehensible, it is rampant among the educated.

Perhaps 'educated' is a misnomer. Can one describe a man or woman who keeps his or her child out of the health-giving sun, plasters its face with poisonous bleaching agents (home-made or otherwise) then selects for it a suitably fair mate—as educated?

Isn't it paradoxical that this same educated person should trouble to take up arms against colour prejudice abroad? That this educated person— who makes public his indignation about segregation in the West, should permit it in the form of all-white clubs and swimming pools in a free and independent... *and coloured India*! That this educated person who orates at great length in the U.N. Assembly against colour consciousness, overlooks the fact that permanent employees at the U.N. are required to state the colour of their skins on the employee's application forms! That this educated person who relishes the news of a white American marrying a coloured American, or who reluctantly permits his child to marry a foreigner would die a thousand deaths if one of his progeny decided to marry a negro!

Something is rotten. Not somewhere... *but here*!

There is little to add to this heart-warming outburst. I have not seen matrimonial advertisements in Pakistan like those discussed by Miss Sen, but, despite the ideal of Islamic equalitarianism, I have little reason to believe that Pakistan is different from India in respect to color.

I do not intend to condone my own nation's failure to achieve its announced ideals by saying, "You, too." Little Rock and all it symbolizes has been a near-traumatic experience for me as it has been for millions of Americans, and it continues to be. What I am pleading for is a single standard of international morality—intellectual honesty on both sides, if you like.

Color is an aspect of materialism, and pride in color is just as much a property value, a "thing" value, as anything mundane can be. In all these respects, then, both Pakistan and India are materialistic—painfully so—and, to end this Great Debate, I will cite that very able Indian journalist and biographer of Nehru, Frank Moraes:

> There is nothing to substantiate the claim, often heard in India and in other countries of the Orient, that the East is more spiritual than the West.... Materialism and the worship of Mammon exist equally in the East and the West; but alongside these manifestations there also exists in both spheres a life of the spirit and of the mind.[8]

I say, "Amen."

Chapter Seven

Sports in Pakistan

A Common Denominator

A trip around the world reveals, among many other things, that one common denominator which can make for mutual understanding among nations and peoples is sport. If a person happens to be interested in athletics (as I am), it is easy to gain the impression that the East, as well as the West, is sports-mad. The evidence is seen everywhere: in playing fields, volley ball nets, tennis courts, basketball courts, cricket pitches, football fields (called soccer in the United States), field hockey nets, and, in Japan, baseball diamonds on every vacant lot. Even if one paid no attention to these physical aspects, the amount of newspaper space devoted to sports in all of the nations we visited would be conclusive evidence in itself. So it was in Pakistan, in India, in Ceylon, in Singapore, in Thailand, in Hong Kong, and in Japan. One picture among many remains in my mind. In Singapore I saw, from a window of the famous old Raffles Hotel, a lively basketball game across the street, featuring a well organized, fast-breaking offense, while on adjacent courts a club tennis tournament was going on in which women were competing against men.

This universal addiction to competitive games is one of the healthy aspects of Pakistani culture. From the youngest schoolboy to the former president of the nation, General Iskander Mirza, the male Pakistani, given the opportunity, will play some game with truly fanatical and religious zeal. From our hotel terrace in Abbottabad in the morning, we used to watch the boys creeping like snail unwillingly to school and sharpening their footwork on anything which would serve the purpose—an old tennis ball, a cheap rubber ball, a tin can, or any cover stuffed with rags. Unfortunately, footballs were expensive. One of the cheapest and most effective things the Pakistan government or private philanthropy could do would be to provide every primary and secondary school with more athletic equipment. As for the president, he, like most army officers, is a keen sportsman. The Frontier Sports Shop in Abbottabad (in which the old marker, Kaka, had an interest) displays a highly prized photograph of the finalists in a tennis tournament held at the local officer's club back in the Thirties, and Mirza is prominent in it. I was told that he still plays a good game.

The Games

For economic reasons, soccer football (shall we say foot football?) is the number one sport in Pakistan from the point of view of participation. All that is needed is a field and a ball; goals can be improvised out of sticks and stones. The schoolboys play on the streets, roads, and in the public parks. The armed forces apparently first lay out their playing fields for football and field hockey, and then they proceed to take care of less important matters like billets and kitchens. The government-run railroad systems have innumerable teams; so do the various government offices; and, relatively speaking, I judge that there are more sports clubs in Pakistan's urban centers than in the United States.

The tournaments are endless. Colleges which are affiliated with the various universities play each other for the university championship. For instance, I saw a game of football between Abbottabad and Swat in the course of the Peshawar University competition. The boys from Swat, that isolated principality which we later visited, knocked off our team with a stylish display of organized passing. After the intra-university championship is settled, the universities each pick an all-star team from the personnel of the component colleges (à la Oxford-Cambridge) and play for the All-Pakistan university championship. So it is in cricket too, and Abbottabad was very proud of one lad who was chosen as an alternate wicket keeper for the University of Peshawar team.

The armed forces follow this pattern also. The inter-service rivalry in various sports is just as intense as it is between the Navy, the Army, and the Air Force in America. The struggle for the North Western Railroad championships in football and field hocky was no less fierce, and I used to wonder when the railroad men who played on these teams got any work done, but then I often wonder how college students on big-time American football teams get any studying done between September and the Bowl games. A closer parallel, perhaps, may be drawn between the special treatment given to athletic stars on railroad, police, and club teams with that accorded basketball stars who play for the so-called amateur national AAU teams like Denver and the Peoria Cats. My students in Pakistan told me tall stories about ringers on other college soccer football teams, and the arguments about eligibility and officials' decisions ("We wuz robbed") sounded just like home.

From the point of view of numbers engaged, field hockey is probably the most popular game next to football in Pakistan. During one period, however, field hockey became the number one interest of almost the whole nation. This was during the Olympic games when India and Pakistan were the finalists. In the end, India won by one goal to nil (as they say on the sports pages on the subcontinent), but the result was generally regarded as a great moral victory for Pakistan, since the Indians have historically monopolized victory in this game. Both nations, it seemed, suspended business of all kinds during the tournament and hung on the radio, waiting for returns from the front, just as if the two teams were settling the fate of Kashmir. On the way to the finals, the Indians beat the Americans 16 to 1, but, I take it, the American public was not particularly disturbed by this result any more than it was over the results of the Graeco-Roman wrestling. All nations, it would seem, have a good-natured contempt for those sports in which they do not excel.

At about the time we left Pakistan, the most important sport was cricket. This was so because a Pakistani team in Karachi defeated the visiting Australian test team (on its way home after losing to England). With great good sportsmanship, the Aussies refused to alibi for their defeat, as well they might have, because the bowling

179

was done on matting rather than on grass. A fair analogy to this epic triumph in cricket would be to see a Pakistani team knock off the Yankees or the Braves in baseball. It is impossible to overestimate the psychological impact of this victory. The Pakistanis badly needed—and still need—something to bolster up the national ego, and this sports upset served the purpose, for a time. Fazl, the Pakistan bowler (pitcher, in our vocabulary) became a national hero, as did his team mates to a somewhat lesser extent, and all Pakistan basked in glory.

Now, cricket is something of a snob game. It takes a good deal of leisure time and much expensive equipment to play it properly. It has always been popular in India and Pakistan among those fortunates who could afford it. But the great win over Australia had the same result that Ike's devotion to golf has had on this side of the water: a large increase in the popularity of an already popular sport. In my observation, more and more Pakistani kids improvised equipment and set up wickets in improbable places just as American kids play stickball in the New York streets, handball against brick walls in any American city slum, and touch-football games on city streets everywhere in the United States.

In our provincial devotion to baseball, American football, and golf, we have no understanding of the power of cricket to command the devotion of millions of fans wherever the British are or have been. The urge to win is just as strong in the cricket world as it is in the football worlds of the Western Conference and the Pacific Coast League. It is for this reason that the lineups of the English county cricket teams are speckled with Indian and Pakistani names. The best players of the subcontinent are recruited for big-time cricket as all-state high school players are sought after here by college coaches.

Therefore, it came as no surprise to Pakistani cricket fans when Fazl, the bowler, went to England. His own nation could not match English offers for his services. As in our own country, proficiency in sports is one way to attain economic security, and it is one of the very few ways in which the underprivileged in Pakistan can do well for themselves. When one of my best boys at Abbottabad, Khetab, told me, in a theme, that he proposed to become a professional cricket player, I could only say, "More power to you."

I myself have played cricket twice, and I learned what other Americans have found out about the game—that batting and bowling are much tougher than they seem to be. Any American who has played much baseball will have no difficulty in fielding, which aspect of the game, I thought, was the major weakness of the players I observed.

Cricket is played with all the punctilio developed for the game in England. For example, batsmen are clapped on and off the field. However, I was somewhat jolted when a visiting team from a Peshawar college, after having lost unexpectedly to the Burn Hall boys, left by bus directly after the match without any farewells at all. It did not seem to be quite cricket to me.

Among other Pakistani athletic heroes was a non-commissioned officer in the Pakistani army, Abdul Khaliq, who was rapturously billed as The Fastest Man in Asia. He made a creditable showing in the Olympic games against the best runners in the world. He qualified for the finals in the hundred meter dash, though he did not place, and he just missed making the finals of the two hundred meter event, after winning a preliminary heat. He was truly a picture runner, reminding me in style of the great Jesse Owens. Khaliq's army connection was not accidental. The armed forces in Pakistan are nearly the only mechanism in the nation which has the resources to train track and field prospects methodically. This fact was brought home to us when we attended the Olympic trials—luckily held at Abbottabad where, as the reader may remember, we met the salesman for Ovaltine who was tying in his advertising campaign with the advent of the Olympic team. The trials were largely an army show. It is true that individual students in the colleges and universities go in strongly for "athletics" (the Pakistani term for track and field), but they cannot go far for lack of competent coaching. The army had hired an English professional to do the job for its men. Having talked with him after the trials (at the club, of course), I found him able and dedicated to his job, but my opinion was not shared by my Hitler-loving student, himself the captain of the college track team, who later angrily denounced the Britisher for sabotaging the Pakistani team.[1]

Despite the apparent similarities, there are some important differences between the American and the Pakistani school sports patterns. Full-time coaches are rare. Our college had one man in charge of the entire physical education program, and he could not possibly coach all sports—though he tried. Usually, a given sport is handed over to some interested faculty man who becomes the incharge. (One enthusiast went so far as to suggest that I should take over the field hockey team!) Practices are held informally, and the whole operation is much more casual than it is in the United States. Moreover, although there is a good deal of interest in certain matches, Pakistani students on the whole are not victims of spectatoritis. There are no organized cheering sections. The teams compete intensely, but the students are interested only insofar as they have a special fondness for a particular game or because their close friends are involved. During my tenure at Abbottabad, on just one occasion was the entire college community—faculty and students—urged to turn out for a match, and that was for the football game with Swat. The whole approach was based on what might be fairly called the Do-It-Yourself policy.

However, the service men were intensely interested in the fortunes of their unit teams, and they turned out in large numbers to cheer their comrades on.

Here on the North American continent we are accustomed to raucous shouts of "Kill the Umpire!" from baseball fans and to threats of violence to ice hockey officials—especially in Montreal. Occasionally, steps are taken toward these desirable ends. From my study of the sports pages in Pakistan, I concluded that such measures against sports officials were taken quite often. I found myself marveling at the valor of Pakistani gentlemen who were willing to accept duty as arbiters. At times, officials were rescued by the police, and, often enough, matches broke up either as a result of violence due to a bad decision by an official or in consequence of an outraged manager taking his side off the field in protest. I do not say that this pattern is the rule, but I think that it is something more than exceptional.

Such behavior is, of course, "American," too. Similar incidents occur in any organized competitive sport, but it may be that the Pakistanis are somewhat more intense than we are in their reactions to what happens on the field of sport. Perhaps they are more like what Mexican and Cuban baseball fans are reputed to be.

Football Riots in Dacca

Consider, for example, what happened in Dacca in the course of a national soccer football tournament as reported in *Dawn*, the important Karachi daily, from November 4 through November 12, 1957. A front-page story read in part as follows:

> A large number of persons including women and children were injured here today following what appeared to be a wrong decision on the part of the

referee in the semi-final match of the National Football Championship, played here this afternoon between East Pakistan "Whites" and Baluchistan.

After the match was over the referee was brought near where the East Pakistan Governor was sitting and a police cordon thrown around the place.

A section of the crowd thereupon raised slogans demanding a replay and this was followed by brick-batting from the raised stadium seats.

Police intervened and made lathi [baton] charges during the disturbances which lasted for more than an hour and resulted in clashes between the crowd both in and around the stadium....

The referee was smuggled out from the stadium with difficulty disguised in a police uniform....

Seventy-seven persons including 54 policemen were injured in the clash. The policemen were admitted in the Police Hospital. The condition of four is serious. The number of injured among the crowd is 23, two of whom have been admitted in the hospital....

The situation is now absolutely normal. (*Dawn*, November 4, 1957)

On the next day, it was reported that the chief minister of East Pakistan, Mr. Ataur Rahman Khan, who was also president of the East Pakistan Sports Federation, "appealed to all not to display any passion while watching games and to maintain peace at the stadium or where-ever any game was played."

His statement continued:

If playfields are reduced to battle grounds for hostile demonstrations, then there is no point in organizing sports events such as the one currently run at Dacca on a national scale.

The Chief Minister said that an inquiry committee had been set up to probe into the incidents and urged all to wait for its finding and not to create further controversy. (*Dawn*, November 5, 1957)

The tournament proceeded, and here is what happened:

The final of the National Football Championship between the Punjab Eleven and the East Pakistan Whites had to be abandoned this afternoon as a surging crowd of over one lakh [100,000] football fans overflowed into the the playground.

The biggest crowd ever to turn up at a football match in Dacca was about three times the seating capacity of the Dacca Stadium which can take only about 35,000 people. They busted the barbed wire around the field, and jammed the ground itself. Appeals made by the Chief Minister, Mr. Ataur Rahman Khan, and officials of the Sports Federation over the microphone to the people to clear the ground proved of no avail and the match had to be called off.

183

A friendly match between the two teams was, however, played about an hour and a half later in which East Pakistan defeated the Punjab Eleven by two goals to one.

Since early morning, all roads leading to the Stadium where the football fans purchased tickets were blocked by big queues.

All tickets were sold out about two hours before the match was due to start.

Trains from Narayanganj came packed with people hanging on the footboards.

Just after five minutes of the start of the friendly game the surging crowd rushed to the press gallery. There was a stampede in which the press box collapsed causing slight injury to several reporters. They had to leave the stadium when they found it impossible to remain there. (*Dawn*, November 9, 1957)

On the 9th, the District Magistrate once more appealed for cooperation, plans were made to put other magistrates into the ticket booths to supervise sales, the police banned assemblies after the game, and ultimately the final was played.

After all this, the Punjab Eleven won. (*Dawn*, November 10, 12, 1957)

The Khans Rule the World in Squash

The game in which Pakistan could justly claim world dominance was squash racquets. This pre-eminence was due specifically to the prowess of the Khan family of Peshawar, the brothers Hashim and Azam and their cousin Roshan. Like the old tennis pro, Mir Abdullah of the Abbottabad Club, they got their opportunity as a result of the intense sports-mindedness of Pakistan's well-to-do clubmen and of the armed forces. Hashim, the founder of this dynasty, was once the pro, or marker, at the Peshawar Officers' Club. From what I have read and heard, he was, at his peak, one of the best squash players who ever lived.

In 1956, Hashim defeated his brother Azam for the United States Open championship; in 1957, he defeated his cousin Roshan for the same honor. As it happened, the 1958 championship was played in Detroit, my home city. Unfortunately, as Harvey Barcus of *The Detroit News* reported, Hashim, then 43 years old, was prevented from trying for three crowns in a row by leg cramps. However, cousins Roshan and Azam created a sensation with their play. Barcus wrote as follows:

184

After two rounds of play Saturday the fifth annual U.S. open squash racquets tournament showed signs of again becoming a family affair for the the Khans of Pakistan.

Top-seeded Roshan and his cousin, Azam, second in the draw, won their matches without too much exertion, amazing the packed gallery at the University Club with their agility and stroke execution. (January 5, 1958)

Then, much to everybody's surprise, the American amateur champion, Henri Salaun, defeated Azam in the semifinals. The amazement expressed in the press was in itself a tribute to the caliber of the Pakistani's play. The final match produced this account:

> Roshan Khan has won many squash racquets championships since taking up the game in his native Pakistan almost 20 years ago, but the biggest of all came yesterday.
>
> The 30-year-old pro defeated Henri Salaun, of Boston, 14–18, 15–7, 18–17, 18–16. . . . The outcome made squash history.
>
> By winning Roshan became the first player to gain a grand slam of the world's major open championships within a one-year period. Roshan previously won the titles in Australia, Egypt, Great Britain and his homeland. . . .
>
> Mohammed Ali, the Pakistani ambassador, came from Washington to see the championship match.
>
> "The Khans are far better goodwill ambassadors than I am," he told the audience when the awards were made. (Harvey Barcus, *The Detroit News,* January 6, 1958)

It is worth noting (with Fazl, the bowler, in mind) that Roshan was described as squash instructor of Pakistani naval officers in Karachi and that Azam "now plays out of London." I do not know Hashim's current affiliation. Very probably, when he is not on the international tournament circuit, he is a marker either in England or at his home club in Peshawar. The point is that this family of true champions, in effect, could never have achieved their status in the squash world without the patronage of Pakistan's armed services and that, as in the case of Fazl, the bowler, sports stars, very likely, do better abroad than at home. Another point to re-emphasize is that the interest of Pakistan's officers in squash (regularly played, for example, at Kakul, the big base near Abbottabad) again illustrates the officer-gentleman concept discussed above.

Indeed, Pakistanis are good at any racquet game. As I have already noted, they play tough tennis. There is no reason why Pakistan should not be represented in Davis Cup play—except one: money. During my stay, there was discussion (*The Pakistan Times*, May 21, 1957) of a program to develop the nation's best young players for this international competition, but unfortunately nothing has come of it to my knowledge.

I also observed, both in person and in the press, that there was great interest in badminton. At Abbottabad, students and faculty played this game, and they played it aggressively, delighting in smash and drop shot. So did the officers at the club who played indoors in the ball room during bad weather. The sports pages regularly chronicled tournaments in Karachi, Lahore, and other urban centers, and Pakistani internationalists have played all over the East where badminton seems to be taken much more seriously than it is here in the United States.

Likewise with table tennis. A visiting Japanese team which stopped off in Karachi in April 1957, on its way home from a triumphant tour of Europe, excited tremendous interest, and, although Pakistani players did not win many matches against the friendly invaders, they made a pretty good showing. What interested me particularly in the press reports of this visit was that Pakistani young women played against their Japanese sisters. Up on the Frontier, as I have indicated, girls do not participate very much in sports.

Volley ball was another favorite game; it was played everywhere. Of course, the army men played it and so did the students. But, in addition to these groups, the young men of Abbottabad, neither soldiers nor students, used to battle nightly in the vacant lot across from our hotel terrace.

In Dacca, East Pakistan, in the courtyard of the good Shahbagh Hotel, between the modern guest rooms and the servant's quarters, a marathon volley ball game took place every afternoon, lasting until dusk. Soldiers, workmen, and hotel servants drifted in and out of the game which was played, as in the West Wing, with much good-natured enthusiasm and wisecracking.

Other Games

Basketball, another truly international game these days, was also popular in Pakistan, notably in the schools and in the armed forces. I read accounts of some tournaments held in Lahore. The game is almost invariably played outdoors. At Abbottabad college, our industrious physical education man had erected backboards, but he had been unable (as yet) to obtain rings, nets, or balls for the game.

Although some interest in baseball, our national game, may have developed through the leagues organized by the American colonies in Lahore and Karachi (composed of teams from consular and embassy staffs, military missions, and ICA personnel), interest in baseball is minimal. Sports-minded Pakistanis know about the game, but they do not play it. The same generalization holds true for American football, and it was surprising to me not to find any evidence whatsoever of activity in "rugger" football, the English ancestor of our own version of the sport.

One of the truly distinctive sports in Pakistan is kabbadi, a kind of team wrestling match not unlike our professional wrestling free-for-alls, but on a grander scale. One of my colleagues at Abbottabad, referred to covertly by his co-workers as The Peasant, or the Jat, had won some respect from these scoffers by his prowess in this sport, if not for his intellectual attainments. I have not had the pleasure of seeing kabbadi, but, since the West has furnished so many sports to the East, it seems only reasonable that we should look into this one. From all accounts, it is a first-class conditioner.

The matter of borrowing brings polo to mind. The origins of the game are lost in history, but surely India and Pakistan are, if not the parents of the game, closer to its birthplace than is the West. The grand tradition of horsemanship holds on the subcontinent, which still produces some of the best riders and polo players in the world. But sports involving the ownership or use of horses are completely beyond the reach of most people, as they are here in the United States. As a result, they are largely restricted to the scions of the few remaining princely states, to the sons of good families like the Afridi, to the officers of the armed services, and to the few remaining cavalry units which have not been mechanized.

However, at the great annual horse show in Lahore, perhaps the most glamorous of all Pakistan's social and sporting events, the traditional equestrian skills are still much in evidence. The climax of the horse show held in 1957 while we were there was the polo series with India. As might be expected, victory or defeat in these matches was taken very seriously—as seriously as the Olympic hockey match. Emily Hahn has given a vivid account of both the sports and social activity involved in the horse show in a *New Yorker* piece called "Tent Guest" (February 1, 1958). For another lively description of the horse show, see "Pomp and Pageantry in Pakistan," by His Excellency Mohammed Ali, Pakistan's ambassador to the United States, in *Esquire*, May 1959, pp. 77–81.

There is not much golf played in Pakistan for obvious reasons:

grass is a rare and precious thing; arable land is at a premium; and golf equipment is expensive. There used to be a golf course in Abbottabad under the English regime, but it is no longer maintained. Even so, some of our British friends at the club used to try to play it of a Sunday morning.

A great many Pakistanis are enthusiastic hunters and fishers— or they would be if they could afford the equipment. Although in the tribal areas, every man or boy carries some sort of a gun, generally speaking, a shotgun is a luxury item. The economic elite hunt and fish in such places as the Kaghan Valley, a very fine region for such pursuits, and, on the other side of Pakistan, in East Bengal, tiger hunting is a big-league sport, even dangerous enough for Ernest Hemingway. However, the average man simply cannot afford this kind of recreation any more than the average American can afford to play polo. There is nothing in Pakistan to compare with the annual exodus of thousands of auto workers from Detroit, Flint, and Pontiac to northern Michigan when the deer or trout season opens. I rather think that this mass migration of factory workers—in their own cars, with their own guns and fishing equipment, working their own national forests and streams—would probably impress many Pakistani visitors more than anything else they might see in the United States.

Women in Sports

Let us recur for a moment to the question of women in sports. In dealing with this subject, we must, once more, make a distinction between the Frontier Province and the more sophisticated urban centers. Not once in Abbottabad (it has to be said again) did I see any Muslim women engaged in any sport. At the Abbottabad Government College for Women, my wife saw girls play volley ball and engage in races in which they carried pottery on their heads, but these sights were denied to males.

This is not to say that Pakistani girls do not play games. I have already spoken of their competition against Japanese girls in table tennis; they also competed in Karachi tournaments. (*Dawn*, November 10, 1957) College girls in the big cities, no doubt, engage in field hockey, tennis, badminton, and volley ball; and I assume that advanced young ladies may even compete openly at the impressive Lahore and Karachi Gymkhanas, though I did not happen to see any of them in action. My Fulbright colleague, Miss Effie Adams, who was assigned to East Pakistan, speaks of a brilliant young tennis star who, quite in the American manner, came to Dacca from Karachi for the national tournament.[2]

Yet I think that Pakistan's girls are much in the same position of our Gibson girls at the turn of the century in respect to both the playing of games and the costumes in which they play—that is, full dress. It is inevitable, in the light of the strength of purdah and the tradition of the *burqa*, that they should be behind in sports, as they are in education. As far as I know, there was absolutely no attempt made to organize a woman's team for any of the sports conducted in the Olympic games.

India is different. In New Delhi, where I watched a tennis tournament, I was impressed by three things: Sikhs playing, with their beards done up in hair nets; the potential displayed by the Indian Junior Champion (male); and by the very short shorts worn by Indian young girls, members of the club, who were merely playing for fun.

Perhaps the brevity of their attire came as a special shock after some months in Pakistan where the women were clothed voluminously. A Pakistani girl in such shorts or in a one-piece bathing suit would be a very rare sight indeed.

It is patent that the relationship of Pakistani women to sports depends on the social system as a whole, and, as this system evolves slowly towards equality of opportunity in education, so, in time will they have more freedom in the realm of sports.

Be that as it may, there is no doubt that male Pakistanis are thoroughly dedicated to competitive athletics—fiercely so.

Sports Behavior and What it Means

Another measure of this commitment to sports which I observed with much interest was the large number of "letters to the editor" on sports matters. These were frequent, long, passionately argued, and generally literate. They denounced the selection committee which chose the Olympic field hockey team; they berated the government for not subsidizing sports more adequately; and they discussed every conceivable aspect of the policies and operations of the bodies responsible for the control of cricket. They "viewed with alarm" and "pointed with pride." Americans would be surprised and impressed by the amount of space devoted to such contributions, but they would be more astonished at the letters in which officials and members of sports clubs heatedly washed their dirty linen in public. These polemics were intensely personal in tone under a crust of pseudo-good-manners, and they abounded in crimination and recrimination. The issues were usually elections, technical questions of official representation, and club finances.

There is no doubt of it, the sports world in Pakistan, both on and off the field of battle, is very much alive. In fact, it is a Donnybrook Fair, for the Pakistanis are as much interested in the politics of sport as they are in sport itself.

All of these patterns—intense interest in sports of all kinds, the idolizing of athletic heroes, explosive reactions to official decisions, and the bitter debates in the letter columns of the press—have their counterparts in the United States, and for much the same reasons. The fundamental difference in the two national psychologies may simply be one of degree, not of kind, but the difference is there nonetheless, and it is significant enough to warrant some probing.

Sports are fun in themselves, and I believe that there is a strong esthetic element in all games of skill which should not be discounted. Furthermore, as the psychologists tell us, sport is the moral (or immoral) equivalent of war—a way of working off aggressions in a sublimated, socially acceptable kind of way. Also, sport is a way of escape from the less pleasant realities of daily life—akin to drugs, alcohol, sex, or the movies—those other characteristic vehicles of flight in modern society. In all these respects, the Pakistanis and the Americans are alike in their responses.

If, as I have suggested, the difference in intensity of response is one of degree, then the causes may be found in the greater degree of frustration in the lives of the Pakistanis. They are, I found, a very unhappy people, and they have many reasons for being so, both national and personal: Kashmir, a limping economy, the basic problem of adequate food supplies, a shaky political structure, and regional rivalries. The Pakistani wanted to be proud of his nation, and he found little ground for pride as he reviewed the past years—notably those since the death of Liaquat Ali Khan. He saw little chance for improvement of his social and economic lot. He was understandably thin-skinned, and he exploded either at a political rally or at an athletic contest, or in compulsive play.[3]

The United States is in a similar position as we are forced to take stock of our failures in economics, education, foreign policy, and internal race relations. Under such circumstances, tensions develop. They are greater in Pakistan, and therefore they erupt more often than they do here—as in the Dacca football riots.

190

There is one other reason, I believe, for the pattern of violence and disorder in sports in Pakistan. Ever since the end of World War II (to take a handy date), the Pakistanis have been in the habit of demonstrating either against the British or against the Congress Party. This conditioned reaction is hard to break, as the perennial student strikes demonstrate. It does not make much difference, it would seem, that they are rioting against their own government, against their own vice-chancellor, or against sports officials who are their own countrymen. Given any provocation, in their exacerbated state of tension and frustration, they will riot. From this point of view, the sports psychology of the Pakistanis is a symptom of a national malaise.

Chapter Eight

Politics in Pakistan

Basic Data

I shall not attempt to give a systematic account of Pakistani parliamentary politics. As events have demonstrated, such an effort would have been outdated by the time it got into print. Rather I shall deal with certain basic patterns, forces, and elements in the political process as I observed them at the grass-roots level in Abbottabad, in a careful reading of the Pakistani press, and in discussions with my Pakistani friends. In the last section of this chapter, I will summarize the results of the patterns which culminated in the establishment of the current dictatorship.[1]

One book on politics deserves special attention. It is *Pakistan: A Political Study* by Keith Callard, associate professor of political science at McGill University, published in 1957.[2] Like the work of his McGill colleague, Professor Wilfred Cantwell Smith's *Islam in Modern History*, it is indispensable for an understanding of Pakistan. Professor Callard has made the enterprise of discussing Pakistani politics much easier because his study provides a solid base of sound historical reference for such complex and important matters as the decline of the Muslim League, the history of the Constituent Assembly, the operations of cabinet government, the federal structure, the position of the minorities, and the role of the public services.

Some basic facts must be recapitulated as a foundation for what I want to say. Pakistan became an independent nation in 1947. A constitution was developed and finally adopted by the Constituent Assembly on February 29, 1956.[3] On the whole, despite its theocratic overtones, it was a liberal document in the tradition of Western parliamentary government. It is not now in operation because, unfortunately, no general election was held under its provisions and because the military dictatorship has abolished the system of parliamentary government. In this respect, Pakistan's history is in sharp contrast with that of her neighbor: under its new constitution, India, a nation of approximately four hundred million people, has had two general elections since 1947; Pakistan, a nation of approximately eighty million people has had none. This fact was not lost on the Pakistanis in 1956–57. They were painfully aware of it. A general election was regularly promised, and it was promised by every politician of every party. It was the crucial question. The whole political future of Pakistan, one way or the other, depended on the outcome.

It must always be kept in mind that Pakistan is composed of two wings, separated by some thousand miles of Indian territory: East Pakistan, carved out of the dominantly Muslim portion of the old province of Bengal in southeastern India, and West Pakistan, composed of the Pakistani share of the pre-partition province of the Punjab, Sind, Baluchistan, the entire old Northwest Frontier Province, the Mekran, a desert region running down to the Arabian Sea, the tribal areas, and some semi-independent states like Swat, Chitral, Hunza, and Gilgit.

East Pakistan has its own government with its capital at Dacca. West Pakistan was, in theory, one political unit with its capital at Lahore. However, the One Unit system of administration came under heavy attack, and it was not beyond the bounds of possibility that, before the advent of dictatorship, demagogic forces, allied with strong, deeply rooted provincial loyalties, might have broken it up. The capital of the federal government as a whole is Karachi.

The only communication between East and West Pakistan is by air or by sea from the sole West Pakistan port of Karachi to the only East Pakistan deep water port of Chittagong. It is theoretically possible to travel by rail across the thousand miles of India, but the mutual hostility, which exists between the two nations, expressed in passport and customs regulations, and the sheer physical energy and time consumed in rail travel make such a course very difficult for all practical purposes.

In these circumstances, Pakistan faces as troublesome problems, merely to exist as a nation, as any nation on the face of the globe, not excluding the new Egyptian-Syrian state. Furthermore, aside from geography, Pakistan has every other problem known to man—economic, social, and political.

The geographical situation inevitably makes for separatism. The East Pakistanis, a majority of the nation's population, speak Bengali. They are language and cultural nationalists and they strongly resented the attempt to make Urdu alone the national language. They feel that they are neglected by the far-off federal government in Karachi, and they are not convinced that their best interests are served by the Pakistani state. This feeling is strengthened by the fact that East Pakistan furnishes the nation with a substantial portion of its foreign exchange through its jute industry. The uneasy relations between the two wings are not helped by the assumption of superiority made by the West Pakistanis over their Eastern brothers. This assumption is not generally stated in public, but it is nevertheless very much present. I sensed it in my students and colleagues in Abbottabad.[4] In fact, it seems to me that the only common bonds between the two wings are Islam; fear, suspicion and jealousy of India; and the English language. These may not prove to be enough.

The Forces of Separatism

Inside West Pakistan there are also dangerous currents of separatism. In part, these are founded on language and related cultural provincialisms, such as the Sindhi's love for his own language and literature, the Punjabi's love for Punjabi, and the frontiersman's devotion to Pushto. I had evidence of the latter at the educational conference I attended at Peshawar, December 1956, during which there was strong opposition to any emphasis on English as the medium of instruction—opposition which, I felt, was much more intense in the minds of many educators present than the overt expressions of it.

Another separatist force is the movement for an independent Pukhtunistan, a movement strongly encouraged by the Afghans, in the past at least. This movement sought to establish a new state composed of Pushto-speaking peoples on both sides of the Afghan-Pakistan border. As a practical matter, it was an impossibility, but as an idea, it caused the government of Pakistan great trouble.[5]

But perhaps the most dangerous of all the forces making for a loose federation of provinces rather than for a strong central government was plain, down-to-earth opportunistic politics. In the first half of 1957, a significant number of dominant political figures in West Pakistan who formerly supported One Unit came out for a return to the old provincial divisions. This reversal of position was open, sudden, and naked, and many observers concluded that it was simply a demagogic appeal to the strong local sentiments of the Pakistan electorate—somewhat akin to the extreme states-rights position advocated in our own country by politicians in South Carolina, Georgia, Mississippi, Alabama, and Arkansas.

As one of my knowing friends in Abbottabad put it, "Well, with One Unit we have only one ministry with twelve or thirteen ministerial posts; with four provinces, we would have four times that many."

The point, if not sufficiently clear, is that ministers of the West Pakistan government had many perquisites of office—salaries, personal staffs of secretaries and servants, and the right to sport a ministerial flag on their automobiles.

Whether this cynical explanation is justified or not, it does sum up the prevailing attitude taken towards both the Legislative Assembly in Lahore and the National Assembly in Karachi by intelligent Pakistanis of my acquaintance. Generally speaking, their representatives were considered simply as power seekers changing their party affiliations and their principles to suit the occasion. There was no really responsible party structure in Pakistan, and for this reason it is difficult to discuss its past politics in terms of parties such as the Muslim League, the Republican Party, or the Awami League, perhaps the three most important political groupings.[6]

Again and again I asked my colleagues and my friends in Abbottabad to explain the differences in the parties and their own choice of party in the forthcoming promised general elections. Without exception, they shrugged their shoulders and said, in effect, that there was not any real difference, that they had no real choice, and that they would have to make up their minds at the time of election on the basis of the personalities standing for office.

Furthermore, I found that very few Pakistanis seemed to know much about the basis on which their representatives to the West Pakistan Legislative Assembly and the National (Constituent) Assembly were chosen. This absence of knowledge was exasperating. It was if a Pakistani professor, teaching in an American university, could not get clean-cut answers from his American colleagues as to the method of choosing representatives and senators for the state legislatures and Congress. The only Pakistani I met who had any clear idea about electoral procedure was the brigadier general who was the station commander in Abbottabad when we left.

There was, of course, some justification for this prevailing lack of information about the political structure of the nation, which was complex. To begin with, the most important point is that the representatives in the provincial assemblies who, in turn, elected the members of the Constituent Assembly, were not chosen by a majority of an electorate composed of voters having universal adult suffrage from districts apportioned by population.[7] Rather, the political course of Pakistan was largely determined by the provincial elections of 1945–46 before either independence or partition had been conceded. Here is Professor Callard's description of these elections:

> The franchise for participation in provincial elections was narrow. The details varied from province to province, but the right to vote was based on education and property, and it is unlikely that anywhere more than 15 percent of the total population was entitled to vote. A number of special constituencies existed for such categories as landowners, university voters, organized labour and women. More important were the provisions for communal separate electorates and reserved seats. Muslims (and in some cases Christians and others) were entered on separate rolls and voted for candidates of their own community. The Scheduled Castes, while not being placed on separate rolls, were provided with a number of seats reserved for members of that community. (pp. 77–78)

It was through this system that the First Constituent Assembly, largely elected by the provincial legislatures, came into being on August 10, 1947. The Second Constituent Assembly, which met in July 1955, was composed of eighty members, seventy-two of which were to be chosen by the provincial assemblies and electoral colleges for Karachi and Baluchistan.[8] These assemblies performed two functions: enacting legislation and making the constitution.

In short, Pakistan was still playing the game of parliamentary government under the old pre-partition rules. Under the new constitution, there was to be a national assembly of three hundred seats with ten additional seats provided for women for a period of ten years. Provincial governments were to be organized on almost exactly parallel lines. The most important point of all is that the franchise was to be extended broadly.

Is some respects, the situation in 1958 before the scheduled general election (which was not held) was like that which existed early in our own history when the franchise was drastically limited and senators were chosen by state legislatures. Current MLA's and MCA's were far removed from the mass electorate. They constituted an oligarchy: the legislative posts were simply the property of a small number of landowners and the like.[9] The situation today might have been different if legislative districts had been set up and representatives, both for provincial and national assemblies, had been chosen by an across-the-board vote of all Pakistani citizens entitled to the franchise under the new constitution.

Another negative element in the Pakistan political situation was the absence of national leadership. Men like President Mirza, Chundrigar, Firoz Noon, and Mohammed Ali had quite impressive records of education, training, and experience, but nobody, I think, would hold seriously that they approached the stature of Jinnah or Liaquat.[10]

Suhrawardy: Politician-Statesman

My favorite political figure in Pakistan was Suhrawardy. He was prime minister from September 1956 to October 1957. Suhrawardy was a very shrewd politician, and, given a chance, he might have been a statesman. He had sharp intelligence, a sense of humor, and a cat-like capacity for landing on his feet in the political rough and tumble.

One measure of the man is an article which he wrote for *Foreign Affairs*, April 1957, called "Political Stability and Democracy in Pakistan." It is the best piece of its kind written by a Pakistani which I have read. Since it was written for an international audience of his peers, it was something more than a political speech, and it was marked by a tonic and refreshing good sense. In this article, Suhrawardy rejected any excuses for Pakistan based on its "youngness as a polity"; said that a nation could earn respect due to maturity only by acting maturely; called for mature and honest self-appraisal in place of self-praise; acknowledged Pakistan's debt to the British for lessons taught in administrative integrity and in constitutional

197

procedure and proprieties; held that Pakistan's goal could only be achieved through elections; denied that the authoritarian path was the answer to Pakistan's problems; and cited, as assets and milestones in Pakistan's progress, the adoption of the constitution, the judiciary's right to issue prerogative writs, and the creation of One Unit out of six for West Pakistan. The article was the work of a practical politician and a political philosopher as well.[11]

Suhrawardy's most effective work was done in the field of foreign policy. He consistently adhered to a pro-Western policy including support for SEATO, close cooperation with the Baghdad Pact powers (which held one of their meetings in Karachi, June 1957), and maintenance of close relations with the United States, practically an outright necessity for Pakistan, inasmuch as the United States was carrying a large share of the national budget.

In the struggle over Kashmir, his administration gained credit for UN support of Pakistan's position, and he managed to support the Egyptian cause during the Suez crisis without going all out for Nasser's extremism after UN intervention. In so doing, Suhrawardy came in for very harsh criticism from the opposition (notably from *The Pakistan Times*) which saw an opportunity to capitalize on this inflammatory issue, but his policy gained ground steadily after Nasser refused Pakistan's offer of an army contingent for the UN forces, launched a polemic press campaign against Pakistan for its allegiance to SEATO, lined up with India generally, and went far towards an outright alliance with the USSR.

After the Suez crisis, Suhrawardy spent much of his time on state visits around the world, including a successful tour of the United States, during which his cheerful sense of humor was much in evidence. The objection to this globe-trotting was that Pakistan's major problems were—and are—internal. It is easy to understand why Suhrawardy, as well as other Pakistani officials, sought every opportunity to make foreign junkets, as our own congressmen do, but the basic problems of finance, agriculture, irrigation, water, land reform, health, industry, and education had to be met if Pakistan was to survive, and they were not being met because the home work was not being done.

Nevertheless, Suhrawardy commanded my admiration by his continuing support for the principle of One Unit government for West Pakistan and by his courageous stand against electing representatives for provincial and national assemblies on a communal or religious community basis. In Pakistan this issue was referred to as "joint" or "separate" electorates. Suhrawardy came from East Pakistan, which has a substantial minority of Hindus—close to ten million; Hindus in West Pakistan are few.[12]

The issue of joint or separate electorates was an explosive one. The nation calls itself officially the Islamic Republic of Pakistan, but its constitution pledges full toleration for all religions, and responsible leaders have preached the doctrine that its citizens owe their allegiance to their country, and conversely, that the country owes the obligation of guaranteeing full citizenship to all its people. This is to say that Muslims, Hindus, and Christians alike are asked to think of themselves as Pakistanis first and as members of a religious community second.

All of this would strike Americans as being sound doctrine. However, since Pakistan was founded as an Islamic state, it is inevitable that theocratic and religious issues should be present in its politics. Out of a combination of sincere religious convictions and political opportunism, comparable to our America-First extremism, a good many Pakistani politicians have raised the specter of danger to Islam if the joint electorate principle should obtain—that is, if candidates should run for public office without distinction as to religion.

Under this system, obviously, Muslims would win in predominantly Muslim regions, and Hindus would win in those very few areas in which they are a majority. Under the other plan, that of separate electorates, a certain number of constituencies would be set up for Hindus and Christians. The argument was advanced that this plan would insure these minorities some representation, and certain minority leaders accepted this view. However, this kind of compartmentalization was clearly dangerous in that it would have accentuated the communal religious differences which produced the blood bath in 1947, and no responsible Pakistani (or Indian) would want a recurrence of those horrible events. There are some forty to forty-five millions of Muslims in India and, patently, what the Pakistan government does to Hindus has inevitable repercussions in India in respect to Muslims, and vice versa.

It is this mutual awareness of the awful holocaust of 1947 which tends to temper Indo-Pakistani relations, and I want to digress, for a moment, to point up its enduring meaning. Nobody knows how many Sikhs, Hindus, and Muslims were killed in 1947. I have heard first-hand reports from missionaries which attest to the truth of the stories of corpses piled roof-high and of the killing of whole trainsful of people. I can think of no parallel in history for the blood lust

199

which resulted in the deaths of so many people—more, I am sure, than were ever killed before in a similar period outside of a major war. The point is that both Indians and Pakistanis are deeply ashamed of the whole business. They are haunted by the memories of the corpse-littered streets of Lahore and Calcutta. They no longer blame each other. Both sides say that both sides were to blame, and even the disposition to blame the British and Mountbatten for pulling out too early is half-hearted. I conclude that blood guilt is on the consciences of the two nations and that this blood guilt is an important, though not much discussed, factor in Indo-Pakistani relations. Never for the rest of my life will I forget the tears welling to the eyes of a young Pakistani officer (the brother of the lady doctor in Abbottabad) when he told us how, before his very eyes, a Sikh friend of his was murdered by a mob in Lahore, how he managed to save the life of a Hindu schoolmate by passing him off as a Muslim, but how the Sikh's long hair and beard marked him for death. Similar stories in reverse, I am certain, can be heard on the other side of the border.

The religious issue produced some strange shifts in Pakistan's politics. In October 1956, the National Assembly decided that East Pakistan, with its large Hindu minority, should have a joint electorate, and that West Pakistan, which is overwhelmingly Muslim, should have separate electorates. In April 1957, this decision was reversed, and joint electorates were decided upon for both wings. Before 1957 ended, two successive ministries in turn changed this basic decision. Of course, after the military dictatorship was established in October 1958, the whole matter of election procedures became meaningless.

Naturally, where religion is involved, passions run high. At the height of the debate, during our stay, the politicians made a lot of hay in the fundamentalist regions of West Pakistan, of which Abbottabad is one. The reader will recall my earlier account of the student strike on this issue.[13]

But, while the politicians of the Muslim League and their allies were saving Pakistan from a nonexistent Hindu threat, Suhrawardy held steadfastly to the principle that the only right course was to permit the holders of the franchise to vote as Pakistani citizens, not as Hindus, Muslims, or Christians. He argued the case boldly and ably in West Pakistan, on occasion at the risk of personal injury, and in so doing he sounded like a twentieth-century voice, whereas his opponents often sounded like voices out of the so-called Dark Ages—as do the Hindu right-wingers in India.

In 1957 Suhrawardy was the only figure on the Pakistani scene who gave any evidence of the kind of parliamentary political leadership which Pakistan needed to make some progress towards its own defined goals. If the general elections had been held in November 1958, he might have mustered up a coalition, based on his strength in East Pakistan, which would have given him the power to carry out an effective program on the home front as well as in foreign affairs. It is a lamentable fact that no other practicing politician showed any indication of becoming a truly national figure.

At best, Suhrawardy's chances were not good. He was not particularly palatable to the fundamentalist Muslims in the West Wing, not only because of his stand for joint electorates, but also because he was caught dancing in public during one of his tours in the Far East, an incident which caused a comic furore back home, just as publicized attendance at Washington cocktail parties is dangerous for some congressmen in our own Bible Belt. His being an East Pakistani was both an asset and a liability. In public, West Pakistanis must be careful of the sensibilities of their Eastern brothers because of the superior numbers and economic importance of the East Wing. Great care must be taken to balance between East and West any official delegation, any committee, any national appointive body, or any Fulbright or ICA grants. But, in private, West Wingers (to repeat the point) have a good deal of condescending contempt for East Pakistanis, and I am sure that they would prefer to have a West Pakistani for Prime Minister.

Suhrawardy resigned as prime minister for a number of reasons: the electorate issue, the One Unit issue, and, perhaps just as important, the feeling of the West Pakistan politicos that he was getting too powerful. What happened is a fascinating case history in Pakistani politics, and I will summarize it briefly for its relevance to the major questions of the all-important general elections and the matter of the past operations of the political parties in Pakistan.

Suhrawardy was forced to resign on October 11, 1957. I. I. Chundrigar, a Muslim League leader, formed a coalition cabinet which was sworn in on October 18. This cabinet moved to reverse current preparations being made for elections on the joint principle and to substitute a communal, separate electoral system. The Republican Party, an important component of the Chundrigar coalition, which had hitherto more or less supported Suhrawardy and his Awami League, then apparently had second thoughts about the election issue, and withdrew its support from the Muslim League, which was a minority anyway. Chundrigar then resigned, and Malik Firoz Noon, a Republican stalwart who had gained increased stature in Pakistan through his presentation of the Pakistani case for Kashmir in the UN, became Prime Minister late in December 1957. Noon's ministry then pressed for a general election to be held in November 1958 and to be based on a common voters' list, irrespective of religion.[14]

There are two points to be made: the first is that politicians and political parties in Pakistan did not stay put, and for that reason, "turncoatism" or switching of sides and positions, was an important issue in itself;[15] the second is that, in the face of the political maneuverings, it seemed unlikely that the complicated arrangements necessary for a general election could be completed on schedule. So it turned out.

It is reasonable to assume that the Election Commission, which had been ordered to prepare the rolls of voters on the joint or single principle under Suhrawardy, on the communal principle under Chundrigar, and then again on the joint principle under Noon, had been badly hampered in its work.[16]

Political Parties

This short case history illustrates the difficulty of discussing political parties in Pakistan. In the minds of the electorate, parties were not meaningful entities. Taken as a whole, they have lost the respect and confidence of the Pakistani masses because of their irresponsible behavior in both provincial and national assemblies. For one of many reasons, there was an almost comic tendency among politicians to change parties and positions on important issues which has produced the term "turncoatism." These reversals were duly recorded in the press either in the form of formal announcements or news stories, and they have led the layman to impute the worst motives to such switches.

In the United States, we are accustomed to unedifying and unmannerly debate in our legislative halls, particularly in state legislatures. But the conduct of the West Pakistan assembly, as joyfully recorded in the communist-line *Pakistan Times* of Lahore during the hot fight which led to its suspension by President Mirza, was an amazingly childish performance. It is one of the reasons why I have suggested, after watching my own Abbottabad students' hair-splitting use of *Robert's Rules of Order*, that the elders were imitating the youngsters.

As for the parties themselves, the Muslim League, which once was the Pakistani equivalent of India's Congress Party in that it was credited with the foundation work for the Islamic state, had forfeited public esteem and confidence and became a minority party.[17] However, in such areas as Abbottabad, the League still commanded a certain measure of support (especially among my students) as the defender of the faith. The Awami League was largely Suhrawardy's own political vehicle in East Pakistan, although he had to fight hard on occasion to retain control of its local apparatus; the Awami League did not have proportionate support in West Pakistan. The Republic Party was started by Dr. Khan Sahib, former chief minister of West Pakistan (who was murdered in May, 1958),[18] but where the Republicans would stand on any given issue was hard to predict. The Pakistan National Party was in itself a coalition of six minor parties (no great harbinger of unity), including Mian Iftikharuddin's group and the Red Shirts of Abdul Ghaffer Khan. The latter, Dr. Kahn Sahib's brother and a former Congress Party stalwart, was an exponent of Frontier and provincial autonomy, and he spent at least six years in jail for political reasons. The result was that the central administration was embarrassed by virtue of long drawn-out court proceedings involving this tough old fighter.[19]

At any one time, these parties would take a stand on current issues like One Unit or joint electorate, but it was useless to try to forecast what they would do in the future. One of the great virtues of the scheduled general election was that the parties would simply have had to come out for something meaningful. They would have had, in Pakistani idiom, "to chalk out" a program.

Of course, all parties supported the lowering of the cost of living (which has shot up almost catastrophically in recent years),[20] honest government, the liberation of Kashmir, and Islam. These were the Pakistani equivalent of the American politician's stand for the flag, mother love, sunshine, lower taxes, a balanced budget, and strong opposition to sin. But one thing Pakistani politicos were conspicuously lukewarm about was any program of land reform. This was understandable inasmuch as a substantial number of MLA's and MCA's were landholders or zamindars, and, in many cases, their tenants were in a feudal relationship to them. The zamindars proposed to protect their vested interests, and they took a dim view of any measures which would give the central government more power to deal with problems of water-logging, erosion, irrigation, salination, or reforestation on a regional scale. There was much talk about land reform in Pakistan, but very little action.

The large landholders acted as anyone would expect them to act and very much as we would act if we were in their places. But there is a middle ground between expropriation (and/or collective farming) and the extremes of traditional feudalism. Unless there is some progress made, both in the management of the soil and in increasing the income of the average peasant, there is little hope for any real improvement of the lot of Pakistan's millions. Here the reader will remember the strong favorable reaction of my students to the proposition I asserted about the lot of Pakistan's peasants in the course of our discussion of Drinkwater's *Abraham Lincoln*.[21] As for the management of the soil, one statement makes the point: Mr. John O. Bell, former director of ICA in Pakistan, just before leaving his post, said in a public address that, in view of erosion, improper rotation of crops, soil exhaustion, and salination, "if this state of affairs is allowed to continue at its present rate, the Valley of the Indus, within less than half a century, will become a desert."[22]

What enabled the political parties and their representatives to get away with it? Remember that MLA's and MCA's constituted small groups of oligarchs. They did not represent any broadly based electorates when they first achieved office.[23] They had not been held accountable to any electorate by regularly recurring elections. Altogether they acted like the proprietors of pocket boroughs in eighteenth-century England before the Reform Bills. Under these circumstances, it is easy to see why current office holders were not eager for general elections and why so many literate and intelligent Pakistanis despaired of the political process. The importance of the scheduled general elections should also be crystal clear by now.

In the light of the politicians' fear of what would happen when an outraged electorate went to the polls armed with general adult suffrage, I hazard the conjecture (not discounting the profound religious convictions at work) that some of the pulling and hauling on the separate or joint electorate issue was parliamentary obstructionism, intended to postpone the Great Day of Reckoning. I think that the "ins" proposed to stay in and therefore, as I watched the course of Pakistani affairs, I doubted that the November 1958 deadline for the general election would be met.

Political maneuvering and turncoatism, as well as doubts about the materialization of that lovely mirage, a general election—all these had created a psychological gap between the legislators and the people of Pakistan. Political corruption was omnipresent and was reflected almost daily in the press. Indeed, Prime Minister Chundrigar, in his first broadcast to the people, felt compelled to make this statement about it: "... corruption has become very widespread, and this evil must be put down with a heavy hand." (*Dawn*, October 19, 1957, p. 1) Very few political speeches in Pakistan failed to denounce corruption.

As a result of all these factors, there was frustration in politically aware Pakistanis which amounted to either an existentialist nihilism in the sophisticates or a fatalistic pessimism in the faithful. Very few individuals had any faith or confidence in the political processes of their country, and, what is even more appalling, very few had any personal sense of responsibility for what was going on. Very few felt that anything they could do would make any difference.

Part of this pervasive pessimism stemmed from corruption in such elections as had been held. I got first-hand reports on these from some of my younger colleagues in Abbottabad who had been election officials. They told me that pressure had been put on them by the police and government officials, that lines of voters for opposition candidates had been held up to prevent their ballots from being cast before the polls closed, and that ballot boxes, presumably containing "wrong" votes, had been filled with ink or otherwise spoiled.

They spoke with admiration of an Englishman (the lecturer in a Peshawar college whom we met at dinner later) who, being in charge of what we would call a precinct, resisted all pressures and insisted on conducting an honest poll. As my colleagues talked, it was clear that they had tried to keep their own operations clean. Moreover, they told me of the mass purchase of votes by wealthy candidates. It appeared that votes were cheap in Pakistan because the people are very poor, and a rupee or two for a vote (the equivalent of a day's salary or more) was a convincing inducement to vote "right." I was reminded of voting practices in eighteenth-century England, as immortalized by Hogarth, of our own Tammany Hall politics, and of Lincoln Steffens' muckraking.

These reports threw a good deal of light on the reactions of the Abbottabad community to President Mirza's suspension of the West Pakistan legislative assembly and ministry in Lahore, early in 1957—a suspension which was revoked in July 1957. The president had the legal right to perform this act, although its justice was questioned by his political opponents. Under this suspension order, executive power was vested in the governor of West Pakistan, Mushtaq Ahmad Gurmani. One explanation of the coup was that the administration forces, led by Dr. Khan Sahib, had lost their majority in the assembly by virtue of defections on the One Unit issue and that the only way in which the opposition could be prevented from forming a new ministry was to suspend the assembly.

This was the opposition's story, accompanied with many charges of unilateral dictatorial action on the part of the Republican party and the president of the Republic. Certainly, the assembly had been both disorderly and ineffective, but it *was* an elective body.

I neither attack nor defend the suspension. Rather I am concerned with the way in which it was received in Abbottabad. Without exception, it was greeted with satisfaction. Yet I do not believe that this general approval represented a pro-administration allegiance; it was a let-that-be-a-lesson-to-all-politicians and a-plague-on-both-your-houses reaction. Nor did all the executive power concentrated in the hands of the governor disturb my friends one bit. Far better that way, they seemed to think, than in the hands of the "politicians."

The inevitable question arising from this complex of political fact and psychological reaction was: Did Pakistan really want a dictatorship? Or, worded another way: Would Pakistan inexorably become a dictatorship?

Before dealing with these questions, I must restate some important general considerations. Pakistan is a new nation; it does not have a democratic tradition; a big majority of the old Indian Civil Service—officials who had been trained in the tradition of government by law—were Hindus; and the Pakistanis, taken as a whole, have been conditioned to accept authority, as witness their rigid social and economic hierarchy. Here in the United States we are just beginning to realize fully that other nations and peoples do not share our primary taken-for-granted assumptions about the virtues of democracy. That fact was brought home to me dramatically by the student debate on dictatorship and democracy,[24] and it underlined the validity of the propositions set forth by Peggy and Pierre Streit in an article titled "Five Mideast Illusions That Befog Us" in the *New York Times Magazine* of August 3, 1958. The two illusions which are most relevant to Pakistan are these: "That the Middle East is ready for Western representative government" and "That the Middle East thinks, as we do, that authoritarian government is evil."

One prime example of the readiness to accept authoritarianism in Pakistan is the position of the "D. C.," the Deputy Commissioner, who, in his district, is very powerful. He has, among other preroga-

206

tives, the right to suspend municipal corporations in much the same way that the president suspended the West Pakistan assembly. That right, by the way, was exercised in Abbottabad on grounds of corruption, and it excited very little comment in the town. I found out about it casually. Nobody cared. Another way of putting the point is that, tribal regions aside, there has been no local tradition of self-government in Pakistan comparable to our New England town meeting. An attempt is being made to encourage panchayats, or village councils, but how successful this is, I can not say.[25]

Although Islam emphasizes the equality of all men before God, a democratic idea which was once powerful in the conversion of thousands of low-caste Hindus and which is still powerful in the Muslim missionary effort in Africa, this concept does not necessarily result in the conviction that political democracy is a good thing. The students at Abbottabad voted overwhelmingly for dictatorship over democracy.

This emotional disposition towards acceptance of the strong man is one aspect of the Pakistani problem. Another is what has lately been called (with an air of great discovery) Arab nationalism. From the Pakistani point of view, a better name for it would be Muslim nationalism. It can be illustrated by what happened in Abbottabad during the Suez crisis. Everybody literally went wild with enthusiasm for Nasser and the Egyptian cause. The faculty of my college assessed itself a day's pay for Egyptian relief, a very considerable sum proportionately. For a time, it looked as if the British in Pakistan would be in real trouble. A Dacca mob burned down the British Information Center. Britons in Lahore and Karachi were asked to stay indoors. I was fearful for our English friends in Abbottabad: the captain in charge of the Pakistan Army Music School; the fathers out at Burn Hall; and especially the six specialists in civvies from the British War Office who lived at the Abbottabad Club. However, nothing much happened. The arguments in the club bar were heated, and deep feelings were involved on both sides, but there were no overt incidents of any consequence.

As for ourselves, Uncle Sam took the "right" position, and our personal stock went up in Abbottabad. However, the unpleasant fact was that the Russians got most of the credit for the withdrawal of the Anglo-French-Israeli troops, a fact which the All-Pakistan Inter-Collegiate debate on the internationalization of the Suez canal made all too clear. If that public demonstration of gratitude to the USSR had not been sufficient, my students' themes would have been enough to prove the point. Although Nasser's stock was considerably lower when we left in May 1957 for reasons summarized above,[26] we heard a good many Pakistanis say, both during and after Suez, "That's what we need—a man like Nasser." I am sure that a large number of Pakistanis still hold this view.

In summary, then, when we consider the alarming distrust of political processes, the general lack of confidence in the government, the disposition towards authoritarianism, the relative absence of any opportunity to practice democracy in elections, and the failure of the government itself to take effective action in respect to basic problems, it appeared that Pakistan was indeed ripe for dictatorship. And, to top it all off, the president of the country was a general with political ambitions.

But, as always, there was another side. Countervailing forces did exist, which, in the long run, might have prevented Pakistan from becoming a dictatorship. But, before we take up these positive factors, let us first look at the former general-president, Iskander Mirza.

He was a formidable person having as assets a Sandhurst education, plenty of experience, charm, and military prestige. If this combination suggests an American parallel, so be it. Moreover, like General De Gaulle, he advocated a strong presidency on the American model, rather than the original conception of the office which was supposed to be above the political battle, like the monarchy in Britain.[27] Furthermore, in respect to democracy, he was on record as saying: "... people of this country need controlled democracy for some time to come."[28]

Nevertheless, it was even then problematical whether Mirza could become and remain the chief power in Pakistan. Having taken an active part in politics, he had created powerful political opposition, and a story in the *New York Times* indicated that he was by no means sure of having everything his own way. It was assumed that Mirza wanted to be re-elected president in the general election scheduled for November 1958, but indications were that he would not necessarily have been a shoo-in.[29] He was not a sacrosanct character. Back in October of 1957, Suhrawardy even called for his impeachment. (*Dawn*, October 28, 1957, p. 1)

Now, we should consider the other counterbalancing forces. Pakistan had a constitution. The mere fact of its existence was a strong force towards its implementation. Powerful elements delayed its operations, but, in the long run, however reluctantly, the current crop of "ins" might have had to bow to its mandates. Another one of Pakistan's assets in the struggle for responsible government, as Suhrawardy stated in his *Foreign Affairs* article, was a judiciary which was strong, respected, and independent of the executive arm. The rulings of the High Court were accepted. I have read accounts of judges in lower courts who did not hesitate to berate the police for brutality and third-degree tactics, and I have observed in action a judge in Abbottabad who conducted a complicated land tenure case with the utmost decorum and dignity and who wrote decisions which were models of lucid prose. Indeed, the judicial system is one of the British legacies for which the Pakistanis might well be thankful.

Notwithstanding the fact that few Pakistanis seemed to take any personal citizen's responsibility for political action, political discussion and debate in the press were comparatively free and unrestricted. It is true that political opponents of the regime had unlikely laws invoked at their expense, and it is true that the *Mirror* of Karachi was suppressed, but it is also true that ten editors of Karachi vigorously protested this ban as a violation of the freedom of the press.[30] At times repercussions in the press forced government officials to retract arbitrary actions. I found that nobody of my acquaintance seemed to have any fear of castigating the powers that be nor did we have the feeling that we were living in a police state from day to day.

There was one other factor which worked against dictatorship in Pakistan. The intelligentsia I encountered seemed to take no personal responsibility for politics, but, nonetheless, great numbers of Pakistanis did turn out for political rallies and they did not hesitate to give vent to their views in violent demonstrations. Three examples will serve to make the point.

On October 31, 1957, the high command of the National Awami Party, Maulana Bhashani, Khan Abdul Ghaffar Khan, the Red Shirt Leader, and the left-winger, Mian Iftikharuddin, were mobbed at a political rally in Rawalpindi and had to be rescued by police baton charges. The NAP stood for provincial autonomy. Supporters of One Unit threw stones and shoes at the three leaders and ultimately captured the dais, completely disrupting the meeting. (*Dawn*, November 1, 1957, p. 1) The same pattern was followed at Sarghoda and Lyallpur, resulting in an appeal by Prime Minister Chundrigar for freedom of speech. (*Dawn*, November 3, 1957, p. 1) On November 29, 1957, both Suhrawardy and Dr. Khan Sahib were victims of hooliganism as the result of a giant rally in favor of separate electorates in Karachi, and once more the prime minister, a staunch Muslim Leaguer, condemned these acts of violence and indecency, as did the editors of *Dawn*. (November 30, 1957, p. 1 and editorial)

This is not to say that every political meeting in Pakistan led to a riot any more than every football game produced one, but it does indicate that the boiling point of the Pakistani urban people was low. The explosive quality of the man in the street might have forced the administration to conduct the general election in spite of themselves. As matters turned out, this emotional tension was, very likely, one of the factors which caused the military to step in.

As for the military, observers generally credit the armed forces, which Mirza symbolized if he did not actually represent them, with being the true stabilizing power in Pakistan. Yet, in my view, the services, unlike their South American counterparts, did not want to usurp political power. They did so because, by their lights, they felt compelled to, not because they necessarily liked it that way.

The armed forces are an amazing phenomenon. They are even more important as social institutions than as instruments of war. The officer cadre was trained in the Sandhurst tradition which stresses a good deal of non-military education, good manners, and, of greater import here, the idea that military men do not meddle in politics. I met many army officers, ranging from lowly lieutenants fresh out of PMA through captains, majors, colonels, brigadier generals, and one chief of staff. And, though I have the traditional American suspicion of militarism and brass-hatism (not lessened by recent American history and my own twenty-eight months service in World War II), I was impressed with the caliber of these men.

A number of the older field officers had been trained in the British Army, some of these at Sandhurst itself. Several had had tours of duty in the United States. But most of the younger generation were graduates of the Pakistan Military Academy, which, until early in 1957, had been under the direction of a British brigadier from the old pre-partition Indian army, General Souter, a whole story in himself. He was both popular and respected. The only criticism I ever heard of him was that he tended to be a little too easy on his boys.

There was a time, not long ago, when Pakistan's army, air force, and navy, like PMA, were headed by English officers of the Souter stripe; today they are all commanded by Pakistanis. In the near past, the army insignia were British crowns and pips; today they are crescent and stars. I still remember the changeover day when, in the dining room of the Palace Hotel, a Pakistani captain pridefully showed us his new badges.

As a result of their training, their satisfying careers, the prestige in Islam of military glory, and their own undeniable capacity, the Pakistani officers were "keen" and able, healthy in mind and body, and possessed of a sense of mission which was in sharp contrast with the spirit of other professional men we encountered. To use a badly worn but still useful word, I would call them "integrated."

In conversation with these officers, the matter of the military's relationship with the body politic often came up. From the lowest to the highest, the responses I received indicated, both explicitly and implicitly, that they had no political ambitions for the army or for themselves. There are two reasons for this point of view: the first is a profound hostility to politics and politicians; the second is that the services were already getting everything that Pakistan can possibly afford—and more. The officer cadre seemed to realize this.

Though not directly pertinent to the present issue of dictatorship, two matters have been raised which demand discussion: the services as social institutions and their effectiveness in case of war.

As to the first, the armed forces, under the Ministry of Defense, are probably the most efficient social mechanism in the country. Their enlisted men are well fed, well cared for, well trained, and relatively well paid. For these reasons, Pakistan has no difficulty in keeping up its armed strength; it relies wholly on volunteers, and, I was given to understand, there is a waiting list of recruits. The cantonments, those areas of Pakistan's cities and towns under military control, are noticeably better taken care of as regards municipal housekeeping than the corporation areas. The armed services are careful about water and sanitation, and it may be that they are making their grestest contribution to Pakistan's future in these areas. Most Pakistanis are not yet convinced that a little thing like germs in water or food can do any real harm. Moreover, the cantonment schools for army "brats" are better housed and better staffed than the public schools.

The army educates its enlisted men to the extent of teaching them to read and write, another major contribution in a land which has an appalling rate of illiteracy—only 13.8 percent of the population being literate, according to one official source.[31]

From the sociological point of view, the army's program of technological training may ultimately be of far-reaching importance. Thousands of Pakistani enlisted men get their first acquaintance with

The Machine. The basic example is the matter of learning to drive a jeep, a staff car, a truck, or a tank, but many other mechanical skills are also taught. And before these men are fed back into civilian life, the army attempts to give them some vocational training. The consequences of this program should be highly significant. Finally, the officer corps is one of the most advanced segments of Pakistan's life, in its awareness of the outside world and differing social patterns. In the slow move away from purdah, the social life centering in the officers' clubs is, very likely, a factor of consequence. It is so recognized by the conservative elements in the country who constantly decry mixed parties and drinking.

In regard to the effectiveness of the Pakistani services as fighting instruments, I know nothing about the navy's potential, nor much about the air force other than the impression that Pakistani pilots are good. Furthermore, I made it a practice not to be nosy about vital military statistics. I do not know how many men are in service; I know nothing about fire power, numbers of planes or ships, nothing whatever about the presence or absence of tactical atomic weapons, and nothing about Pakistan's planned tactics or strategy in the event of war.

However, I believe that anybody who has lived in Abbottabad for any length of time—in the middle of an important military sector—would agree that the Pakistan army is well officered and that the rank and file are very tough customers; they can march, they can shoot, and they can endure in the field with short rations in all kinds of weather; and their morale is good. In these respects, marksmanship possibly excepted, the Pakistanis are probably better than our own troops.

On the political side, I found that both officers and men were thoroughgoing, almost fanatical, anti-communists, but perhaps the most important generalization to make is that the army is, above all, a *professional army*. The officers struck me as being very cool and objective in their attitudes to both India and Egypt—two countries which might be expected to produce passionate and contrary emotions. They have no love for Bharat, and they do not rule out the possibility of armed conflict with their neighbor. Yet they are not fire-eaters or swashbucklers. I doubt that they will permit the tribesmen to undertake another campaign to "liberate" Kashmir, and I heard no "On to Delhi" talk. They are confident that, man for man, they can outfight the Indian army, yet they were not overly enthusiastic about the prospect of war with India which, as one officer pointed out calmly (much to my surprise), would almost certainly begin with the loss of Lahore, indefensible as it is on its open plain near the Indian border.

As for Egypt and Nasser, like all Pakistanis, the army men had a strong emotional affinity for what they consider to be the Arab-Islamic cause, together with a traditional anti-colonialism, which means dislike, coupled with respect, for the British, and hatred of Israel.

Nevertheless, the officers did not go overboard for Nasser as my students and colleagues did, perhaps because, as military men, they did not think that Nasser put up much of a show. As the Egyptians progressively pursued an anti-Pakistan policy, these officers manifested a quiet kind of I-told-you-so view.

In sum, ardently nationalistic, ardently Muslim, and thoroughly suspicious of India as they were, the leaders of the Pakistan army struck me as being highly realistic "pros." In conclusion, I venture to say that any attempt to force the historic passes of the frontier Himalayas would encounter rough going indeed, but whether the Pakistani economy could sustain its army in the field for any length of time is a moot question of total logistics.

Perhaps the real question should be: What is the true function of the Pakistani army—what is it *for*? The same question applies to the Indian army. Both nations are spending more on their defense budgets than they can afford (as which nation is not?). The obvious reason for the arms competition of the two nations is Kashmir, and the tension created by this issue is great, as a recent saber-rattling speech by the normally moderate Mohammed Ali testifies.[32] But even if the Kashmir issue were settled reasonably, I suspect that, as a matter of national pride, Pakistan would insist on having substantial armed forces. The armed forces themselves would probably insist on being large in numbers and well fed. I find it hard to visualize any Pakistani regime cutting the service budgets drastically.

After drawing up this trial balance of forces which could have made either for or against dictatorship in Pakistan, I came to these conclusions: if the general election had been held as scheduled in November 1958 or in a reasonable time thereafter, there would have been hope for an orderly development towards a functioning parliamentary government and for some systematic improvement in the economic lot of Pakistan's masses. Since the election was not held, since it was systematically postponed on one pretext or another, popular pressures generated an explosive situation, and the military was forced, somewhat against its will, to take over and to administer the country as a more or less benevolent dictatorship.

These were not the only alternatives but they were the more probable ones. It was also possible, for example, that Pakistan might have fallen apart as the result of the secession of East Pakistan and the disintegration of West Pakistan into a loose federation of former provincial units, but I rather believe that national pride, Islam, and the military prevented that.

Americans keep asking me whether it is at all possible for Pakistan to rejoin India on an autonomous basis, but this, I think, is plainly not in the realm of possibility. And I believe that, even in the remote event of war over Kashmir (or over the Assam border) with an Indian victory, the Indians have no desire to take over Pakistan; they have enough troubles of their own. However, if India should go communist, then Pakistan would be under great pressure. This statement brings us to that perennial American question: Could Pakistan go communist?

The Communist Party was banned in Pakistan, but that law did not prevent its operating in one way or another. However, insofar as I could tell, communist power in the political field was in no way as strong as it was in India where the communists took over Kerala State in a free, democratic election. The most powerful instrument for the forces of communism was *The Pakistan Times*, published in Lahore, and this daily paper (put under government control in April 1959) must be taken into account by any student of Pakistan's history. The owner and the management of the *Times* were generally regarded by my Pakistani friends as being either communists or close followers of the party line, and my friends were not exactly hysterical about the situation either. American officials in Pakistan were categorical in private about the *Times'* communist line. I have no first-hand knowledge of the facts in the case. I do know that Mian Iftikharuddin, an MLA, was spoken of by my Abbottabad acquaintance as the power behind the *Times*, and I observed that he got plenty of space in the paper without, however, being identified as the head man. Iftikharuddin has been identified by Professor Callard "as the most persistent and wide-ranging critic of the policy of successive governments . . . who took an extreme left-wing position."[33]

The *Times* was a big paper. A typical issue ran to twelve pages with seven columns to a page, and, since its column was wider than that of a standard United States daily (*The Detroit News*, for example), its pages were likewise wider. Such a daily takes considerable newsprint, and one statement to me was that, whereas the other newspapers might have trouble getting basic stock, the *Times* always had enough—from Czecho-Slovakia. I cannot attest to the veracity of this report; it is significant in that it typifies the way in which the *Times* was regarded in Abbottabad, but nonetheless read for all that.[34]

With substantial resources at its disposal, the *Times* printed news about every aspect of Pakistani life, including, in its Sunday magazine, reviews of books, radio programs and movies, in addition to cultural articles which were not necessarily Marxist in line or content. Moreover, it was generous in its "Letters to the Editor" column wherein the man in the street was given a chance to air his gripes and his opinions at greater length than John Q. Citizen can do in the United States.

My favorite letter was one sent to the *Times* by a Mr. Z. D. Qureshi who had earlier sent an inquiry to B. G. Brooks, professor of English at the University of Peshawar, about the meaning of Dylan Thomas' "Poem in October." Professor Brooks answered at length, and Mr. Qureshi sent his explication to the *Times* which printed it in full on May 13, 1957.

The *Times* struck me as a formidable institution. Literate and fairly well edited technically, it tended to blanket all of northern and western Pakistan, and, because the Karachi papers like *Dawn* arrived too late to be fresh and useful, except editorially, most people on the Frontier who read English language newspapers were driven to the *Times* in spite of its editorial policy.

As mild competition for the *Times*, there was the old Lahore *Civil and Military Gazette*, for which Rudyard Kipling once worked. The *Gazette* was attempting a revitalization program under a new editor in the first part of 1957. However, even those who wished it well and sought to encourage it (like myself) found themselves forced back to the *Times* for fuller coverage of internal stories of great importance —like the suspension of the West Pakistan assembly, for example.

What made the *Times* a hair shirt for Americans in Pakistan (and the former *Times* management will take this as the highest compliment) was its slanted foreign news and its party-line editorials, particularly on foreign affairs.[35] It had a field day during the Suez crisis, playing down the pro-Egyptian stand of the United States; it made capital out of any statement by an American in an official capacity in Pakistan, usually charging interference in the nation's affairs; it gleefully played up any misdeed of American personnel in respect to traffic accidents or financial chicanery, some instances of which are bound to happen whenever relatively large missions are established in an allied country; and it consistently attacked the whole system of American aid to Pakistan. Hungary? The *Times* used the unfortunate event as the basis for a serious heart-to-heart talk among comrades— another instance of that almost ritualized self-criticism which says, not that the USSR occupation or suppression of the rising was morally wrong, but that the boys in charge had not been running a good show: therefore the revolt.

As for internal affairs, the *Times*, as chief public enemy of the then current regime, did not have to slant its news; only the application of a selective principle was necessary. The conduct of Pakistani politicians made its task easy. All it had to do was to report *verbatim* the parliamentary debate in both the provincial and national assemblies, and it did so with almost full pages of transcript. Furthermore, the factual reporting of the numerous cases of corruption, involving Pakistani officials and the anticorruption police, spoke volumes. In these circumstances, editorials on domestic affairs were easy to write, and the result was that the *Times* gained some prestige as spokesman for all the justifiably disgruntled Pakistanis who were not and probably never will be communists. The prevailing mood of apathy and pessimism which I found to be characteristic of Pakistan's literate citizens may be traced in some degree to the daily news of its government—an observation which is not to be taken as an argument for the censorship of the press.

Despite the power of the *Times*, it was not strong enough to bring communism to Pakistan itself. The countervailing forces were Pakistan's strong feelings about Marxian atheism, the dominance of the landlords, the zamindars, the strong anticommunism of the bureaucracy and the armed forces (most of the leaders of which come from "good families"), the growing strength of the industrialists and the entrepreneurs, and the fatalist resignation of Pakistani peasants, which may be, it seems to me, in sharp significant contrast with the volatile political psychology of the urban masses.

All in all, I think there was little chance for an internal movement in Pakistan which could have resulted in the establishment of a communist state. I do believe, though, that in a free, honest, general election, the voters would have manifested the same kind of agrarian and labor protest which produced American Populism in the 1880's and the New Deal in the 1930's, but such a result would not necessarily have been communist inspired; it would have been a natural consequence of things as they were.

Of course, knowing what we know about communist tactics, it is a sure bet that the crypto-communists would have sought to mobilize such a national protest to their own ends. If, as I have noted, India should slip into communism, the osmotic pressures on Pakistan's society would be tremendous. There is, of course, the remote possibility of outright invasion of the Indo-Pakistan subcontinent by either the USSR or China or both, an eventuality which, in light of the threat of nuclear warfare and the very great problems both Asian giants are facing internally, is possible, but not probable. On the whole, I do not think that there is much chance of Pakistan's becoming part of the communist orbit in the near future.

But we can not rest comfortably with this conclusion. It is not enough that our friends and allies should be anticommunists or noncommunist. The ultimate question, to my mind, is whether the masses of Pakistanis and Indians are to have some chance of eating better, living better, and having a way of life which will permit them simple human dignity. Manifestly, communism, despite the great scientific and technical progress incarnate in Lunik, can not provide the dignity which comes from freedom. Its record of failure lies in the news about the execution of Imre Nagy and other Hungarian "rebels." Likewise the failure to grant the elementary recognition that a man must live is plain in most, if not all, the so-called Arab states—a fact which incandescent nationalism with all its momentary triumphs can not conceal for long. Nasser has given millions of Arabs the illusion of dignity, and the Iraquis are glowing in their revolutionary triumph, but the intoxication will wear off and the hangover will be painful. When this happens, millions of Muslims will be saying, "Glory is great, but what's in it for me?" There had better be an answer then, and a police state will not be a long term answer.

I still believe that the only course which can afford even a fighting chance for economic progress yoked with political liberty is the path of parliamentary democracy. My opinion is relevant to the question at hand because it would be easy to conclude from what I have written that democracy has failed in Pakistan. Many Pakistanis said as much, and I answered, *This is not true. Democracy has not as yet been tried in Pakistan.* The general election was *not* held. Given the opportunity so richly promised in the Pakistan constitution, the nation could have produced a government which would have made significant progress. I do not blame the military for what happened; the politicians who were afraid of democracy are responsible.

This conclusion was documented by a front-page editorial in the special Republic Day issue of the *Star* (March 23, 1957) a weekly published in Lahore. It was not a left-wing journal. Its political orientation was made clear by a box on the front page which called for support of the coalition government (headed at that time by Premier Suhrawardy) and for general elections before Republic Day of 1958.

The editorial itself was something more than a party pronouncement; it is the best summary I have read of the prevailing point of view held by the educated community in Pakistan at that time. It will illustrate much of what has been said in this chapter so far. When I first read it in Pakistan, it moved me, and it moves me still. It was written by the editor, Aziz Beg. Captioned "God Save Pakistan," it is given here in full:

> This is the second anniversary of the Republic Day. But how many realise the sanctity and significance of this day? West Pakistan's warring politicians and their servile stooges have made a mockery of democracy and thrown all consitutional proprieties to the dogs. In the circumstances, President Mirza had perhaps no option save to take over the administration of the province in the hope that this respite might create in them a saner mood and impart some sight to their failing vision.
>
> But many of our readers may not like to share our optimistic note, as the Common Man in Pakistan has come to believe that it is a case of political myopia! How can we expect them to show foresight when they seem to have lost even sight? Perhaps the Common Man is right, for we see today a situation which only the enemies of Pakistan would love to create. They have proved that the real enemies of Pakistan are not without but within the country. What we see today is the ghastly spectacle of a people who fought for freedom, who won freedom and who are prepared to stake their all to guard their freedom, but who have been betrayed by the very men who were loudest in their professions of allegiance to the spirit that created Pakistan. Our eyes can see today the very hands that reared the mansion of Pakistan and prayed in mosques for the glory of Islam and the greatness of Pakistan, digging the grave of eighty million children who inhabit this holy homeland.
>
> We say so because every member of an elected house who agrees to sell his conscience for the advantage of an import license or a permit is guilty of shameful betrayal to the ideal which should determine his political conduct. Every M.L.A. who shifts his loyalty at the sight of the slightest stir in the political whirlpool is an evil agent, out to destroy the fabric of political stability. Every act of corruption committed by a public man is a bullet in the heart of Pakistan. Every minister, who refuses to resign in spite of being publicly condemned, exposed and even abused is like a monster who will wreck the chair before abdicating it. Every member of a political party who is opposing One Unit after supporting it is reviving the demon of provincialism. But this time, we assure them, the demon will devour all those who come within its ominous orbit.

218

All this is happening and being justified in the name of freedom and democracy, for the sake of Islam and Pakistan. But, little do they realise that the Common Man is not interested in sermons but service, not in promises but performance, not in declarations but deeds. He has been fed too long on vain hopes and vain dreams.

Let this Republic Day remind us of the problems and pitfalls we face today. Let it remind us of empty stomachs, shivering bodies and bare, blistered feet that belong to millions and millions of Pakistanis. Let it remind us of poor parents who have no means to educate their growing children. Let it remind us of the sick, the ailing and the diseased who cannot afford to pay the fee of a doctor or buy a medicine. Let it remind us of those brave but starving sons of the soil who love the land we call Pakistan, but have no land to cultviate. Let it remind us of our enemies across the border who have never concealed their designs to destroy Pakistan. Let it remind us of Kashmir, without which Pakistan is like a man without a head and a house without a roof. And, let it remind us of those office-hungry, power-thirsty, intrigue-ridden and inflated politicians who should be cut down to size before they cut us to pieces.

The Road to Dictatorship: the Last Mile

As a result of the forces summarized in the *Star* editorial, events in Pakistan culminated in the establishment of a dictatorship (however benevolent), headed by General Mohammed Ayub Khan and supported by the armed forces.

In July 1958, a conference of political party leaders presided over by Prime Minister Noon postponed the general election promised for November 1958 to February 1959. Nobody was surprised.[36]

In September 1958, a more hopeful event was the visit of Prime Minister Noon to New Delhi for two days of talks with Prime Minister Nehru. This trip was hailed by American observers as a promising augury for the improvement of relations between two nations whom we fervently desire to be friends. Before going to New Delhi, Noon declared that he would never lead his country to war against India, and, after he got there, the two chief ministers of state managed to settle the troubled question of the undemarcated boundaries of East Pakistan and India which had led to ominous shooting affrays. Noon's policy in respect to India may or may not have been a factor in the sequence of events which led to military dictatorship, but the mission is too important an event to omit.[37]

On September 25, 1958, the deputy minister of the East Pakistan provincial assembly, Syed Zahid Ali, died as the result of injuries inflicted on him by opposition members in the legislative chamber itself. This murder and the postponement of the general election led the *Manchester Guardian* to print an editorial in which it was pointed out that these two occurrences were evidences of parliamentary government in degeneration and that the disease in Pakistan was "social even more than political."[38]

On October 8, 1958, President Iskander Mirza, the former general, put Pakistan under martial law and abolished the existing government. He outlawed political parties; annulled the constitution; dissolved the central and provincial governments; and abolished the national and provincial assemblies. At the same time, he pledged Pakistan to honor all international commitments; that is, in essence, to continue the nation's pro-Western foreign policy.

Mirza named General Mohammed Ayub Khan, commander-in-chief of the Pakistan army, as chief administrator of martial law and placed all armed forces under him. There were no disturbances.

In justification for his act, Mirza said that the constitution of March 23, 1956 had proved unworkable, though, in fact, it had not really been tried, and he promised a new constitution better suited to the genius of the Muslim people. He also cited corruption, a ruthless struggle for political power, the exploitation of the masses, and the prostitution of Islam for political ends as other reasons for his decision.

A day later, Otober 9, 1958, in a joint interview with Elie Abel, New York *Times* correspondent, the following points were made by President Mirza and General Khan: that the authority for the takeover was revolution; that there was no sanction in law or the constitution, only Mirza's conscience; that it was a joint decision with General Khan for which Mirza had taken the initiative; that General Khan had urged Mirza to take such steps in private conversations over the preceding year in order to save Pakistan from misrule by corrupt politicians; and that Khan had told Mirza that if he, the president, did not take action, the army would be forced to.

Both leaders insisted that Pakistan wanted good relations with India, provided that outstanding questions were settled in accordance with international agreements. General Khan added that, if there was war with India, it would be of India's making.

When questioned about the promise of elections in February 1959, Mirza said, "It was clearly unrealistic to expect healthy democracy on a Western pattern in a country where only 16 per cent of the population could read and write. Democracy without education is hypocrisy without limitation."

Mirza defined his aims: to establish order in Pakistan's chaotic economy; to make the country self-sufficient in respect to food; and to crack down on black-market hoarders and bribe-taking civil servants. He advised people guilty of malpractice to get out of the country, and he singled out one politician, Maulana Bashani, leader of the National Awami Party, accusing him of high treason for the interesting reason that Bhashani had gone to Cairo and made "direct contact" with Nasser.

The first reports indicated that the Mirza-Khan takeover was a success. There was no opposition. The ensuing crackdown on malefactors, public and private, was, apparently, popular with the man in the street and, hardly to my surprise in the light of the Abbottabad community's reaction to Mirza's earlier suspension of the West Pakistan assembly and the endemic suspicion of and contempt for politicians, Pakistani public opinion seemed to be content with the new regime, on the surface, at least. Very probably many Pakistanis said, "Good riddance."[39]

Then (to complete the journey to dictatorship) on October 27, 1958, President Mirza resigned and handed over the presidency and all powers to General Ayub Khan. The chief reason given was that any semblance of dual control was likely to hamper the effectiveness of the new government. An interesting sidelight is that an Indian cartoon, reprinted in the *New York Times,* predicted this event by showing Mirza as a ventriloquist's dummy seated on General Khan's knee. The Indians took no great satisfaction in what was happening in Pakistan, some of them seeing foreboding parallels between the current Indian situation and the Pakistani situation before the Mirza-Khan coup.[40]

Now, what of the future? The important fact is not so much that a general is in charge but that the Armed Forces are in charge. I have paid my respects to the military services: I have said that the forces, taken altogether, constitute the most effective social mechanism in Pakistan. We may well expect that the day-to-day administration of Pakistan will be more efficient and less corrupt. However, running a country is quite a different task from running an army. It will take more than honesty, patriotism, devotion to Islam, and a professional sense of duty. The chief problems of Pakistan are social and economic. Among the gravest are the compelling need to give the peasant a better break and to save the land itself from erosion, salination, and the like. To solve these problems, the vested interests of the great landowners must be challenged. It is a question whether the generals, conservative by virtue of family origin, education, and professional training, will have the imagination, the knowledge, or the will to effect the major changes needed to make Pakistan a truly going nation. Yet, one of the first acts of President Ayub Khan was to direct the Land Reform Commission to prepare a comprehensive land-reform plan. At least, this is a recognition of the basic problem and a happy sign.[41]

One phase of the troubled drama of Pakistan's history closed with the banishment of President-General Iskander Mirza to England, leaving General Ayub Khan in complete control. But a big question now arises: Is General Khan the leader or the prisoner of the armed forces?[42]

Whatever the answer to this question will be, it is pleasant to record that General Ayub got off to a good start. He made a favorable impression on two such different—and experienced—American visitors as Ernest K. Lindley and Averill Harriman, neither of whom may be charged with any fondness for dictators.[43] Moreover, he has elicited favorable editorial comment from the highly respected *Manchester Guardian Weekly*. (June 18, 1959, pp. 8–9) This editorial is a good summary of Ayub's philosophy and intentions, and it provides some basis for judgment of the political future of Pakistan; therefore, I quote it in full.

On Pakistan Day in March the President, General Ayub Khan, expressed his belief that "the introduction of a representative form of government in due course is vital to enable us to achieve our destiny." He has spoken in similar vein on other occasions, since the early days of his seizure of power, and from time to time he has promised that a commission of "the best brains in the country" shall prepare a constitution. This will be submitted to referendum by indirect vote and, he hopes come into force within two years. But he has also been insistent that the constitution which emerges must be nothing like the previous one, which was so disgracefully used: "Let me make it quite plain that the bulk of our population in villages as well as in town get the creeps when there is any mention of the politicians coming back into power again."

That is the sort of thing that any military dictator might say, but there is good reason in Pakistan why it is very likely true. President Ayub wants first to push through his programme of reforms that the old politicians should have tackled—agrarian, legal, educational, administrative—and even the sternest opponents of military rule must agree that he is keeping his word so far. When the new constitution is drawn up he wants the President to remain out of reach of the politicians. As he said early in December: "The people should be given the right to elect a President either by universal suffrage, or through electoral colleges. But once the President is elected, he must be given fairly wide powers to run the affairs of the country, so that there is no leg-pulling by the legislatures every day." The legislatures, in fact, should stick to legislating, and not interfere in administration.

Now, for the first time, President Ayub has made a move to associate the governed with government. Plans have been announced for the setting up of "basic democracies"—in four tiers, with village panchayats (or councils) at the lowest level. Each tier will have elected and nominated members, and there will be panchayat representatives on each. If the forthcoming constitution should provide for indirect election, it is stated, the panchayats may form the electoral colleges. This fits in with President Ayub's well-known belief (not borne out in other states) that predominantly illiterate electorates cannot be expected to make responsible decisions. The "basic democracies" are to take part in development schemes and police functions. Ironically, this is just the sort of arrangement that Mahatma Ghandi thought more suitable for Indian conditions than Western-style democracy. Some of the strictest of his followers still recommend it. But whereas representative democracy as we know it in the West has not failed in India, it has in Pakistan; and it will be interesting to see whether it can strike grass-roots from the bottom up, since it did not grow downwards from the top. It is at any rate a worth-while attempt, and while it will not satisfy the President of the Karachi Bar Association and other brave critics of the dictatorship, it is much better than a continuation of the gap between Government and people which has existed, in different forms, since Pakistan became a state.

I have already registered my dissent against the proposition that democracy has failed in Pakistan. My view is that the much maligned constitution of 1956 never was given a chance to go into full operation on the basis of a general election in which full adult suffrage was exercised. Still, the views expressed by General Ayub do afford some hope that Pakistan may, in the future, establish some form of representative government.

Chapter Nine

An Indian Interlude

We spent some six weeks in India, from Christmas 1956 to the middle of February 1957, on our leisurely way to an educational conference held in East Pakistan's capital, Dacca. We were able to enjoy this Indian interlude because the college at Abbottabad closed down for the winter about December 20 and did not re-open until March 1.

It would be presumptuous to write anything at all about India but for two factors: the first is that this trip was sandwiched between two periods of living in Pakistan and it gave us perspective to the Pakistani way of life; the second is that I had opportunity to face some Indian audiences, and what happened in those situations may prove helpful for Americans who seek to understand that pivotal nation.

We will dispose of the tourist aspects of this interlude briefly. We spent a month in New Delhi at the Janpath Hotel, constructed by the government for the UNESCO conference and then maintained as a public hostelry for official, semi-official, and non-official visitors. It was, by the way, the best hotel in our Indian experience. Then we did the usual tourist circuit in northern India: Agra and the Taj Mahal; the famous Red City of Fatehpur Sikri, not far from Agra; Lucknow with its carefully preserved memories of the Mutiny; Banaras, the holy city of the Hindus; Patna; Calcutta; and Darjeeling, the storied hill station, a center of the tea industry and the home of Tensing of Everest fame.

Aside from the pleasures of shopping at the fascinating government handicrafts center and at other impressive private establishments, of sightseeing, and of a reverent pilgrimage to Ghandi's simple monument, the Delhi sojourn was notable for several quite different matters.

We very soon began to feel like long-time citizens of this cosmopolitan city. This was an interesting psychological reaction, certainly not warranted by the length of our stay, but nonetheless pleasant. What accounted for it was a daily reading of the Delhi newspapers, the interest taken in us by the hotel staff, and the similarity of the city's patterns to those we had experienced in Karachi and Lahore (though Delhi is better planned and better administered than either). We quickly achieved a sense of familiarity (justified or not) with what was on the minds of the Indians—which turned out to be quite like the things on the minds of the citizens of New York, Washington, or Detroit: civic problems, sports (particularly a national tennis tournament), the world of arts and letters, the coming elections, the domestic economy, international affairs, and, above all, the question of Kashmir, then nearly ready for debate in the UN assembly.

Another enlightening and absorbing pastime was watching the rapid flow of guests through the hotel dining room: the personnel of a Russian circus then playing in Delhi; members of a Russian mission putting on a film festival in the capital; delegates to an international medical convention including some top-flight American doctors and some very sharp-looking representatives from Red China who, in manners and appearance, at least, made their Russian allies look like country cousins; members of the entourage of the Dalai Lama of Tibet, who was making an important state visit to India; and a mixed bag of Americans like ourselves—tourists, Fulbrighters, ICA technicians, or members of cultural missions of one sort or another. After a week or so, we had a kind of seniority in the dining room where we always ate at the same table with the same waiters and were made to feel at home. Moreover, as the head waiter came to know us, it was a rare day on which he did not point out to us an important Indian minister or political figure at lunch or dinner.

The Russians in New Delhi

Since the Russians are obviously making a big play for India, some comment on the Russian circus and the film festival is in order. The circus personnel, our daily companions in the dining room, struck us as being patently citified peasants. They spent most of their free time shopping for (or examining) consumer goods in Connaught Circle, Delhi's mercantile center. As for their professional performance, it was no better than bush league, on a par with the small outfits which used to travel the small-city route in the United States in the early part of the twentieth century. I think it was not highly rated by the Indians. They were polite, but even the ardent party-liners in the audience could not generate more than mild enthusianm for the show; I am making due allowance for the fact that, in keeping with traditional mores, Indians do not customarily applaud any more than Pakistanis do, and that is not much.

The jugglers got through their acts without dropping anything, but just barely. The trapeze performers did not fumble any of their team mates, but it was usually a close thing. Altogether the performers lacked the precision and apparently careless grace which were taken for granted in the great Ringling and Barnum and Bailey shows. Knowing how hard the Russians work on their Olympic teams, their ballets, and other show pieces for the outside world, I was surprised that the Comrade-Commissar for Circuses let this one out of the country. I do not propose to criticize the arts (and the circus is an art form) from the ideological point of view; that is a Russian principle. And so I will modify this adverse review by reporting that the one clown, whose function was to tie the acts together by a series of running gags, was the best thing in the show. He was a genuine comic.

There was some unintentional humor, too. Both at the circus itself and at the hotel, we were brought to realize that saxophone players are brothers the world over, in clothes, sophistication, and manners, and it is ironic that the Russians should officially condemn jazz while the Russian circus band of five pieces ground out music which was 100 per cent American in origin and, in its riffs and arrangements, was strongly reminiscent of stock jazz recordings of the Twenties as imitated today by high school boys.

The Russian movie people were more sophisticated, but, nevertheless, their leading lady, a blonde star well known in the Soviet Union, looked like an effective caricature of Marilyn Monroe. The movie festival ran for about a week. We read the press commentary carefully, and we went to see the Russian production of *Twelfth Night*. As for the reviews, it was clear that Indian critics were not taken in by the overt propaganda of the Russian films. They were carefully polite, but certainly not particularly impressed. The *Twelfth Night* was a refreshing surprise. The technicolor was good, the costumes charming, the direction adequate to good, most of the scenes were filmed outdoors in lovely settings, the lines were read intelligently, and Malvolio was first-rate. This straightforward presentation of a classic was marred by the short film which preceded it—a grossly sentimental presentation of a combined school and TB sanitarium which was designed to show how kind Mother Russia is to all her children.

Mixed Grill

Before coming to grips with the central concern of this chapter, American-Indian personal relations, I can not resist commenting on four quite unrelated topics: Christmas at the Janpath; the Indian concern for tourism; the Pakistani attitude towards the Taj Mahal; and the sari makers of Banaras.

On Christmas Eve, a group of carolers appeared at the Janpath. Most of them were Christians of Indian origin, and never in our lives have we heard a more variegated group sing *Silent Night*. They differed in sex, age, costume, and ethnic background. There were men and women, young and old, in saris and dhotis, in European attire, and in a mixture of both European and Indian clothes. It would have touched the heart of Old Scrooge himself. On Christmas Day, the Janpath went all out to serve the most traditional of traditional English Christmas dinners. This was one celebration of the birth of the Prince of Peace which we will never forget.

Indian efforts to encourage tourism first became apparent to us at Palam Airport, New Delhi, in the courtesy of the customs officials and in the attention given us by the official government tourist aid. This initial impression was strengthened when a young lady in the Delhi government tourist headquarters gave us, without hesitation, a complete set of quite expensive and most imaginative travel posters, simply because we expressed admiration for one of the set. The policy was demonstrated beyond doubt when we were interviewed in Banaras by a polite and bright young man who was conducting a survey of tourist opinion for his government quite in the manner of our own sociologists. In the course of our conversation with him, it developed that the Indian government was proposing to send cooks abroad for training in Western cookery for the benefit of future tourists, but to—of all places—England! It should be evident all through this book that we came back from that year abroad with respect, admiration, and affection (in varying degrees) for the British whom we met in India and Pakistan (not to speak of our gratitude for the handsome hospitality accorded us by the British colony in Hong Kong), and, therefore, I hope they will forgive me for saying that the worst cultural legacy the British Raj left behind was its culinary tradition. We urged our Indian researcher to recommend that India send its students of cookery to some other European country.

I will spare the reader any rhapsodic appreciation of the Taj Mahal. What may be a fresher and more interesting point is the reaction of our Pakistani friends to the fact that we had *seen* it. They thought of the Taj as a personal possession, as a Muslim achievement. Their response to it and to the love story which it incarnates was another piece of evidence showing how deeply romantic they are—something which we had seen earlier in their kindred response to such movies as *The Last Time I Saw Paris* and to Pakistani movies. Before we left for India, we were ordered to see the Taj by moonlight, and the first question asked upon our return was: "Did you see the Taj by moonlight?" Unfortunately, it was impossible to arrange our visit to Agra to coincide with a full moon, and so, having been made uncomfortably aware of this lunar fixation, we did the next best thing: we rose very early in the morning and saw the Taj at the breaking of the dawn. Very few (relatively) can make this claim. Therefore, armed with the knowledge of this morning pilgrimage, we took the offensive, in the face of the implied reproaches of our friends because we had not seen their beloved symbol at its best, reproaches which were, perhaps, a form of compensation to make up for the fact that they had not seen it and probably never would. However, this stratagem was at best regarded as an unsatisfactory substitute for moonglow, and we were made to feel that we really had not seen the Taj at all.

The spectacle of Banaras—with its myriad temples and burning ghats—literally beggars description. A careful study of it would probably throw more light on the inner recesses of the Indian psyche than any other comparable enterprise. Furthermore, Banaras dramatizes the conflict between Hindu and Muslim religious values and demonstrates why that conflict is inevitable. We could not cope with Banaras at all in its spiritual aspects; it is simply overwhelming. However, on a more mundane level, we found that even a standard tourist visit to one of the Banaras sari-making establishments was a most impressive experience. There the age-old traditions are maintained in a genuine way. It is wonderful to see how intricate designs are translated by hand into silken artifacts of great beauty on looms which have nothing to do with our machine age. In the process one sees that the traditional skills are being handed down from the middle-aged master to the younger journeyman and to the youngest apprentice, lads who are not even in their 'teens. Good honest hand craftsmanship has a hard time surviving in this era of mass production, but it is pleasant to think that the Banaras sari (and its Dacca counterpart) will, very probably, be in demand as long as women and men love beauty in fabrics.

Indians and Americans

When we arrived in India, we had reason to suspect that we would find some evidence of latent or overt hostility. Indians did not (and do not) approve of our foreign policy, particularly in respect to the admission of Red China to the UN. They did not like our close relations with Pakistan nor our support of Pakistan's position in respect to Kashmir, then just on the point of coming up for debate in UN, and they particularly resented (as they still do) our military aid to Pakistan. They felt that, despite our action at the time of the Suez crisis in support of Egypt, we were still lined up with the old imperialist powers, France and England. They did not like what appeared to be firm support of Portugal in respect to Goa. In general, Indians were opposed to massive retaliation, brinksmanship, nuclear-bomb-brandishing, and all the ideas of John Foster Dulles. Pursuing a neutralist course, they were, nevertheless, more sympathetic *emotionally* to the Russians and the Chinese than they were to Americans for the primary reason that they were suspicious of the West and all its works. History has made them so. The point here is not whether the Indians were right or wrong in these attitudes; it is rather a simple summary statement of the state of mind we thought we would encounter.

Moreover, we were Americans coming from Pakistan in what could be regarded as a semi-official position, and we thought we might possibly be suspect as willing workers for an "enemy" state. As tourists, we guessed that these considerations might not mean much on the surface; after all, nearly every country wants to treat tourists decently because it is good business to do so. But, insofar as any closer relations with Indians could be attained, the factors cited, we thought, were very likely to come into play. In sum, we expected that anything but formal contact with Indians was likely to be difficult or unpleasant and that, quite possibly, we might encounter resentment or dislike in public.

It did not turn out that way. I have already recounted the evidence of the desire of the Indian government to treat tourists well, and, to cite one cogent example of unofficial and non-commercial friendliness, at the Red City of Fatehpur Sikri we met whole busloads of Indian school boys and girls from Bombay whose eager warmth and cordiality are still memorable. They even wanted autographs!

But more compelling than these manifestations was what happened at the Janpath itself. We became acquainted with one of the assistant managers. He learned that I was a Fulbright professor from Pakistan. He asked whether he might introduce us to a friend of his, a lecturer in English at S.N. Das Gupta College, which prepares students for various university examinations and competitive examinations for the civil services and the armed forces. The college was founded in Lahore in 1931, and shifted to Delhi after partition. Of course, we were happy to meet the friend of our friend. We invited both young men to tea. They came, and it was a very pleasant occasion. The lecturer then invited me to speak at his college on American literature, and I did so.

Before I touch on that lecture and its context, I wish to comment on certain aspects of the conversations we had with these two Indians. In the first place, their attitude toward Pakistan was hardly what we had expected. They were largely uninterested in their neighbor state. It made little difference to them that I was teaching in a Pakistani college. Indeed, I got the impression from them and others in India that they think a great deal less about Pakistan than the Pakistanis do about India. By and large, Indians tend to view Pakistan condescendingly and contemptuously. Contrariwise, the Pakistanis seem to be highly conscious of India, and not only because of Kashmir. I believe that the Pakistanis have an inferiority complex in respect to "Bharat," a complex which produces all the usual angry and emotional reactions characteristic of all such complexes.

It ought to be made clear, however, that no Pakistani of our acquaintance seemed to think that we had in any way been "disloyal" in spending our vacation in India; in view of the strong feelings against Hindus, expressed by some of our Abbottabad friends, this point is worth making. Whatever they felt about Indians, they had nostalgic sentiments for many places in India, specifically Lucknow and Allahabad, and they seemed to be pleased for us and, perhaps, a little envious that we should be making the trip. On the way back from Dacca on a Pakistani plane, the purser took particular pains to announce that we were passing over Lucknow, renowned for the quality of its Urdu, and every adult Pakistani on the plane went to a window to see what he could of that city. For a moment there was an atmosphere of hushed reverence. Likewise, we also met Indians who had similar feelings of nostalgia for certain places in Pakistan, especially Lahore, and it came as something of a shock when, after hearing that we came from Abbottabad, one young Hindu in Delhi quietly told us that his family used to own the Palace Hotel there, our home.

To come back to our conversations at the Janpath, the two Indian gentlemen did not seem to be very curious about the United States, in which respect they were like many of our Pakistani acquaintances. We asked a great many questions about India, but the corresponding questions were not raised, nor did they seek to discuss foreign policy or Kashmir, possibly out of courtesy. They talked about literature, Delhi, and Indian politics, and they talked about these very freely and with evident enjoyment. We were especially interested in what they had to say on the latter point. A general election was imminent, the Indian press was full of campaign activity, and, in these face-to-face conversations, we were able to check and confirm, in part, what we had learned from the papers. Our most important conclusions were that the political process in India was vital and meaningful and that the Congress Party was in trouble.

As for the lecture at S.N. Gupta College, the most significant aspects of that function were these: it was conducted with the same kind of formal punctilio which we had become accustomed to in Pakistan; the staff and student body seemed to be grateful that we had come, though we were just as grateful for the invitation. The audience, save for the faculty, was composed largely of young girls, and, after having lived some months in the Purdah Belt, it was pleasant to see them enjoying a degree of social and intellectual freedom which was denied to most of their Pakistani sisters. The girls, most appealing in their saris, seemed very young and frail as compared to American girls. In the question period, it developed that Indian students of literature were just as much interested in "criticism" as were their Pakistani counterparts.

Encouraged by these first contacts with Indians on other than purely tourist terms, and growing tired of the routine of sight-seeing, I went to the United States Information Service center on our arrival in Calcutta and volunteered my services. By pure accident, the Cultural Affairs officer of USIS was a former English instructor at my American university and an old friend. He was in the process of organizing a seminar on "The United States in Mid-Twentieth Century" to which were invited Indian politicians, academicians, publishers and editors, labor leaders, and business men. The seminar was composed of a number of panel discussions of such subjects as "The Continuing Social Revolution," "Mass Education and Intellectual Values," "The Changing Role of Government," "The Foundations of American Foreign Policy," "The New Economic Synthesis," and "The Role of the Intellectual in an Industrial Democracy." The format of the panels was first a talk by one of the panel members, then a discussion of the issues raised in the opening speech by the other panelists, and then questions to the panel from the audience. Among the most notable of the American participants were Professor Foster Rhea Dulles of Ohio State University, Professor Fowler Harper of the Yale College of Law, and Mr. Robert L. Crowell, president of the Crowell Publishing Company and a well known Thoreau enthusiast. I became an added starter on two of these panels.

It is difficult to assess the worth of this enterprise. The Indian guests raised some shrewd and searching questions, but they seemed to be "under wraps" to some degree, perhaps out of politeness, and I had the impression that they were not really speaking their minds nor asking the tough questions they really wanted to deal with— excepting the Kashmir issue.

The highlight of the four-day session, in my opinion, was the performance of Professor Dulles who had to carry the brunt of Indian questioning of our foreign policy. He happens to be somewhat distantly related to John Foster Dulles. In the course of his opening speech, he made certain things very clear: that in some important matters he did not agree with his kinsman and that he understood India's neutralist position and the reasons for it. Then, in a quiet manner and with solid knowledge, he made an effective defense of the broad outlines of American foreign policy, especially since World War II, contrasting it sharply with Soviet policy in the same years. In the question period he was challenged in respect to the American position on Kashmir, and with good humor, dignity, and firmness, he explained to the Indian audience what America and a good part of the outside world thought about that burning question. He managed to do this apparently without offending the sensibilities of his audience, though, of course, they were not exactly converted. Here and elsewhere in India, Professor Dulles was in a tough spot, but he acquitted himself nobly.

I judge that the audience was intrigued by the spectacle of an American professor under semi-State Department auspices taking issue with some of that department's policies, and thereby making his defense of our basic positions all the more effective. As I have remarked to my Pakistani friends, apropos of comparable circumstances, can anybody imagine an official or semi-official Russian cultural ambassador taking issue with *any* of his country's policies? There is a moral here, but I will not labor it.

At the close of this seminar, the delegation from the University of Patna in Bihar State invited me to come to their institution for some lectures, probably because I had tried to face up honestly to the question of McCarthyism in one of the panel discussions. This Patna expedition was surely the highlight of our Indian interlude. The university, we found, was a highly sophisticated community— a fact which did not prevent the Indian students from celebrating the festival of the Goddess of Learning, Saraswati Puja, with ritual processions through the streets, ending with the commitment of statues of the Goddess to the waters of Mother Ganga, the sacred Ganges. This delightfully "pagan" ceremony was, on the one hand, a traditional religious observance; on the other, it may have been a form of insurance against flunking examinations, which are just as important to the careers of Indian students as they are to Pakistani students inasmuch as both countries have the same kind of university systems.

The Patna program included a lecture on Jonathan Swift, a lecture on American literature, an open discussion of literature in America with another Fulbrighter and the head of the Patna University department of English, a session with the students' United Nations Association, and trips to two neighboring institutions, Jain and

Maharajah colleges. All of these functions were accompanied by ritual teas and receptions exactly like those we had been given on the other side of the border.

Some of these functions can be disposed of quickly. The Swift lecture was carefully listened to by both men and women students because Swift was in the sacred curriculum and because it was novel to have an American lecture on him. The American literature lecture was not so new in content to the Patna audience because this university prided itself on being more advanced than other Indian universities in that it required a paper or two on American literature. The discussion with the English department head became a test of the visiting Elks, and it had its points of interest. The faculty attended in a body, and, considering the conflict in timing with the great religious festival, the students were there in fair numbers. Our host elected to discuss the tragic spirit in America. It was a rather peculiar choice because he had not read much American literature, having received his training at Cambridge, England. The discussion became a little like a doctor's oral examination in reverse in that the two American examinees knew a good deal more about the subject than the Indian examiner. At any rate my American colleague and I were able to exploit the resources provided for us by Hawthorne, Melville, E. A. Robinson, Maxwell Anderson, Arthur Miller, Eugene O'Neill, and others. We enjoyed the give-and-take, and, at the ceremonial tea which followed, we were given grounds for believing that the faculty as a whole had also had a good time.

The meeting of the United Nations Association was a very lively affair. It was made so by the high spirits, *joie de vivre*, wit, and humor of the Indian students who, in this context, seemed to be much more vivacious and sophisticated than my boys back in Abbottabad. They wanted to hear about student life in the United States, and I gave it to them off the cuff—getting in a few licks about the dignity of labor in the process.

As pleasant as this Patna experience was, it was less consequential in respect to the central concern of this chapter, Indo-American personal relations, than three other events which took place in the neighborhood of Patna. These were appearances before audiences at Jain and Maharajah colleges and a picnic which turned into a lecture. In these three situations, we felt that we were closer to the heart of India than we had been in Patna. After all, though profoundly Indian, our academic hosts at the university were, almost without exception, worldly gentlemen educated in the Western humanistic tradition.

Academically, at least, we spoke the same language. We were not strange to them, for they were accustomed to Englishmen and Americans. The Patna setting did not seem particularly strange or different to us. But this was not so in the other three places.

Jain College was a short rail trip from Patna. Surely, we were not the first European or American couple to appear there, but the intensity of response to our presence produced the impression in us that we were visitors from another planet. It can only be described as startling and heart-warming. We were made to feel that we had conferred a great favor on all concerned by the mere act of coming to the campus. The fervor of the reception far exceeded the requirements of courtesy to foreign guests. It was as if we had received the physical impact of an electrical current of friendliness flowing out of the hearts of the entire college community. Schmaltz? Sentimentality? Perhaps so, but we were not prepared for it, we were not looking for it, and it happened. This condition of happy tension reached its peak when, for a tour of the campus, my wife was gallantly handed into a rickshaw by her escort, a young faculty man, who then sat beside her. Their vehicle followed the one in which I was seated with our official host for the day, a lecturer in political science who had attended the Calcutta seminar. As we drove off, there was an explosion of delighted laughter and applause from the whole student body. I do not know how to account for this reaction. The mere fact that my wife's escort was a young bachelor may have had something to do with it, but not enough to explain it completely. Could it be that this body of Indians still remembered memsahibs of the Kipling type who would not have ridden with an Indian in a rickshaw?

As for the total reaction to our visit, these factors may help to make it understandable: both Jain and Maharajah are country colleges, more isolated from the main stream of world life than the more urbane Patna University community; foreign visitors were, evidently, rare; and the people themselves were less armored by sophistication and more spontaneous (and genuine?) than city folk. We were told that most of them came from villages, that they were poor, and that they were eager for education. There was a quality of direct simplicity in them which was most attractive. Many of my students in Abbottabad had this quality too, but their manners, their whole cultural conditioned responses to social relations with strangers were more formal, and, of course, they were less accustomed to the presence of women. Both Jain and Maharajah colleges were coeducational.

235

The program of the day was routine in outline except for one novelty which will be described later: tea with the principal, a tour of the campus, a sidetrip to the nearby Maharajah College, lunch with the lecturer in political science and his housemates, a speech in the afternoon, more tea, and departure for Patna.

The novelty was that our official host had earlier asked me to speak on the political process in America from precinct to presidency. I was sceptical of this subject. Was that what the students really wanted? Did he set the subject because he happened to be a political scientist?

He insisted. He understood that I had had some experience in this area—which was true. I had been twice a candidate for the Common Council of the city of Detroit; had served as precinct delegate in the Democratic Party; had worked on various party committees; and both my wife and I had been active in the 1952 Stevenson campaign— she as executive secretary of the Detroit Volunteers for Adlai. I did not deny all this, but I still wanted to know why this subject would be of interest to the Jain people. What about American or English literature?

Nothing shook him. He wanted American politics, the more explicit the better. And, remembering that the Indians were just then on the verge of their second grand election, I agreed.

That afternoon I spoke to the college community—about four or five hundred—for two hours in the open air. I talked about the precinct structure and about struggles for control of precinct organizations, about county, state, and national party conventions, about the hard political facts of life which go to make up "availability" (the Congress Party knows all about this). I spoke about the two Democratic parties, south and north; about the two Republican parties, the right wing and the Eisenhower wing; about the 1956 election and its significance; and about the 1960 election, discussing the issues and the potential candidates in both parties.

I never had a more attentive audience. They listened with great concentration, and, in the question period, they asked sharp and discerning questions. We could hardly get away. They wanted more, and the meeting finally broke up only because tea was a ritual which could not be omitted and because we had to catch a train back to Patna. It was an amazing experience.

Would the students of any one of the hundreds of small denominational colleges in the United States listen to a detailed account of internal Indian politics for two hours on a hot day, and clamor for more? I wonder.

The sidetrip to Maharajah College was quite different. My Jain host had generously conceded a small part of our time to his neighbor institution, but he nevertheless rode herd on us pretty closely. The result was that there was no time for any formal lecture or speech, and so I volunteered to face questions fired by the audience, consisting of the whole college packed into a hall. I made one reservation: since I was at that time a guest of India and since I had been and would be again a guest of Pakistan, I regretted that I could not decently discuss the Kashmir question. I expected some disapproval of this statement. On the contrary, it was greeted with loud applause.

This was a good beginning, but I did not get off easily. The questions came thick and fast, and, for the first time in India, I sensed hostility in the person of one questioner. The questions were tough enough, and their very phrasing expressed disapproval, but only in this one instance did the asker project personal hostility. I will dispose of the main issues raised from the audience and then come back to this case.

As I had expected all along, the first big question was about segregation in the United States. I dealt with it as I had done in Pakistan: not glossing over the facts or attempting to explain them away; stressing the force of the Supreme Court decision; pointing to the progress made in such places as St. Louis, Missouri and Louisville; describing conditions in Detroit in terms of my own experience; and the like. Then I made the point which I made earlier in this book. Granting that an evil in one country does not excuse that same evil in another, I drew a parallel between our problem in the United States and the Indian caste problem. India has abolished caste distinctions by law under its constitution. How long, I asked, will it take before these caste distinctions will disappear in practice? I suggested that by the time the Negro in America is wholly integrated into American life, caste will still exist in India because the power of religious and social custom is so great. And I repeated a plea which also has been made before in this book: let us not have a double standard of morality in the matter of color and race relations—one for India and another one for the United States.[1]

What was the reaction of that audience to this line of argument? Applause! The case would have been harder to argue after Little Rock, and I do not envy Americans abroad today who must face up to that symbol.

Next big question: What about the admission of Red China to UN? Answer in summary: The Indians think we are wrong on this one; conversely, a great many Americans think that India is wrong in its neutralist policy. Conclusion: disagreement on such issues does not necessarily make India the enemy of the United States nor the United States the enemy of India. We can like and respect one another without total agreement in respect to foreign policy.

Next question: What about our military aid to Pakistan? Answer: the United States will not tolerate the use of American military aid for aggressive purposes, and a good many Pakistanis think that the United States is giving too much aid to India.

Finally, we came to the question which seemed to be asked with hostile intent: *Is the United States really a peace-loving nation?* In this question, we may see the impact of the communist peace line, though I do not assume that the student who asked it was a communist. At any rate, he was aglow with an angry intensity which might have been either party-line fervor or simply burning normal conviction.

Answer: Of course we are a peace-loving nation. The Korean War, however necessary, was probably the most unpopular war in our history, and it played a large part in the election of Eisenhower. We did not declare war against Japan; Japan started that war at Pearl Harbor. Germany and Italy declared war on the United States, not we on them. Moreover, since the charge of imperialism is very closely allied with the charge of war-mongering, what about our conduct *after* the war? We withdrew our occupation forces from Germany and Italy as soon as possible after World War II, and we helped both nations to establish free governments by free elections; we likewise withdrew our occupation forces from Japan soon after Japanese defeat; and where in the world are our troops stationed without the consent of the countries concerned? Can the Russians say as much? What occupied lands have they ever retired from? And, in conclusion, what about the crushing of the Hungarian revolt?

More applause.

It is easy to delude oneself under such circumstances. The audience *sounded* good, and the USIS representative from Patna who accompanied us on this trip, a tough-minded Indian pro not given to flowery speech or compliment (according to his American boss), said we did all right. A year later he took the trouble to look me up while he was touring the United States, and I rather doubt that he would have done so if we had not made a good impression. But I

238

am reasonably sure of this conclusion: despite the pointed questions and despite the incandescent young man, the Maharajah college community, like its Jain neighbor, was warm and friendly because its members wanted to think well of us and of the United States. They too seemed to be extraordinarily pleased with the mere fact of our appearance.

Now, to conclude this account of the Patna expedition, I shall briefly describe the picnic, which turned into a lecture. At the close of our three days of hard and pleasant work, my university host, another political scientist who knew a good deal about American politics, as well as India's, decided that we should have a holiday trip to Nalanda, a famous old Buddhist seat of learning. He brought with him one of his colleagues, a lecturer in art and archeology, to give us the historical background of the ancient monuments. We traveled by automobile this time. On the way, we stopped in a pleasant, tree-lined field for a tea break. The field was adjacent to a high school, and we were soon surrounded by eager Indian schoolboys. Shortly thereafter, the principal and his faculty appeared. We were pressed to speak to the whole school, and we agreed to do so. Classes were dismissed; a holiday, in effect, was declared; the students were drawn up in semi-formal order on the grass; a table was brought outside by the inevitable peons; the faculty was marshalled behind the principal; and the show was on. After the talk, we had to stay for tea and refreshments, quickly procured from the neighboring bazaar, a notable feat of catering on short notice.

Again, what happened was not important—I talked about American education and answered some questions. It was the atmosphere of the occasion that was important, with its current of friendly feeling. From the principal, a man of rare spirituality of countenance and gentle courtly manners, down to the youngest lad present, we were given (for the third time on this Patna trip) the feeling that we had conferred a great favor on all concerned. It should be apparent by this time that, in every case, we felt that the debt was on our side. That kind of reaching out—that kind of emanation of affection—simply does not happen very often.

This is not to imply, by the way, that the same behavior did not occur in Pakistan. It did happen on occasion, though, on the whole, the Pakistanis seemed to be less emotional in such circumstances because, as I have observed before, the manners and public deportment of Muslims, except with close friends, are perhaps more formal and punctilious than those of Indians who are not Muslims.

With close friends and relatives, the Pakistanis are most warmly demonstrative. But, under the crust of decorum, the same kind of fire burns, and it would flame up every now and then. Naturally enough, the strongest instance of this parallel phenomenon came during the college function which was, in part, our formal farewell to the Abbottabad college community when everybody (including ourselves) became quite emotional. After that function, a laboratory assistant said quietly, "My prayers go with you." It might have been a conventional remark, but it certainly did not seem so. One other example was a very formal tea party given in my honor on the eve of departure by three students at a local restaurant. The whole affair was conducted with the highest dignity, and, to cap it, the host arose and read a highly rhetorical tribute to his visiting professor, through which the underlying feeling glowed. I still have it as a prized possession.

Some Personal Conclusions

Having set down what I conceive to be the most significant aspects of our Indian Interlude, I venture to make some generalizations, admittedly personal, admittedly based on a short-term experience, but nonetheless vividly enforced on me. Much of what I will say has been said before by other observers, but I believe that these things have to be said over and over again in every possible way, from every possible point of view; they must be brought home to enough Americans to make a difference in the way in which we see ourselves and other peoples, and then we shall have to translate the fresh vision into action if we really want to achieve what we hope to be in the eyes of the world and in our own eyes at home and abroad.

I think that the Indians are disposed to like Americans as individuals, but they are sceptical and worried about our conduct as a nation. I believe that this ambivalence stems from a deeply felt desire on their part for the United States to live up to its stated ideals. They do not want us to fail. They want us to succeed in the sense that our national behavior, both internally and externally, may be worthy of the love and respect which they have for such American figures as Lincoln and Franklin Roosevelt. I do not believe that they are eaten up with envy or jealously of our economic well being, and I do not believe that the most important aspect of American life, from their point of view, is our technology. Mingled attitudes of respect and envy exist, but as secondary factors, not as primary ones.

Much of Indian exasperation and disappointment with our national record in recent years is indicative of the feeling that the United States is, potentially at least, one of the great hopes for mankind. The Indians have a fervent wish to see one large political entity on the face of the globe achieve a great-hearted ideal in practice as well as in theory. Their disappointment—and the manifestations of it in the form of pointed questions, newspaper comment, and UN debate —is, then, the result of frustrated love rather than of hate—of the betrayal of great expectations.

The Indians, though reasonably proud of what they have accomplished since 1947, are certainly worried about the future. Despite their great commitment to their own varied cultures, especially in respect to religion, they look abroad for a working ideal to emulate in other respects, and I think that they would rather look to the United States. They are, it seems to me, far more ruggedly individualistic or familistic than they are collective-minded. But if the ideal of their almost instinctive preference fails, then perforce they will turn to another, and there is no need to identify that other.

There is one more factor which makes for the possibility of establishing an honest rapport with the Indians, and, by rapport, I do not mean 100 per cent agreement; I mean a friendly and sincere respect for and understanding of convictions grounded on principle. This factor is the willingness of the Indians to listen to plain talk, provided that it comes from people of demonstrated good will and is not characterized by complacence, arrogance, or implied superiority, of which the peoples of Asia have had a bellyful.

Not that the Indians are innocent of these all too human failings. A great many of them have a double standard of international morality; many of them are as guilty of racist views and color prejudice as the deepest-dyed follower of Faubus; many of them evince an unshakable conviction of moral superiority; and many of them, out of the same kind of ignorance of the United States which parallels our ignorance of India, have greatly distorted views of such matters as American art and scholarship.

Nevertheless, I am convinced that the assets on the side of genuine amity between both nations far exceed the liabilities. If we take the trouble to understand the Indians in their terms, we will set in motion a reciprocal process whereby the Indians will come to understand us in ours. The result could be a friendship which acknowledges necessary differences and an alliance based on something more than the demands of *real politik*.

India and Pakistan

I said earlier that comparisons are inevitable. In making one between India and Pakistan, certain basic facts should be borne in mind. They are so much taken for granted that often they are not taken into account. India is much the larger in people, area, and resources. India inherited most of the great cosmopolitan centers, notably Calcutta and Bombay. India had the advantage of a much greater proportion of trained administrative talent when partition came because, for a variety of reasons—economic, political, and religious—the Muslims were a minority in the Indian Civil Service.

In consequence of all these, when Pakistan started in 1947, it had very little to start with. These facts will serve to explain, though not necessarily to justify, much of what has happened in Pakistan since. Before 1947, the Muslims in India thought of themselves as a disinherited and repressed minority; that is why a great wave of Muslim nationalism created Pakistan to begin with. It now remains to be seen whether the Muslims in their own state will continue to be a disinherited and repressed majority—under their own rulers.

The two nations have much in common. It could not be otherwise after living together as they have for centuries. Coming from Pakistan, we did not find India as strange or exotic as we expected it to be. Still, the similarities may have been more apparent than real, and it is quite possible that the more one knows about both countries, the greater the difference between them will seem, and the difference will probably grow greater as each pursues a separate course.

Let us look at the similarities first. Both nations have a common denominator of surface mores inherited from the British. It is seen in the English language press—not in what is said but in the format and in the style of the writing. It is heard in the speech of those who know English. It is apparent in the clothes of those who wear Western dress. It is manifest in the mutual enthusiasm for sports of all kinds. It is evident in the organization and educational philosophy of their universities and in formal education generally. The British stamp is on the public services, on the military services, and on the operation of clubs and hotels. It is well to remember that many of the leading figures in both nations went to the same universities at the same time, or served together in the armed forces before partition. This state of affairs will doubtless not be true of the next generation of administrators and officers.

Strongly in evidence as this body of common practice is, it is not as important as the similarities in such matters as the family system and the agricultural system. They are alike in their reliance on the family as the universal shock-absorber and in the great, all-important fact that both countries rest on the village—as even a casual trip through the country-side in either nation will demonstrate. And, insofar as West Pakistan and North India are concerned, they are alike in the fundamental color of the landscape: it is not green; it is dun, and, at best, the green of the crops seems barely to cover the primordial sandy soil.

Economically, both countries are in desperate straits, and the contrast between the luxurious houses of Lahore and New Delhi and the terrible poverty of the city and rural masses is nothing less than shocking. In India, one feels that the forces of government are at work to do something about it. In Pakistan there was much less evidence of effective governmental action. Surely, there is wide-spread corruption in both countries. The Congress Party has suffered for it at the polls in India, and any party in power is likely to suffer for it in the future. In Pakistan, corruption has so eaten into the heart of the country's administration that Iskander Mirza made it one of the primary reasons for establishing dictatorship with the support of the armed forces. It remains to be seen whether this endemic corruption can be halted in India, short of a similar result or regional separatism, but, for all its faults, government in India is still a going concern. It may be so because the political process there is also a going concern. Elections are held under the constitution; campaigning is hot and bitter; the voters seem to know the difference between parties and to have some sense of what they are voting for; the ballots are, on the whole, honestly counted; and the results are respected. One of India's greatest achievements is the holding of two general elections since partition with a very impressive record of voter participation. Pakistan can not match this; it has not held one, and now the whole matter of elections is meaningless because President Mirza and Ayub abrogated the constitution, dissolved political parties, and suspended the legislative bodies.

However, in respect to the basic problem of national economics, anything more than the provision of a bare subsistence for millions seems out of the question, and it would not make much difference if both countries were administered by political angels. I fear that both are doomed to defeat by one great natural cause: the birthrate.

In the face of rising tides of population, Five Year Plans and the like (even if they reach their objectives) will be less than adequate. Quite simply and tragically, there are too many mouths for too little food. The pressure of population on the subcontinent, from Peshawar to Calcutta, is palpable. It is physically felt in cities like Lahore, Karachi, Delhi, and, above all, in Calcutta. It is no less sensed in somewhat different terms as you ride through the mountains around Nathia Gali or drive through the country beyond Mansehra. In such places, people seem to materialize like magic in the most un-likely places—in areas which strike one as *necessarily* uninhabitable. Then you take another look at the arable land and compare it with the population which it supports, and you wonder: how do these mil-lions live, and what do they live on? They do live, and they will some-how continue to exist, but the terms of such a life are not pleasant to contemplate. "The Population Explosion" worries demographers all over the world; the meaning of what they talk about is brought home to the visitor in India and Pakistan.

Alike in these respects, the two nations differ in that India has a much more open society than Pakistan has. The reason is obvious. Pakistan is homogeneous; a vast majority of its people are Muslims. The varieties of culture and belief in India are amazing, and, how-ever fanatic one group may be in respect to religion or language (and there is much fanaticism), the presence of so many who think and live otherwise makes for an overall national tolerance in general practice, though it is violated often in specific instances. In India, Hindus, Sikhs, Muslims, Christians, Buddhists, Jains, Parsis, and variations of each sect have to live together in order to live at all. For this reason India declares itself a secular state, an idea which was given powerful support by Nehru in principle and practice. In Pakistan, the minorities are so minimal in size (excepting the sub-stantial number of Hindus in East Pakistan) that they do not really color the dominant social atmosphere in any significant way.

This is not to say that right-wing Hindus are any less fanatical than the fundamentalist Muslims of the Northwest Frontier Province. In Pakistan I saw the powerful emotional commitment to a faith which helped me to understand the blood lust of the partition mas-sacres. I saw its counterpart at Banaras. India is a sophisticated country, more so than Pakistan, but the primitive fires of zeal burn very near the surface in both nations, and they could easily erupt in holocaust again—over Kashmir.

244

Conclusion

Make no mistake about it: India and Pakistan have their own fascinations. The hold they have on the English is more than historical habit. In decent weather, few cities are as charming as Delhi, few as exciting to walk in as Calcutta. Nobody, having been there once, will ever forget the Himalayas at Darjeeling, or the mountain people in the marketplace with their dignity and likeableness. The Ganga, like all great rivers, is something to conjure with wherever one sees it, and the Deer Park at Sarnath communicates an unearthly serenity.

On the other side of the border, Lahore is still a queenly city; the Indus is a history lesson in itself; the Vale of Peshawar and the city of Peshawar speak to something in the heart which cannot be defined in words; Nathia Gali and the nearby brooding Nanga Parbat tell us that we are close to the center of an ancient mystery, but they never tell us what it is; and, when we came back to the little mountain town of Abbottabad after those weeks in India, we felt that we had come home."

Abbreviations

APWA—All-Pakistan Women's Association
ICA   —International Cooperation Administration
MLA   —Member of Legislative Assembly
NAP   —National Awami Party
NWFP—Northwest Frontier Province
PIDC —Pakistan Industrial Development Commission
PMA   —Pakistan Military Academy
SOP   —Standard Operating Procedure

Notes

I

1. Karachi's growth is dramatized by the following figures: In 1941, according to the *Encyclopaedia Britannica* (1956), the population was 359,492. In 1951, according to *Pakistan: 1954–1955* (Karachi: Pakistan Publications, 1955), p. 130, the population was 1,126,000.
2. This estimate is given in *Webster's New World Dictionary,* College Edition. *Pakistan: Basic Facts* (3rd ed.; Karachi: Pakistan Publications, 1955), p. 7, gives 849,000. The million figure is no doubt more nearly correct today.
3. However, Benjamin Gilbert Brooks, professor of English at the University of Peshawar, who knows Pakistan better than I do, takes a dim view of Kipling's interpretation. See his very interesting essay, "Three English Novelists and the Pakistani Scene," in *Crescent and Green: A Miscellany*

of Writings on Pakistan (London: Cassell and Company, 1955), pp. 120–30. Professor Brooks discusses Kipling's *Kim*, E. M. Forster's *A Passage to India*, and A. E. W. Mason's *The Broken Road*. He finds both Kipling and Forster disappointing, and he rates Mason higher than both of the better known writers.

    Crescent and Green was one of the useful items sent to me by the Pakistani Embassy in Washington, D. C. before our departure.

4. See three essays on Iqbal in *Crescent and Green*: Alessandro Bausani, "Iqbal: His Philosophy of Religion, and the West"; J. J. Houben, "The Individual in Democracy and Iqbal's Conception of Khudi"; and Alessandro Bausani, "Dante and Iqbal."

5. An interesting sidelight is the fact that the Pakistan government hired a French architect, M. Michel Ecochard, to design the plant for the new university at Karachi. See *Dawn*, the important Karachi daily, November 14, 1957, p. 8. Also see *Dawn*, November 17, 1957, p. 6, for an account of student concern about the alleged mishandling of the project.

6. See Sir Mortimer Wheeler, "Pakistan Four Thousand Years Ago"; and V. Gordon Childe, "Pakistan and the West" in *Crescent and Green*.

7. In *Crescent and Green*.

8. See Abul H. K. Sassani, *Education in Pakistan*, Bulletin No. 2, Office of Education, United States Department of Health, Education, and Welfare (Washington, D. C., 1954), p. 54. This is the best single source I have found on the subject of Pakistani education.

9. The figures for Kansas derive from United States Census data as given in *World Almanac: 1958*; the figures for the Punjab are taken from *Pakistan: 1954–55*, p. 225.

10. See below, p. 117.

11. The statistics on Abbottabad, Nathia Gali, and Murree are cited from a brochure issued jointly by the Information Department, Northwest Frontier Province, and the Public Relations Department, North Western Railway. The publication is in itself an indication of Pakistan's pioneering attempts to exploit its potentialities for tourists.

II

1. See below, pp. 66–67.

III

1. On Aligarh, see Hector Bolitho, *Jinnah: Creator of Pakistan* (London: John Murray, 1954), pp. 41–43. Jinnah also left bequests to Islamia College at Peshawar and to the Sind Madrasah in Karachi where he had been a schoolboy. Bolitho's book is useful, but a definitive biography of Jinnah is needed.

2. Dr. Khan's bibliography of seventeen items is listed on the inside cover of the reprint of his lecture, "Philosophy and Education," which first appeared in *Kaghan: The Journal of Government College, Abbottabad*, December 1957. In addition to a copy of this reprint, he also sent me reprints of two

other articles which he had written: "Differences of Moral Ideologies: Western and Islamic," *The Islamic Literature,* August–September 1952, and "A Critical Exposition of Mohiuddin Ibn Al Arabi's Sufism," *The Journal of the University of Peshawar,* No. 3, December 1954. The former is the most challenging to the Western reader.

3. On this problem of the returnee, see "Pakistan's Lost Talent," by Nasim Ahmad (*Dawn,* London correspondent) in *Dawn,* November 10, 1957, p. 7. Mr. Ahmad says in part:

> Another problem that faces young Pakistani scientists and technicians, and my meetings with many of them in this country and in America bear testimony to it, is that after a brilliant academic career they find themselves "jobless" in Pakistan. This may be due to intrigues on the part of older, but less qualified, Pakistanis in eminent scientific and technological positions who do not want to be eclipsed by brilliant young men. The difficulties afflicting qualified scientists and engineers in Pakistan can also be due to the lack of highly developed plants and institutions that can put their talents to proper use.

> See also John Useem and Ruth Hill Useem, *The Western Educated Man in India* (New York: Dryden Press, Inc., 1955). In large measure the findings of the Useems apply just as well to Pakistan as they do to India. I would endorse most of the Useems' recommendations made on pp. 189–228, notably those which deal with the utilization of the foreign educated, pp. 216–25, and those which warn against any lowering of American academic standards for the benefit of foreign students out of good will, pp. 208–09.

4. In *Horned Moon* (Bloomington: Indiana University Press, 1955), p. 13. See also Stephens' "Appendix I," which reproduces a magazine article in which the term was first recommended.

5. See Peter Mayne, *The Saints of Sind* (New York: Doubleday, 1956), pp. 31–35.

6. For a discussion of APWA and its program, see below, pp. 156ff.

7. See also pp. 180–81, below.

8. See also pp. 206–07, below.

9. See also pp. 207–08, below.

10. See pp. 198–200, below.

11. See above, n. 4, Chapter I.

12. See Mayne, *The Narrow Smile: A Journey Back to the Northwest Frontier* (London: John Murray, 1955), pp. 83–84; and John Masters, *Bugles and a Tiger* (New York: Viking Press, 1956), pp. 191–92. Masters quotes an old Pathan proverb: "A woman for business, a boy for pleasure, a goat for choice." He also quotes a famous Pathan song which begins with the words, "There's a boy across the river with a bottom like a peach, but, alas, I cannot swim."

> See also Philip Deane, "Afghanistan—A Wild and Woolly Land," *The Globe Magazine* (Toronto), August 23, 1958, pp. 8–9. Discussing the Afghan hill men, who are much like their brothers on the Pakistan side of the border, Deane says, "This kind of homosexual relationship is common in Afghanistan and is attributed by some to the extremely strict purdah laws, which keep young men and women apart."

13. See Chapter VI, "The Great Debate."

IV

1. See pp. 96–99, below.
2. See Abul H. K. Sassani, *op. cit.*, p. 80.
3. See p. 46, above.
4. See Sassani, *op. cit.*, p. 81.
5. See *ibid.*, p. 82.
6. See *ibid.*, pp. 80–83.
7. See *ibid.*, p. 79.
8. See p. 159, below, for Begum Liaquat Ali Khan's somewhat similar proposal.
9. See above, p. 82.
10. On color consciousness, see below, pp. 172ff.
11. At the time of the debate on coeducation and its relationship to prostitution, I did not have the item from *The Pakistan Times* for April 18, 1957, p. 3, which read as follows:

    The General Secretary of the Mardan Prostitutes Union has been arrested together with two other alleged prostitutes by the order of the City Magistrate. They were sentenced to one month's imprisonment and Rs.30 fine each or in default of the payment of fine, to undergo a further one week's imprisonment.

    All of them were charged with violating the order of the Deputy Commissioner, Mardan, which prohibited under Section 144 the attendance of dancing and singing women at any private function for two months. The accused, however, it was alleged, danced and sang at a private function in contravention of the order.

    See also Mary Jean Kennedy, "Panjabi Urban Society," in *Pakistan: Society and Culture,* Stanley Maron, ed. (New Haven: Human Relations Area Files, 1957), p. 92:

    The practice of polygyny is defended as a man's natural privilege because of his biological nature, and as an alternative to the prostitution of the West—an argument which overlooks the flourishing areas of prostitution in urban Panjab.
12. (Karachi: Government of Pakistan Press, 1956), par. 162.
13. See below, p. 205.

V

1. See Wilfred Cantwell Smith, *Islam in Modern History* (Princeton: Princeton University Press, 1957), pp. 228–29. A very important book. Anybody interested in Pakistan should read all of his Chapter V, entitled "Pakistan: Islamic State," pp. 206–55.
2. See the collection of articles entitled *Pakistan: Society and Culture.* Of these, I found that the following illuminated my own experience in West Pakistan: "Panjabi Village Life," by Zekiye Eglar; "Panjabi Urban Society," by Mary Jean Kennedy; "Pathans of the Peshawar Valley," by Herbert H. Vreeland, III; "Pathans of the Tribal Area," by James W. Spain; and "Women in West Pakistan," by John J. Honigmann. On the tangled subordi-

nate question of what a "Pathan" is, see Vreeland, p. 105, and Spain, p. 137. In my practice, I have called anybody a Pathan who thought of himself as one.
3. See above, p. 59.
4. See *Dawn,* November 11, 1957, p. 1, for the protest of ten editors of Karachi against the banning of *The Mirror;* and p. 3, for ex-prime minister Suhrawardy's protest. See *Dawn,* November 13, 1957, p. 4, for a report on the government's prohibiting the export of the November issue of *The Mirror.*
5. For the Afridi raid on Peshawar, see Stephens, *op. cit.,* p. 227.
6. See above, p. 122.
7. Smith, *op. cit.,* pp. 246–47.
8. See Chapter VIII.

VI

1. See p. 159, below. See also Mary Jean Kennedy, "Panjabi Urban Society," p. 91.
2. See above, pp. 76–78.
3. On the position of women in Pakistan, see also the interesting survey "Women in Our National Life," *The Pakistan Times,* March 23, 1957, the Republic Day Supplement, pp. XVIII, XX. However, in order to see what the dominant male view is, see Muhammad M. Siddiqui, *Women in Islam* (Lahore: The Institute of Islamic Culture, 1952), *passim,* and especially pp. 188–94. See also I. H. Qureshi, *The Pakistani Way of Life* (London: Heinemann, 1956), especially pp. 17–18 in Chapter II, "The Family."
4. (Karachi: Mirror Publications, 1956), pp. 67–68.
5. (New York: W. W. Norton and Company, Inc., 1957.)
6. (London: Victor Golancz, 1954), p. 37.
7. June 1957, p. 15.
8. See *Yonder One World* (New York: The Macmillan Company, 1958), p. 6. See also C. L. Sulzberger's comments on Moraes in the *New York Times Book Review,* April 13, 1958, p. 6. I owe the Moraes reference to this review.

VII

1. The pride taken by the Pakistanis in their squash, cricket, and track achievements is spoken of in two articles in the special Republic Day Issue of the weekly *Star,* Lahore, March 23, 1957: "Pakistan Sport Forges Ahead," p. 16, and "The Olympic Excursion," p. 17. Strangely enough, the Pakistani field hockey team, which lost to the Indians by only one goal, is not mentioned.
2. See Effie Kay Adams, *Experiences of a Fulbright Teacher* (Boston: The Christopher Publishing House, 1956), p. 77. Miss Adams taught in East Pakistan.
3. For a good summary of these forces and their consequences, see John E. Owen, "Report from East Pakistan," *The New Leader,* October 6, 1958, pp. 7–8.

    Clarence B. Hilberry, president of Wayne State University, has called my attention to John E. Owen's "American and Pakistani Students: A Study in

Contrasts," in *The Journal of Higher Education,* February 1959, pp. 82–86. Mr. Owen was a Fulbright lecturer in sociology at Dacca University, East Pakistan.

VIII

1. The United States Educational Foundation, Pakistan, provided me with copies of *Dawn,* covering the period from May 30, 1957 to November 30, 1957, a crucial time in Pakistan. *Dawn,* founded by Jinnah, was generally independent and often critical of current administrations.

   A. M. Rosenthal's reporting of both India and Pakistan struck me as being sensitive, sympathetic, and accurate. Mr. Rosenthal devoted most of his attention to India, but, on occasion, he wrote perceptive pieces on Pakistan, notably during the cabinet crisis which resulted in the resignation of Suhrawardy. See the *New York Times,* October 13, 1957, p. 2; October 18, p. 1; and October 19, p. 5.

   George Leather's "Prospect in Pakistan," *The New Statesman,* January 11, 1958, pp. 33–34, is a good short piece. Leather's point of view, like Rosenthal's, is sympathetic, and, therefore, it is all the more telling when he says: "Yet I found alongside all this [evidence of progress] a widespread cynicism in Pakistan, and of a rather desperate kind. Nor is it likely to be extinguished in the near future, for it has too much to feed on...."

   See also Alexander Campbell, *The Heart of India* (New York: Alfred A. Knopf, Inc., 1958), especially Chapter 16, "East Pakistan: Moslems Divided"; Chapter 17, "West Pakistan: Moslems United?"; and Chapter 18, "Kashmir: Men in Fur Hats." Chapter 17 includes enlightening interviews with General Iskander Mirza, former president of Pakistan, and Suhrawardy, former prime minister.

2. (New York: The Macmillan Company, 1957.) Callard's book was issued in cooperation with the Institute of Pacific Relations.

   I wish to call particular attention to Callard's "A Note on Pakistani Names," p.[7]. Obviously, I have had to face the same problem. Cf. my "Preface."

   Professor Norman D. Palmer, South Asia Regional Studies Department, University of Pennsylvania, has reviewed Callard's book in conjunction with another important basic work, *The Economy of Pakistan,* by J. R. Andrus and Azizali F. Mohammed (Stanford, California: Stanford University Press, 1958). I have read the Oxford (1958) edition of this work. See "The Problems of Pakistan," *The New Leader,* December 15, 1958, pp. 22–23. Professor Palmer finds that these two books supplement each other admirably.

3. See Callard, p. 121.

4. On the stresses between the two wings, see Callard, pp. 92, 97, 156–57. On the explosive language issue, see Callard, pp. 180–83. Today both India and Ceylon are involved in the same kind of language problem.

5. See *The Pukhtunistan Stunt,* a Pakistan government publication printed by Ferozons, Karachi; there are two editions of this pamphlet: March 1956 and April 1956. My copy is of the second edition.

6. See Callard's Chapter II, "The Decline of the Muslim League," which also discusses the other political parties.

7. I am aware that this is by no means true of the United States either, and that great inequities exist in respect to urban-rural representation by virtue of the failure of our state legislatures to follow equitable principles of apportionment, but it is the general operating principle more or less observed in practice.

8. See Callard, pp. 118–20.

9. For instance, see Callard, pp. 25–26.

10. For Jinnah's stature, see Bolitho, *op. cit.* For Liaquat's stature, see *Dawn,* October 16, 1957, on the occasion of the anniversary of the stateman's assassination, p. 1; the editorial, p. 5; and the article, "The Greatness of Liaquat," by Sharif al-Mujahid, p. 5.

11. XXXV, No. 3, 422–31. See also *Vital Speeches,* October 15, 1956, pp. 6–9, for a characteristic political address.

12. See Callard's "Table I," derived from the 1951 census, p. 232.

13. See above, pp. 61–62.

14. See *Dawn,* October 12, 19, 1957, and the stories in the *New York Times Index* for December 14, 17, and 31, 1957 under "Pakistan: Politics and Government."

15. See *Dawn,* October 14, 1957, p. 1. In the headline for the lead story in this issue, "turncoatism" is obviously misspelled "turn-courtism."

16. Here is the story as it unfolds in the columns of *Dawn.* October 1: the Election Commission announces that the general election would be held in November 1958; October 12: Suhrawardy resigns; October 19: Chundrigar and his cabinet are sworn in. From the latter date to November 20, almost daily stories deal with the electorate issue: bills are scheduled to be passed, establishing religious electorates; strong assurances are given that the new bills, once passed, will not delay the general election; the Election Commission is reported at work under the proposed new dispensation; doubts and hesitation as to the possibility of meeting the deadline appear. Then, as reported on November 20 and 21, the Republican Party reverses its field and withholds its support of Chundrigar and the communal principle on the grounds that the people's wishes on this important matter should be ascertained and that nothing must be allowed to stand in the way of the election of November 1958. The ultimate result is the fall of Chundrigar's ministry and the accession of Noon's ministry late in December 1957. See *Dawn's* editorial, November 21, 1957. It is maneuverings of this kind which, in considerable part, led to the postponement of the general election to February 1959, as reported in the *New York Times,* July 20, 1958, p. 26.

17. See Callard's Chapter II, "The Decline of the Muslim League."

18. See the *New York Times,* May 10, 1958, p. 1, and May 11, p. 17.

19. See Callard, p. 81; and *The Pakistan Times* (Lahore), December 14, 1956, p. 7.

20. On the cost of living in Pakistan, see *The Pakistan Times,* May 21, 1957, p. 1: "The prices of foodstuffs in Pakistan have risen from 25 to 575 per cent during the last two years, as is proved by the table below giving the prices of some of the commodities in daily use."

21. See above, pp. 88–89.

22. See Edward C. Jandy, "A Decade of Socio-Economic Progress in Pakistan," *United Asia,* Anniversary Number, X, No. 1 (February 1958), 25. Professor Jandy, a sociologist, is one of my colleagues at Wayne State

University and he served as a Fulbright Professor at the University of Karachi while I was teaching at Abbottabad.

I well remember the impact made by Mr. Bell's speech. To the credit of the Pakistanis, many of them accepted his plain speaking in the same spirit which prompted it: a sincere concern for the nation's welfare.

23. For example, the West Pakistan One Unit Assembly was elected in January 1956 by the provincial MLA's from each district. Callard says, "Thus from Sialkot 15 MLA's were empowered to return 10 new members." (pp. 61–62)

24. See above, pp. 58ff.

25. On the panchayats, see *The Pakistan Times,* May 28, 1957, p. 3; see also the *Manchester Guardian Weekly,* June 18, 1959, pp. 8–9.

26. See above, p. 198.

27. See Thomas R. Kenyon, "Pakistan: A Land in Search of Nationality," *The Reporter,* November 28, 1957, p. 15.

28. See Callard, p. 142. The quotation comes from *Dawn,* October 31, 1954.

29. See A. M. Rosenthal, the *New York Times,* April 9, 1958, p. 8.

30. See *Dawn,* November 11, 1957, p. 1.

31. According to the 1951 census as cited in a mimeographed reprint of a useful article called "Progress of Education in Pakistan," by the Editorial Staff, *Journal of Education,* Sind University, I (October 1955), 3.

32. See the *New Statesman,* May 17, 1958, p. 622.

33. See Callard, p. 324; see also pp. 74–75.

34. For a typical anti-American speech, see *The Pakistan Times,* May 13, p. 1. Iftikharuddin blasts American economic and military aid as the new imperialism. The occasion of the speech was the celebration of the First War of Independence against the British, the so-called Mutiny of 1857.

    In April 1959, the Ayub government amended the Security Act to permit changes in the management of newspapers in order to prevent the publication of material "likely to endanger defense, external affairs or the security of Pakistan." Under this act the government can remove any responsible agent who may publish information contravening the Security Act "with the aid of funds from foreign sources." This measure was invoked against the publishers of *The Pakistan Times.* See the *New York Times,* April 19, 1959, p. 13.

35. See the editorials of May 11, 1957, on American aid, and of May 28 on the Formosa riots.

36. See the *New York Times,* July 20, 1958, p. 26.

37. For Noon's visit to Nehru and the American reaction thereto, see: *Time,* September 22, 1958, p. 29; *Newsweek,* September 22, 1958, pp. 50–52; the *New York Times,* September 14, 1958, sec. 4, p. 2.

38. See an Associated Press dispatch from Dacca, East Pakistan, September 25, 1958, *The Detroit News,* p. 43. Ali took the chair to replace Speaker Abdul Hakim who was injured in an earlier riot in the assembly. See also the *Manchester Guardian,* October 2, 1958, p. 8.

39. For the initial account of Mirza's drastic actions, see an Associated Press dispatch, Karachi, *The Detroit News,* October 8, 1958, p. 25. For the enlightening interview with Mirza and Khan, see Elie Abel, the *New York Times,* October 10, p. 1; for the reaction of the man in the street and for the immediate results of the seizure of power, see Elie Abel, the *New York Times,* October 12, p. 34; for a summary roundup story, see the *New York*

Times, October 12, sec. 4, p. 2; for a background story and analysis of Pakistan's current big problems, see Elie Abel, the *New York Times,* October 19, sec. 4, p. 5.

For a significant account of the Indian reaction to events in Pakistan, indicating, among other matters, Indian awareness of disturbing parallels in the politics of the two countries, see Elie Abel, the *New York Times,* October 26, p. 6.

40. For the naming of General Mohammed Ayub Khan as Prime Minister and head of a twelve-man cabinet, see the *New York Times,* October 28, pp. 1, 6; and the *New York Herald Tribune,* October 28, pp. 1, 12.

41. For General Ayub's effort to institute land reforms, see the *New York Times,* February 1, 1959, p. 10.

42. These questions are prompted by the analysis of the situation by Elie Abel in the *New York Times,* November 9, 1958, sec. 4, p. 6. This article bears the significant title; "Pakistan Dictator Now Must Prove Worth." It also rings the curtain down on the political career of Mirza with these words: "The morning after the Mirzas had been bundled aboard an airliner bound for London, Ayub Khan took up residence in the President's House."

For a perceptive commentary which contrasts the currently dominant generals in Pakistan and Burma, see *The New Republic,* November 10, 1958, pp. 4–5. In respect to Pakistan, this short article makes the significant point that General Ayub Khan is a Pathan; Army Commander Mohammed Musa is from Baluchistan; and East Pakistan Commandant Umrao Khan is from the Punjab. The conclusion:

> Since most of those in the ranks are either Pathans or Punjabis, military rule looks uncomfortably like the incipient rule of regional groups located in the western wing of a divided country which has more than half of its population in its eastern, Bengali wing. (p. 5)

Be it noted that General Ayub Khan is a Sandhurst product and a veteran of the old British Indian army.

After the dust had settled somewhat, Elie Abel reviewed the whole complex of causes and events which produced the present state of affairs in "What Went Wrong in Pakistan," *New York Times Magazine,* November 30, 1958.

43. See Ernest K. Lindley, "This is Pakistan Today," *Newsweek,* May 11, 1959, p. 45, for a fair-minded report on the Ayub regime and its problems.

W. Averill Harriman has written an understanding account of the dilemma the United States finds itself in as a result of our military aid to Pakistan and our economic aid to India. He finds that our policies have aggravated the mutual suspicion which exists between the two nations. His article is one of a series written for the North American Newspaper Alliance. It may be found in *The Detroit News,* March 28, 1959, p. 17, under the caption: "Strongman Key to Democracy for Pakistanis."

In this connection see also the editorial entitled "Aid, or Waste," *The Detroit News,* June 24, 1959, p. 54. Commenting on Ayub's position that Pakistan needs more American military aid for the sole reason of providing security against India, the *News* says: "... the implications are unmistakable.

Ayub Khan has made it impossible to afford military aid to Pakistan without gravely jeopardizing its own relations with her great neighbor."

See also Selig S. Harrison, "The Case History of a Mistake: India, Pakistan and the US," *The New Republic,* August 10, 1959, pp. 10–17. This is the first of three important articles.

IX

1. In respect to caste in India and its future, one highly intelligent and perceptive Indian, who was spending a year in the United States, has pointed out to me that the Harijans, "The Children of God," the Untouchables, are of the same ethnic stock as the members of the other castes; that is, the Harijans are not different in color from other Indians in any given area. Therefore, as he sees it, the discrimination against the Untouchables, in contrast with discrimination against Negroes in the United States is not founded on color; rather it is a historical development based on the unpleasant and menial occupations which have made the Harijans untouchable for easily understandable sanitary reasons, among others. From his point of view this discrimination will disappear as a combined result of education and the opening up of greater economic opportunities for the Harijans. For example, a Harijan, decently clothed and working in a government office cannot be distinguished from Indians of other castes *by color.* He saw a great advantage in this fact. The generalization, he pointed out, would not hold for the American Negro under similar circumstances. In his view, what the Indians cannot understand (and, by implication, cannot forgive) is discrimination in the United States based on color.

Our Indian friend has a point here, but the fact remains that grave discrimination does exist in both countries and that, whatever the bases for that discrimination may be, in practice the injustices in both countries are likely to strike the objective observer as more alike than different.

As to the issue of how long caste discrimination in India and color discrimination in the United States will endure, one can be sure that both will last longer than men of good will would wish. The rate of speed of social change is the question here. I am not disposed to change my own prediction on this head.

Two recent documents are relevant here. See Taya Zinkin, *India Changes* (New York: Oxford University Press, 1958). Mrs. Zinkin gives a useful and fair-minded summary of the problem in Chapter X, "The Children of God." See also Elie Abel, "India's Untouchables—Still the 'Black Sin'," in *New York Times Magazine,* March 1, 1959.

A very important somewhat earlier work is *The Pitiful and the Proud* (New York: Random House, 1956), by the distinguished American journalist, Carl T. Rowan, a staff writer for the *Minneapolis Tribune.* Mr. Rowan, a Negro, spent four months in India and a month in Pakistan under the auspices of the USIS. He faced many hostile and critical audiences. His observations on the color and caste questions are particularly valuable and significant. See his Chapters I–XIV on India, *passim,* and especially Chapter X, pp. 154–56. Chapters XV–XVI are devoted largely to Pakistan's politics.

Index

Abbottabad, 3, 8, 16, 17, 21–26, 32–35, 55, 64, 68, 73, 75, 107, 120, 123, 124, 133, 136–140, 145, 147, 148, 150, 151, 152, 156, 161, 170, 172, 203, 205, 206, 207, 231, 245, 247

Abbottabad Club, viii, 27, 107–116, 128, 152

Abbottabad Government College, vii, viii, 28, 38–73 *passim*, 92, 104, 106. *See also* College life

Abdullah, Mir ("Kaka"), 109, 110

Afghan-Pakistan relations, 129

Afridis, 127, 128, 130, 250

Ahmed, Anna Molka, 13

Ali, Mohammed, 213

Ali, Syed Zahid, 219

Aligarh University, 42, 43, 247

Allah, modern views toward, 162–167

All-Pakistan Intercollegiate Debate, 57, 60, 207

All-Pakistan Women's Association, 7, 12, 53, 135, 145, 153, 156–165

Ambassador's Report, 173, 174. *See also* Bowles, Chester

American Achievement in Literature, The: 1900–1956, 91

American literature, lectures on, 103. *See also The American Achievement in Literature: 1900–1956*

Americans in Pakistan, 6

Anglo-Pakistanis, 123–125

Arab nationalism. *See* Muslim nationalism

Arif, 47–49, 52, 53, 64

Art in Pakistan, 12, 13

Asia Foundation, vii, 40, 103, 104

Authoritarianism, 206–208

Awami League. *See* National Awami Party

Ayub Regime. *See* Khan, General Mohammed Ayub

Badshahi mosque, 11

Bagdad Pact, 198

Banaras, 12, 113, 227–229, 244

Bearers, 111, 154

Beg, Aziz, 218

Begums (ladies), life of, 133, 134, 154–161

Bell, John O., 204, 253

Bengali: language, 25, 77, 103, 194; people, 173

Bharat (Pakistani name for India), use of, 48, 212, 231

Bhowani Junction, 124

Bowles, Chester, 173

British Council, 77, 78

British Information Center, 62, 207

British in Pakistan, 19, 26, 48, 117, 124–129, 137, 197, 205, 207

British-Pakistani relations, 111, 191

British War Office, 108, 207

Burn Hall School (Upper and Lower), viii, 22–24, 43, 46, 56, 117, 127, 128, 136, 156, 207

Burqa (hooded garment), 3, 36, 60, 68, 101, 122, 133, 136, 137, 140, 165, 189

Buy Pakistan campaign, 111

Calcutta, 5, 6, 232, 235, 244, 245

Callard, Keith, viii, 192, 251–253

Canadian-Pakistani relations, 15

Cantonment, 13, 14, 147, 211

Caste, in India, 175, 237, 255

Christians in Pakistan, 10, 57, 166, 199, 244

Chundrigar, I. I., 197, 201, 204, 205, 209, 252

257

Edited by Esther Ellen Jacoby

Designed by Raymond L. Colby

Set in Linotype No. 21, Alternate Gothic, and Century Expanded
type face

Printed on Warren's Olde Style Antique Wove paper

Bound in Hollistan Zeppelin cloth

Manufactured in the United States of America